# SEARCHINGS

# SEARCHINGS

Essays and Studies
by
## B. C. Butler
Auxiliary Bishop of Westminster


Edited, with an Introduction
by
**Valentine Rice**
Fellow of Trinity College, Dublin.


Geoffrey Chapman

**Geoffrey Chapman Publishers**
an imprint of Cassell and Collier Macmillan Publishers Ltd.
35 Red Lion Square, London WC1R 4SG
and at Sydney, Auckland, Toronto, Johannesburg.
An affiliate of Macmillan Inc., New York.

ISBN 0 225 66052 0

# Contents

# Acknowledgements

Acknowledgement is gratefully made to the owners of copyright for permission to reprint the following studies:

"The Christian Eucharist and the Mystery Religions", originally published as "Christianity and the Mystery Religions", *Report of the Anglo-Catholic Congress, 1927*. London: Society of SS. Peter and Paul, 1929.

"One Aspect of the Christian Fact", *Downside Review,* Vol. LV, January 1937.

"Unification", *Downside Review,* Vol. LV, April 1937.

"Authority in the New Testament", *Downside Review,* Vol. LVII, October 1939.

"The Priority of St. Matthew's Gospel", *Downside Review,* Vol. LXV, April 1947.

"The Duality of History", originally published as "The Value of History", *Downside Review,* Vol. LXVIII, July 1950.

"The Unity of the Church", *Blackfriars* (now *New Blackfriars*), 1950.

"The Catholic Faith and the Bible", *Downside Review,* Vol. LXXV, Spring 1957.

"Newman and Development", originally published as "The Significance of Newman Today", *Dublin Review,* Vol. CCXXXIII, Winter 1959.

"The Absurd and John Chapman", originally published as "English Spiritual Writers: John Chapman", *The Clergy Review,* Vol. XLIV, November 1959.

"The Object of Faith According to St. Paul's Epistles", *Extractum ex Studiorum Paulinorum Congressus Internationalis Catholicus, 1961*. Romae: E Pontifico Instituto Biblica, 1963.

"Spirit and Institution in the New Testament", London: A. W. Mowbray, 1961.

"Collective Bias and the Gospels", *Downside Review,* Vol. LXXX, October 1962, and Vol. LXXXI, January 1963.

"The Constitution on the Church and Christian Reunion", *Downside Review,* Vol. LXXXIII, April 1965.

"Belief and Reason in Science and Religion", originally published as "Belief in Science and Reason in Religion", *Downside Review,* Vol. LXXXIV, January 1966.

"The Aggiornamento of Vatican II", *Vatican II—An Interfaith Appraisal,* ed. John H. Miller, Notre Dame and London: C.S.C. University of Notre Dame Press, 1966.

"Joy in Believing", *The Tablet,* Vol. CCXX, February 5, 1966.

# Introduction

The Abbot of Downside, Dom Christopher Butler, emerged as one of the most significant prelates at the Second Vatican Council. He came to Rome as President of the English Benedictine Congregation and soon attracted worldwide attention by his contributions to debate. In many ways he resembled Newman, though he himself would reject the comparison. Both men came from Oxford and the Anglican tradition; both were members of religious congregations; both came in their maturity to play a leading role in the affairs of the Church.

For many years before the Council, of course, Abbot Butler had demonstrated a concern beyond the confines of his monastery. For almost forty years a stream of books and articles had come from his pen; more recently he had become well-known on B.B.C. radio and television. At the Council he emerged as an original thinker whose ideas were peculiarly relevant to the crisis which beset the Church. He emerged too as a bridge-builder —as a man who, without any sacrifice of his convictions, could earn the confidence of men whose ideas differed from his own. He is today particularly qualified to participate in the reconciliation of the Anglican and Roman Catholic communions.

In December of 1966 Abbot Butler left his monastery to become Auxiliary Bishop of Westminster. This volume seeks to assemble from the journals of many years some of his more important articles and studies.

I

Some biographical information may serve to complement and illuminate these writings. A man's thought is a product of his living. And, for Bishop Butler in particular, the intellectual concerns of later years were conditioned by the problems with which he grappled as he made his way into Roman Catholicism.

Basil Christopher Butler was born on May 7, 1902, in the town of Reading, some forty miles from London. He was the second boy in a family of six children and was baptised Basil; the name Christopher he assumed when he became a monk. The Butler family was lower middle-class and strongly High Church. In 1911 he won a scholarship to the local grammar school; it was nominally Anglican but in practice was religiously neutral. He has never regretted this first initiation into pluralistic living.

Some spiritual crises of his adolescence offer significant indications for the years ahead. At the age of fourteen he was seized with a frightening scruple regarding the divinity of Christ. In order to lay the ghost he turned to the New Testament and sought for a text to settle the matter. He came to the opening passage of St John's Gospel; here, he told himself, was the proof that he needed. Though the text provided him with a working peace, he suspected at a deeper level that the problem had not been solved.

In the following year he felt for the first time a desire for ordination. The sacramental life had always been important to him and he liked to picture himself saying Mass for his people. At one level he thus sought for the epitome of Christian participation; at another he was beginning to doubt the central element in the Christian faith. At the time the two opposing poles were never brought into explicit confrontation. The schoolboy was far too busy.

When he was sixteen a curate in the local church set him to reading Newman. Within a year he experienced his first bout of "Roman fever". He dealt with it by reading Bishop Gore's *Roman Catholic Claims*; the book was so convincing that it seemed only a waste of time to read Abbot Chapman's reply.

In 1920 Butler won a scholarship to St. John's College, Oxford. His life there was academically brilliant but socially undramatic. He read Classics and Theology and obtained a Triple First. In the intellectual climate of Oxford the old religious doubts returned with increased force. By the middle of his undergraduate years he was no longer concerned with the rival claims of the several Christian denominations; instead it was Christianity itself which was at stake. He saw that the truth of Christianity is necessarily dependent on the existence of God. And he saw that, even if one granted both the existence of God and the divinity of Christ, it was still necessary to justify the historical and institutional Church. He found in the writings of Baron Friedrich von Hügel a satisfactory *apologia* for the institutional Church. Here was a

God-intoxicated writer, deeply immersed in the European tradition but equipped with the techniques of scholarly analysis and interpretation. Historical Christianity assumed a new plausibility for Butler when von Hügel convinced him that the mystical element in religion requires to be disciplined and contained by the structures of religious institutions.

It was neither a book nor an argument, however, which made the existence of God seem plausible. In his fourth year at Oxford there grew up a deep friendship between Butler and an undergraduate named Martin Hancock; the friendship has lasted to this day. The reality of the relationship seemed quite unintelligible if the universe were merely a product of blind chance, a mechanistic aggregate devoid of a Supreme Being. "If you intellectualise the thing," Butler commented later, "it becomes a sort of argument from a hierarchy of values, that the thing which is good but limitedly good cannot maintain its metaphysical entity unless you accept behind it the good which is unlimitedly good. But this puts it in too intellectual a form for the experience which I had."[1]

By 1925 Butler had decided that he would be justified in seeking ordination. He was offered a post as Theological Tutor in Keble College and, at the age of 23, he began to teach there in October. The following year he was ordained a deacon of the Church of England.

He was at this time extremely radical in biblical criticism and could not admit the infallibility of Pope, episcopate, Church, or even, he remembers sadly, of Christ's human intellect. He was disturbed by the Anglican insistence upon credal formulae, and was therefore attracted by A. E. J. Rawlinson's theory that the general trend of the Church's mind was "indefectible". Thus, he felt that a false step *here* might be redressed by another *there,* so that, on the whole, the domain of truth could not disappear, but might in fact increase. One aspect of the theory, however, was disturbing. If the Church of England, without any claim to infallibility, could assert that the Churches of Rome, Alexandria,

---

[1] Except where otherwise indicated, reported statements and biographical data in this Introduction are based on tape-recorded conversations which are in the possession of the editor. For a more extended biographical account see my *Dom Christopher Butler*, No. 15 in the series *Men Who Make the Council* (University of Notre Dame Press, 1965).

and Constantinople had erred, was there any reason to suppose that Canterbury was not in error also?

In the summer of 1926 he went to Germany and discovered there for himself a living Catholicism which held the population as he had never known religion to do elsewhere. Henceforth he could view the Roman Church as a living thing rather than as an academic abstraction; he also felt torn in two between an enquiring mind and a basic need for the security of an unquestionable religious authority. Thus, even at the time of his ordination as deacon, he was divided between his intellectual liberalism and deep spiritual instincts which pointed to Rome. And then, in December of 1926, Martin Hancock confessed that he too was profoundly troubled by the Roman question. They decided that the matter must be settled once for all and set about reading systematically. And so began for Butler a spiritual journey which would involve much suffering and anguish.

He approached the matter principally from the point of view of the Church's unity and doctrinal authority and examined these issues in the light of the history of the first four or five hundred years of Christianity. Newman played a dominant role in this historical investigation. He read the *Essay on the Development of Christian Doctrine* several times and came eventually to conclude that the logic of the movement initiated by Pusey, Keble and Newman was inevitably oriented toward Newman's decision of 1845. He decided therefore that he could not honestly go forward to seek ordination as an Anglican priest. As Newman had done before him, he came to feel that his appointment at Oxford involved a moral commitment. And because he knew that it would be quite embarrassing for the authorities at Keble College if their Theological Tutor became a Roman Catholic mid-way through the academic year he went to see the Warden about his resignation.

B. J. Kidd was both magnanimous and understanding. He was sorry to lose his tutor and he asked him what he intended to do for a living. Butler said that he might teach. Kidd recommended that he seek for an appointment in a Catholic boarding school so as to experience Catholic living at first hand. He suggested that he try Downside School and he wrote personally to the Abbot. As it happened, there was no vacancy, but the connection that was established so accidentally was to influence Butler profoundly. The Abbot, Dom Leander Ramsay, was a man of immense learning and a master of English prose. His life had curiously paralleled Butler's own: he had learned his theology at Cambridge; he had been ordained an Anglican priest; eventually he had become a Roman Catholic in 1895. He invited Butler to spend some days of quiet at the abbey, and in the difficult months that followed it was to him that Butler would turn almost exclusively for help. "At a time when you have been forced to break with old associations," the Abbot wrote him, "it is my desire to give some indication as to the possibility of forming new ones to take their place. I have such a vivid recollection of the friendship which was shown me—and at Downside—when I was as you are, that I feel it as a duty, as well as a real pleasure, to hold out the hand of friendship to others."[2]

And so, on July 12, 1927, Butler came to Downside Abbey. He came directly from the Anglo-Catholic Congress at the Albert Hall where he had delivered a paper on the Christian Eucharist and the Mystery Religions.[3] His first experience of the monastery was quite overwhelming and he was tempted to plunge immediately into the Roman Church. Abbot Ramsay he found immensely congenial; they had common ground in their mutual background in Anglicanism and in their interest in the Bible and early Church history. But when he left the abbey the certainty which had seemed within his grasp began to recede. The *a priori* consistency of Roman belief on the constitution of the Church appealed tremendously to his logical faculties, but there seemed to be a gap between what logic suggested and what history presented. He felt it was hard, for example, to do more than conjecture that Christ had intended St Peter to bequeath his primacy, and it was difficult to regard the rupture of 1054 as a mere detachment of members from a corporate unity which remained whole and entire after the secession. Moreover, the evidence for any inherence of the dogma of the Immaculate Conception in the original deposit of faith seemed so scanty that he had to hypothesise, at the very least, a direct revelation of such inherence. Perhaps he ought to trust the Church on such points? But until he could identify the Roman communion as the essential church such confidence was difficult.

2 June 26, 1927. The editor is grateful to Bishop Butler for placing this significant correspondence at his disposal.

3 The paper is reproduced in this collection by courtesy of the Church Literature Association. It was Bishop Butler's first published work.

He found a post as a Classics master in a boarding school in Brighton and began to do some work as an assistant deacon in a local Anglican church. He was still preoccupied with historical difficulties. He felt that the contention that Catholicity ceases when communion with Rome is lost was very hard to reconcile with the fact that the Catholic Church recognised as saints men who had died out of communion with Rome during the Acacian period. This, he conceded, did not particularly lessen the force of the argument for the papacy but it did allow an interpretation of the contemporary situation analogous to the interpretation of the Acacian episode to which Rome seemed to be committed. "What seems to me possible," he wrote to Ramsay on September 15, 1927, "is that the basic Roman position and her doctrinal pronouncements might be true, and yet the East and the Church of England might be held to be dislocated parts of the one true (Roman) Church, and the way back . . . to be by a corporate movement."

Throughout the closing months of 1927 he struggled in silence. Then on February 13 of the new year he sent a carefully-worded letter to Abbot Ramsay. He asked if it was possible to define an area outside of which the Catholic Church did not demand from the faithful an unconditional interior assent to authoritative rulings. He was worried, in particular, about the Church's claim to rule on the conscience of Christian writers and on "dogmatic facts", facts not directly revealed, but connected with the content of Revelation. "I have not troubled you with letters," Abbot Ramsay replied, "as I feel that it is the grace of God, not man's interference, which can put an end to your difficulties. From what you say it would appear that you have made real progress. Two points in your letter give ground for encouragement: (1) You seem to be arriving at a clearer perception that Catholicism is historical Christianity, and that the alternative to this is rationalism. (2) You admit that it is for the Church to decide what falls within the area of authoritative (and infallible) definition. These two points rightly understood and firmly accepted, cover the whole ground."[4] With regard to pronouncements on the orthodoxy of Christian writers such as St Thérèse of Lisieux, he distinguished between the private mind of an author and his mind as expressed; it was on the latter only that the Church ruled. With regard to dogmatic facts, he argued that the office of protecting the deposit of faith must carry with it the power of teaching certain related

[4] February 20, 1928.

14

facts with authority. How else for example could we know the canon of Scripture?

In March of 1928 Butler reached one firm decision. "I came to the position," he recalls, "that if Christianity were true at all, I couldn't see that there was any form of Christianity other than the Catholic version. I still was not quite sure in my discursive mind that I believed in God, but if Christianity sprang from a universally valid intervention of God in human history, then God could not have so contrived things that the ultimate Christian truth resided in the Anglican solution." And so he took off his clerical clothes and began to live as a layman.

On March 27 he wrote again to Ramsay. He was finding things very difficult. For some time past at intervals, but especially and continually during the previous ten days, he had been racked by doubts about the Christian revelation in general. He had been continuing to receive Anglican sacraments on the argument that a sheer suspension of all institutional practices seemed contrary to his deepest beliefs, yet he wondered if in conscience he could still continue to do so. On the other hand, many of the pronouncements of Roman authority on such matters as Hell, Our Lady and the Bible caused him acute and unabated difficulty. "I am like one feeling about in the dark," he continued, "and starting off in what he thinks may be the right direction. Perhaps the situation will be clearer to you if I add that my closest friend decided to become a Roman Catholic ten days ago. I spent a good part of this afternoon in a Roman Catholic church. . . . I am very grateful for your prayers and need them very much."

Abbot Ramsay received this letter at mid-day on March 28, after a night-journey from Ireland. His reply was unequivocal. "In view of what you tell me, and as you are good enough to ask my advice," he wrote, "I have no hesitation as to the answer which I should give to your questions. I think the time has come when you can no longer make use of Anglican sacraments. . . . The ground of my advice is not what loyalty to the Roman Catholic Church demands, but the fact that in the matter of sacraments we cannot act on less than certainty, and that certainty for you is morally impossible. I am aware of the grave responsibility which I take in advising you in the above sense. If you are prepared to accept that advice, I think you would be right in coming to Downside and indeed I urge that you do so. Come when you like and stay as long as you like. You will be committed to nothing by coming and you need no assurance that you will be left free to work out your problems with Almighty God without undue interference from anyone. But I am quite clear that you have reached the stage at which it is proper for you to choose a Catholic atmosphere in which to struggle with your difficulties. Anglicanism has had its chance with you and (as far as you are concerned) it has broken down."[5]

And so, on March 30, Butler arrived on the 4.45 p.m. train to Chilcompton to spend the Easter vacation at the abbey. He arranged to be received as a Roman Catholic on Saturday, April 14. But when the time came he found that he could not go through with it. The Church's apparent attitude towards inspiration, inerrancy and modern biblical scholarship burgeoned into an impossible difficulty; he was closer than we are to the days of the Biblical Commission's reign of terror. So he returned to Brighton and again the whole of Christianity began to be in doubt. In those weeks he was facing the bleak problem of whether he could accept Christianity at all, in view of the apparent obscurantism of that form of Christianity to which he seemed to be driven.

On May 10 he wrote again to Abbot Ramsay. Things again were going badly. His general feeling was that the Christian fact and its evidences seemed tiny in face of the sombre whole of human experience with all of its suffering and sin and godlessness. The doctrine of Hell still troubled him; he had gone to see a priest in London who gave him a brilliant tabloid lecture on the subject, but even eloquence could not remove the thing or make it palatable. On the other hand, he did not feel that the arguments against the Faith were strong enough to justify him in turning his back on Christianity. Perhaps he should ride rough-shod over his difficulties and be received forthwith, praying God to forgive him if he were making a mistake?

Abbot Ramsay thought that Butler should wait; he felt that he was at the time in an undue state of tension and that it would be most unwise to take any major step while in that condition. On May 20 Butler wrote again. He was longing to be inside the

[5] March 28, 1928.

Church and to receive the sacraments; he looked to this to give him the stability he needed. In some ways the hardest thing to talk about was belief in God. On the whole, he kept returning to the position that a theistic philosophy was the most rational. The First Mover argument of St Thomas seemed to probe deeper than the objections which could be raised against it. Furthermore, the moral argument seemed to hold good, and the appalling mystery of evil seemed less damaging to Theism than the moral imperative was to any non-theistic position. The great temptation, of course, was to agnosticism, but he was inclined to think that agnosticism was fairly met by the twin facts of the categoric, absolute character of duty, and by the actuality of religion as a positive efflorescence of personality in the prophets and saints. But he could never feel certain of his position in the same way that he was certain of a friend's love.

As for Christianity-Catholicism, he felt he could honestly hold that Christianity was the highest and deepest of religions. Indeed, in its faith in the Incarnation it seemed to have reached not merely to a comparatively higher position, but to a sort of *telos.* And, in innumerable deep ways, Catholicism seemed to ring true. "There are elements in the Church's teaching," he wrote, "which seem to me profoundly hard of acceptance, but they are, on the whole, I think, not the sort of snags which one can imagine God to rely on for dissuading men from taking a false step. If a religion were untrue, God surely wouldn't let it seem profoundly true in every respect save over (let us say) the Virgin Birth. He would give us grounds more relative than that."

Perhaps the apparent superiority of Christianity among extant religions was merely an illusion of our pervasively Christianised European minds? He honestly did not think so. There must be something in the final religion, he felt, which absolves men from further search and enables them to say: This, if it can substantiate its claim, is what we are looking for. Such an absolute finality seemed to be forthcoming if the Incarnation was a reality.

Abbot Ramsay replied that Butler's difficulties seemed to cover the whole ground, yet at each stage he admitted that reasons for belief predominated.[6] "My reading of the situation is this," he said. "You have a very active mind and the tension of the present

[6] May 20, 1928.

crisis, working upon a marked tendency to intellectual scrupulosity, has caused the will, for the time being, to lose proper control of your mental operations. Reasons for and reasons against are crowding into your mind and dashing against each other, and the will is not working in such a way as to put them in their proper place and to force a decision. You must try to be master in your own house. You must endeavour to show the calmness and firmness of a judge on the bench." He reminded Butler of an old point of Newman's—that with regard to Christianity, it was mathematical, not moral demonstration that is impossible. "The latter kind of demonstration," he continued, "is sufficient basis for the fullest certainty and has to serve us in most of the important things of life. My advice is that you should try to get order in the processes of your mind; that you should, by the exercise of your will, force your reason to face the essential points one by one, and to register a decision on (1) God, (2) Revelation in the Incarnation, and (3) the Church." And when he had done so he should not fail to distinguish between the registered decisions of reason and the consolation or otherwise which he might experience in the region of feeling.

On the morning of Thursday, May 31, 1928, Butler faced up to the three questions. Again, he eliminated agnosticism as a viable solution. He went through a difficult time over the question of God, but decided that experience presupposed an Eternal Reality which is Perfect Being, and that things within our experience, in the measure of their perfection, approach to the nature of the Eternal Reality. Personality and goodness are the most deeply real of our experiences and there seemed to be no doubt that, in treating of the Eternal Reality as infinitely personal and absolutely good, we approach nearer to his nature than by denying him these characteristics. He dealt with the questions of Christ's divinity and of the Church's divine mission almost out of hand. In neither case was the evidence intellectually irresistible, but in each case it was far too strong to make a convinced negative reasonable. With regard to his old problem regarding the Church and biblical scholarship, he made an act of faith that since the Church was true, its *real* doctrine on Scripture must be compatible with the truths discovered by modern scholarship.

He went into a church and said a *Credo* and a *Gloria*. He became a Roman Catholic at Downside in June, 1928, and was received in mental suffering and spiritual blankness. It would be over a year before his new faith brought him any consolation.

After his reception as a Roman Catholic, Basil Butler found a post as a Classics master at Downside school and began to teach there in September of 1928. It was a time for decision-making. He was quite certain that school-teaching was to be merely a temporary arrangement, and already felt that he wanted to be ordained; the essential decision was between the monastic life and the secular priesthood. His friend Martin Hancock opted for the latter and arranged to go to the seminary of S. Sulpice. "My wishes are urging me to be a secular," Butler wrote him in January of 1929, "and are repelling me from monkery; at the same time I am anxious not to be led off the track by mere wishes; and when I get below the region of wishes I am rather in the dark as to what line to take."[7]

It was perhaps loyalty to Newman which brought him to Birmingham to investigate the Oratory during the Easter vacation of 1929. He was shown Newman's wig; the dead hand of the old man seemed to weigh like lead over everything; he thought the country house of the congregation was "musty in excelsis". So he returned to Downside.[8]

In weighing the claims of the monastic life he was influenced by the relative freedom which it would afford for intellectual work and by the consideration that it seemed closer to the Gospel ideal of perfection, provided that one was free to enter it and was capable of living with its demands. In spite of the personal dis-inclination involved, the final decision seems to have come rather easily. "I have decided in favour of Downside," he wrote to Martin Hancock on April, 1929. "I spent some time before the Blessed Sacrament on Tuesday afternoon, and meant to settle it all yesterday, but went to the pictures instead. This morning I went into Church about eleven o'clock and had a colossal think. I decided that my advisers more or less cancelled out. . . . What remained was the fact that I had for so long had the idea of being a monk in my mind and that as things turned out I have been brought into close contact with Downside. . . . So in the end I let that turn the scale."

[7] I am grateful to Bishop Butler and to Canon Martin Hancock for allowing me to quote from their correspondence during this period.
[8] Letter written on Wednesday of Easter Week, 1929.

He entered the novitiate at Downside in September of 1929 and took the name of Christopher. He began to study theology again; in view of his previous studies the normal period of preparation for the priesthood was reduced from six years to three. He found the life of the monastery congenial. On October 12 he wrote to Martin Hancock: "I am certain that it brings real peace to know that everything except sin is a means of union with God, and is in fact a mode or occasion of union." The following February he could write: "You know, I am getting back the old desire to become holy. It seems to me the one thing in life of which the value is certain." A year later he felt that all that mattered was that one take one's religion literally. "Let us pray for each other," he wrote on March 5, 1931, "that we may have courage and grace to stake all our money on Christ as the actual lord of our lives and will within our wills." He began to write for the *Downside Review* and experienced a certain conflict of allegiance between philosophy and scripture. He concluded that his philosophic powers were not as great as his philosophic passion, whereas he had a fair amount of faith in his capacities for biblical scholarship; furthermore, this activity also fitted in well with Benedictinism and the spiritual life.[9]

He was ordained priest in the summer of 1933 and for the following six years he taught Classics at Downside school and Scripture to the young monks at the abbey. He continued to write. Two years after his ordination he went through a difficult time. On September 18, 1935, he wrote: "I am in such 'darkness' as never was—though darkness is not quite the word, for it is rather as though the whole spiritual universe has dissolved into thin air and left one with the daily paper and one's sausage and mash. The angels must think us very weird, mustn't they?" The chores of teaching provided a lifeline. "School started the week before last," he wrote on January 26, 1936, "and as 'dope' it is working. . . . I pass my time between the sane paganism of my school life and the mad misery of the holidays." A year later he was still in travail. On reading a prayer-book for boys by a fellow-Benedictine he would write: "I felt rather like weeping when I saw it, since it brought home to me how my own days have declined like a shadow, my bones grown dry like fuel for the fire."[10]

[9] Letter of April 29, 1932.

[10] December 20, 1936.

By April of 1937 he was buoyant again, doing a little Homer, "enjoying" the Synoptic problem, and talking philosophy and theology with Fr. Mark Pontifex and Br. Illtyd Trethowan. In face of the gathering European crisis be became involved with Catholic Action. He declared that politically he was neither a Fascist nor a Communist; the only *signum victoriae* was the Cross, even if it brought martyrdom. The Church, he felt, should ask much of the laity since "the need to sacrifice one's self, all that is deepest in one, is really a far more tremendous need than the need for food and drink and justice."[11] In December of 1939, he became headmaster of Downside school and continued in that post until 1946. He was happy in the work; it was an anodyne in time of war to be involved in the eternal problems of youth. Life was busy and the stream of articles dried up completely.

Christopher Butler was elected Abbot of Downside in 1946 and was re-elected in 1954 and 1962. When he became Abbot he returned to his writing and began a systematic study of modern Continental theology. He published six books: *The Originality of St. Matthew* (1951), *The Church and Infallibility* (1954), *Why Christ?* and *The Church and the Bible* (1960), *Prayer in Practice* (1961), and *The Idea of the Church* (1962). In 1961 he became President of the English Benedictine Congregation and in that capacity came to the Second Vatican Council.

He experienced the Council as a profound education. He was surprised to find that the Church as a whole was much further to the left than he had imagined it to be. He was particularly impressed by the Uniate Churches. Previously he had met them only on the pages of books; now he found that these churches, so limited in numbers, are a standard witness to the world that Catholicism is something larger than Latinism. His Anglican background enabled him to contribute non-Roman theological insights and was particularly relevant in an assembly which sought for Christian re-union; his life-long concern with the Scriptures assured the biblical scholars of a champion. During the second session he became a member of the influential Theological Commission.

In December of 1966 Abbot Butler accepted appointment as Auxiliary Bishop of Westminster, and assumed particular responsibility for the fifty-one parishes in Hertfordshire. He was

[11] September 29, 1937.

21

already familiar with pastoral work since the abbey at Downside had the care of several parishes. He serves on the Commissions for Theology and Ecumenism of the Episcopal Conference of England and Wales. As bishop he is in daily contact with the flux of events and has found a new appreciation for history as it is being made in all its particularity. Though there is less opportunity than in the monastery for reflection he has been able to complete three new books, *The Theology of Vatican II* (1967), *In the Light of the Council* (1968), and *A Time to Speak* (1972).

## III

Bishop Butler returned from the Council with a conviction that its impetus must be sustained. The contemporary Church is still in crisis. The Council gave voice to pressures and dissatisfactions within the Church and it achieved almost miraculous results. However, the work which it initiated must be brought to completion. And here he professes to be profoundly troubled. At the Council the progressives carried the centre with them by an exercise of holy rhetoric; when these same bishops of the centre are immersed again in the work of their dioceses there is a serious danger that they will succumb to the pressure of traditional associations.

And so the future of the Church is still in doubt. Bishop Butler likes to illustrate its predicament by means of an analogy. In the twentieth century the situation of the Church is like that of a biological species when the moment has come for a new step forward in evolution. When significant changes have occurred in the environment a species is faced with an existential crisis and it may respond in one of three possible ways. It can make itself plastic to the new situation, introducing change and modification within itself, while maintaining only its basic identity intact. Alternatively, it can refuse the challenge and entrench itself ever more firmly within its traditional structures and patterns. It will then go to the wall and perish, and future scholars may one day discover its fossilised bones in the ground. Faith teaches us that this cannot happen to the Church; we have a divine guarantee that it will not perish. But there is a third possibility for a biological species: it can flee from the challenge and take refuge on the borders of natural history, like a blind fish on the floor of the Indian Ocean. And this, he believes is a very real peril for the Catholic Church. "We have a guarantee from God," he has stated, "that the Church will not cease to exist. We have no guarantee that it will not become so irrelevant to the human race that it survives, like the religion of Tibet, only on the margin of the real history of mankind."

The fundamental issue is therefore one of relevance. If the Church is to be relevant to contemporary man and to man of the future it must undertake a process of adaptation in depth. And central to this work must be the elaboration of a new and deepened theology. He believes that the traditional manual theology—on which indeed perhaps the majority of the Church's ministers have been nourished—is no longer adequate. Despite the insights which it enshrines, it has been unduly shaped over the centuries by the twin pressures of Canon Law and medieval thought.

Bishop Butler deplores the situation which has frequently obtained in which Canon Law seemed to control theology. Too many churchmen, he feels, still look at their theology through spectacles of Canon Law rather than adopting the more Christian stance of looking at their Canon Law through spectacles of theology. Canon Law busies itself with exact propositional formulations; it proceeds by deductive methods and allows for exceptions. Its influence has tended to produce a propositional theology, proceeding by deductive means and leaving a number of loose incoherencies at the periphery which have to be allowed for by exceptions. This, he feels, is absolutely alien to the spirit of the Bible and to the spirit of a religion whose revelation consists in an Incarnation of the Word of God.

The restrictive influence of medieval categories is not the responsibility of the men who created the medieval synthesis. The scholastics, in developing a theology, set out from the Bible and tried to intellectualise the evidence which it presented. They conceived of theology as the rational explication of the data of revelation and they were faithful, on the whole, to the principle that philosophy is the servant of theology. In the course of time, however, there has developed a tendency to accept the completed philosophical theology as the starting point. As a result, he insists, the biblical data are partly distorted, partly rejected and omitted, and the criterion of orthodoxy has been the finished product of the medieval synthesis. Very frequently, the traditional theologian is operating within an essentially philosophical framework of thought and, as a result, it is generally the Bible which has to bow to his philosophy.

There must therefore be a return to Christian origins, and the new theology must be a biblical theology. "We must begin by admitting with St Ambrose," Bishop Butler states, "that God has not chosen to reveal himself by a propositional revelation; he has chosen an historical method, and has revealed himself through the historical person of Christ. The right world of discourse, therefore, in which to approach the question of theology, is not that provided by the Hellenic scholastic philosophy, with its non-historical orthodoxy, but the world of discourse provided by the modern study of history. Now the whole of this is uncongenial to a mind which has been formed by the scholastic system. It must all sound terribly vague, because the method of history is not deduction but a convergence of probabilities. It is a trial and error approach, which seems terribly untidy intellectually. Nevertheless, I think it is the kind of approach which is appropriate for a religion which is incarnated in history. We've been trying for too long to stretch Christianity on a procrustean bed of Hellenic categories and concepts."

He differs from many progressive theologians, however, in his conviction that it is not sufficient merely to elaborate a biblical theology. The human mind asks philosophical questions; it reaches toward synthesis. Accordingly, he feels it will be necessary to create a new Scholasticism from the mating of a deepened philosophy with the insights of biblical scholarship. And he thinks that the philosophy for a new and open synthesis is at hand in the philosophy of Bernard Lonergan.

IV

For much of his lifetime Bishop Butler has been engaged on such a programme of new theological beginnings; many of the articles in the present volume are such searchings in theology. These articles span a period of forty years and range from his first published piece of writing to an epilogue written in the wake of the Council. They have appeared in a variety of publications; some may be difficult of access to the general reader. The studies are reproduced here substantially in their original form;

occasional minor alterations have been made principally to rationalise conventions and to eliminate dated references.

The articles are broadly representative of Butler's thought over the period of his published work. Over the years one can discern a variation of tone, from the rather ultra-Catholic stand of the earlier pieces to the confident and mellow Butler of later years. There is also a diversity of approach. Some of these pieces are unashamedly academic and technical; others are aimed at a wider public. There is also considerable variation in subject-matter; indeed, it was tempting to compile from the *corpus* of available material separate collections of scriptural studies, of philosophical pieces, of commentaries and book reviews. No doubt this work will some day be accomplished. However, there seemed room at the present time for a collection which, were the subject-matter of a lighter nature, might be termed *The Best of Butler*.

The editor has therefore sought to identify some of the more important studies without regard to type, and the selection has been approved by the author. There was, of course, a considerable problem of ordering. The articles could conceivably be grouped by theme and category; however, themes overflow from one composition to another and categories could be over-rigid. It seemed best in the end to place the studies in chronological order, attaching the date of composition. This would help to situate them in context and would clarify any development in thought that had taken place over the years.

Beneath the surface diversity of these studies there is, however, an underlying unity of concern. There are two unifying principles —the particular biographical experiences of the author and his emphasis on the necessity for a theological return to the Bible. The second principle is, of course, a product of the first. And very frequently both are operating together.

The first article in the book, "The Christian Eucharist and the Mystery Religions", is a product of Bishop Butler's Oxford years. "The Absurd and John Chapman" flows from his experience as a Benedictine; it is an analysis of the spirituality of a former Abbot of Downside. The pieces on the Council issue from one of the most important phases in his life and manifest his present involvement with *aggiornamento* and Christian unity.

The biblical emphasis, on the other hand, yields first of all several general articles on the Bible. "The Catholic Faith and the Bible", for example, tackles the problem of the role of the Bible in the Roman Catholic Church, and may serve as an introduction to his book on the subject. "The Priority of St Matthew's Gospel" is a convenient summary of a central Butler thesis which receives extended treatment in a separate volume. And "Collective Bias and the Gospels" levels a serious charge against a consensus of contemporary biblical scholarship.

The remaining articles constitute, in terms of volume, the major part of the book. By and large, they bring together existential concerns and analysis of the scriptures: Bishop Butler searches the data of revelation for fresh insight into theological problems, particularly those problems with which he wrestled on his way into the Church. The problem of authority in religious matters was a considerable stumbling-block to the young Butler; in "Authority and the New Testament" he seeks for a scriptural solution. The growth of religious dogmas had occasioned him considerable difficulty; more than once he returns to Newman's theory of development. "Spirit and Institution in the New Testament" is perhaps the most technically mature statement in the whole collection. It reflects the author's longstanding preoccupation with the problem of the institutional nature of the Church, and returns to what von Hügel told the young Oxford tutor many years before—that the mystical element in religion must be disciplined and contained by the structures of formal institutions. Through an analysis of the New Testament Bishop Butler discerns this conjunction of spirit and institution at the heart of the original Christian deposit.

Another central and related theme is to be found in "One Aspect of the Christian Fact" and in "The Meaning of History". We must distinguish between the incarnational and the eschatological aspects of Christianity, he says, and it is imperative that we should not emphasise either to the exclusion of the other. Rather, we must recognise them as two co-penetrating elements of the one reality, and "the key to the understanding of Christianity is precisely this conviction that the beatific future of redeemed humanity is already contained, though not exhausted, in its militant presence."

Concern with the nature of the Church inevitably leads to concern for Church unity. Three studies in the present collection deal specifically with ecumenism; they are "Unification", "The Unity of the Church", and "The Constitution on the Church and Christian Reunion". They manifest a development in thought, from the detached and philosophical tone of the first to the pragmatic optimism of the last. Though the context of "The Unity of the Church" is pre-conciliar, the article is significant for containing the first articulation of an idea which Bishop Butler would later develop in *A Time to Speak*—his suggestion that doctrinal reunion must involve the quest not for a Highest Common Factor but for a Least Common Multiple, which, by integrating all that was positive in the various traditions, would yield a synthesis richer than that of any tradition taken on its own.

Finally, there are those essays which are concerned with the ultimate basis of all Christian involvement—faith. "Belief and Reason" explores the notion of faith from a philosophical standpoint and manifests the unmistakable influence of Bernard Lonergan. And "Joy in Believing" accepts both the mystery and the experience of religious faith in the second half of the twentieth century.

As editor of this collection I wish to thank Bishop Butler for the privilege of working with his materials. The idea for the book was Michael Glazier's; throughout the progress of the work he has never failed to provide encouragement and support. And I wish to express to Miss Vera Burke and to my wife, Ellen, my sincere gratitude for their assistance in the preparation of the manuscript.

Trinity College                                         Valentine Rice
Dublin.

# The Christian Eucharist and the Mystery Religions

1927

A sacrament may be described as a ceremony in which an outward sign is used as a means of conferring grace, and a sacramental religion is one in which grace is believed to be given, if not by any means exclusively, yet specially and assuredly, in connection with ceremonial actions and formulae or sacred things. In this broad and general sense, of course, sacramentalism is almost coextensive with religion itself, and it is clearly necessary, for the purposes of this paper, to make a selection from the material at our disposal. We will therefore restrict our attention to ceremonial eatings and drinkings, in what are known as the "Mystery-Religions" of the epoch and region in which Christianity took its rise.

I

What were these mystery-religions? They were in the main sectarian and un-Hellenic cults making their way out, each from its own primitive national setting in Persia, Asia Minor, Egypt, or elsewhere, into the Mediterranean cosmopolitan culture of the centuries immediately preceding and succeeding the commencement of the Christian era. They made their appeal, not to society in its collective aspect, but to individual men and women, without respect to sex or class or nationality. And the supreme boon which they claimed to ensure to their adherents was a blissful immortality in the presence of the gods after death. In fact, we may say that the idea of immortality played a role in the mystery-religions as central as that of ethical holiness in Judaism. Their vogue was probably in large measure due to the supersession of the old national or city-states, first by the great supernational monarchies of the Hellenistic age, and then by the Roman Empire.

The old religions had been bound up with the old political forms and entities, and the overthrow of the states dealt a severe blow to the prestige of the religions connected with them. At the same time the pressure upon the individual of the old, narrow, but acutely self-conscious social life was relaxed, and men began to

28

realize at once their own individuality, no longer as Athenians or Spartans merely, but as men, and also their individual religious needs. Thus the old religions no longer satisfied, and a gap was created which the mystery-religions helped to fill. These cults lacked many of the qualities which we have learnt to associate with sound religion; they were deficient in dogma, and offered myth where we would demand history; the ethical considerations in them, when present at all, were rather accessory than essential, and they had neither the confident monotheism of Judaism and Christianity nor, on the whole, their proud exclusiveness. Nevertheless, they appealed to the populace partly by means of an attractive and sometimes gorgeous ceremonial, by the mystery that surrounded them and the romance of their alien aspect and origin, and again by the hopes they held out of a blessed after-life. Most of them were concerned with gods who were apparently held to have passed through sorrow, suffering, or death to a happiness beyond these woes, and this complex of good arising out of evil was brought home to the heart of the worshipper by ceremonial and ritual, whose ultimate effect may, at least in some cases, have been held, already as early as the beginning of the Christian era, to have included some identification of the deity and his worshipper. At a somewhat later date (c. A.D. 150) Apuleius, in the *Metamorphoses,* narrating his hero's initiation into the Isiac mysteries, tells how at the end, when morning came the neophyte was dressed in a robe and adorned like the sun, and made in fashion of an image, and was made to stand on a platform and solemnly displayed to the congregation; it would seem that here we have an example of identification with the deity.

But it must be clearly understood that our evidence for the mystery-religions is scanty, scattered, often late, and incomplete; that what is true of one such cult in one period may well be untrue of another, or of the same cult at an earlier date; and that though there was in later paganism a confusion of the different cults, and a kind of coalition and unification of the various pagan religions against the growing menace of Christianity, this coalition was yet a slow process, and must not be supposed to have got beyond its initial stages in apostolic times. The great days of the mystery-religions were yet to come; at present they were still alien cults, to a large extent independent of one another, but all involved in the Westward progress which took Christianity also at an early date to Rome.

## II

To what extent were ceremonial eatings and drinkings included among the ceremonies of the mystery religions? This question can best be answered by an examination of the various cults one by one. First, there are two mystery-cults which have a better claim to be considered Hellenic than most of those we have been considering: these two are the Eleusinian and the Orphic.

(a) Clement of Alexandria (*Protrept,* II, 21) gives as the password of the Eleusinian religion the following formula: "I have fasted, I have drunk the porridge (*kykeon*), I have taken from the chest, having wrought (or perhaps, "having tasted"), I have put back in the basket and from the basket into the chest." This porridge, or barley-drink, is presumably associated with the porridge wherewith the Eleusinian mystery-goddess Demeter was said to have broken her nine days' fast of mourning for her abducted daughter. As Dr Farnell says: "It is probable that the votary felt, in drinking the barley-drink, a certain fellowship with the deity, who by the story had drunk it before him." In the broadest sense of the word this may be considered a sacramental act, but of any deeper significance than that of a sympathetic fellowship with Demeter we have no evidence.

(b) The evidence for ceremonial eating and drinking in the Orphic mysteries is of the vaguest. It should be remembered that the common characteristic of the mystery-religions is the secrecy with which the central rites and ceremonies are veiled from the knowledge of the uninitiated. We have thus to conjecture what may have happened from very uncertain indications. For the Orphic ceremonial we may consider three classes of evidence: (i) that from the Orphic mythology, as probably bearing some relation to the ritual; (ii) that from the non-Orphic public ritual of the Orphic god, Dionysos—for the worship of Dionysos was not restricted to the Orphics, but preceded the rise of that sect; (iii) the evidence of some wall-paintings from Pompeii which the Italian scholar, Macchioro, thinks depict an initiation into the mysteries of a conflate Eleusinian and Orphic sect.

(i) The Orphic mythology tells how the infant god, Dionysos, was enticed away from his nurses by the giant Titans, torn in pieces and eaten; he was subsequently born again of the high god, Zeus, and man is sprung from the ashes of the Titans,

whom Zeus slew with his thunderbolt. We are thus compact of
the evil nature of the Titans (identified with our bodies) and
the divine nature of Dionysos, whom they had consumed, our
souls being this divine part of us; and our task and aim are to
escape from the prison-house of the body and live beyond the
grave the untrammelled existence of the immortal gods. It
should be noticed that it was apparently in connection with the
initiatory rites that Orpheus, according to the tradition,
handed down the rending of Dionysos by the Titans (Diodorus,
V, 75, 4).

(ii) There survived in Crete down to the latter days of
paganism the orgiastic worship of a boy-god, among the ceremonies of which, according to the Christian writer Firmicus
Maternus, there took place a rending with the teeth of a "live
bull". We must suppose that Maternus has somewhat misrepre-
sented the performance, and that what actually took place was
the slaughtering of a bull, whose flesh was forthwith eaten raw:
it is hard to imagine a live bull allowing himself to be rent by
human teeth. Another Christian writer (Arnobius, V, 19)
speaks of Dionysiac ceremonies in which the worshippers twist
snakes round themselves, and, "to show that they are possessed
by the divine majesty of god, tear with bloodstained lips the
flesh of struggling goats". There are other indications which
suggest that in some cases the animals thus treated may possibly
have been in some way identified with the god Dionysos, who
was himself held to have been torn in pieces and eaten by
the Titans.

(iii) The wall-paintings at Pompeii show, in one of a series
of panels, a meal at which the person undergoing initiation
takes part; in the next panel, Macchioro thinks he can descry
a female satyr suckling a kid. It is, of course, probable that
the meal has sacramental significance, at least of the very vague
kind suggested for the Eleusinian porridge; and it is conceivable
that the kid is in some sense to be identified with Dionysos.
But in order to make it even probable that the food eaten is
identified either with the kid or with Dionysos, it would have
been necessary for the order of the panels to be reversed; and
it is unlikely that Macchioro has mistaken the order in which
the pictures are to be read. It should further be pointed out
that the double climax of the passion and of the exultant joy

of the neophyte seems to occur at a later stage than that in which the meal is eaten and the kid depicted. Thus the evidence for an Orphic meal of any more than the most indeterminate sacramental significance is so far vague and inconclusive in the extreme. I will add, however, one piece of evidence that might show more than this if it could be proved that it refers to Orphic mysteries and not to non-Orphic Dionysiac rites. A Greek editor's note on Clement of Alexandria's *Protreptikon* (1, p. 433D) says: "Those being initiated to Dionysos used to eat raw flesh, performing this rite as a representation of the rending which Dionysos underwent at the hands of the Maenads." But in the Orphic myth it was apparently the Titans, not the Maenads, who tore Dionysos in pieces; the note, then, for what it is worth, cannot be taken as evidence for Orphic rites or ideas.

(c)    We pass on to the ceremonies of the Attis-religion. This was a Phrygian religion which was extending its influence in the Mediterranean at about the time of our Lord's earthly life, and was probably sanctioned at Rome by the Emperor Claudius (who is mentioned in *Acts* as contemporary with St Paul). A formula of the Attis-religion is preserved by Clement of Alexandria: "I have eaten from the drum, I have drunk from the cymbal, I have borne the sacred basket, I have gone down into the marriage-chamber." It should be observed that drum, cymbal, and basket were among the paraphernalia of the religion. A similar formula is given by Firmicus Maternus: "I have eaten from the drum, I have drunk from the cymbal, I am become a votary ('mystes') of Attis." Here, doubtless, we have in the broad sense a sacramental partaking of food and drink; but it has been argued that the food and drink were actually held by the believers to convey life to the soul. For Firmicus Maternus, from the Christian point of view, asserts that, as a matter of fact, *death* is the sequel to the pagan meal, and recommends, as the true food of life, the Bread and the Cup of Christ. But the contrast of life and death, as following respectively the pagan and the Christian sacramental meal, may have been suggested to the mind of Firmicus by his own remark that the Attis-worshipper uttered the words of the formula "that he might be admitted, *a man about to die,* in the inner parts of the temple". The comparison of Christian and pagan sacred foods goes back to St Paul and recurs in St Justin Martyr, and it is quite possible that Firmicus has exaggerated the similarity of the significance of the two things. In any case, it must be remembered that he is writing centuries after Apostolic times, and that there is still one further step to go, even beyond admitting that the food and drink in the Attis-rite were life-giving, before it could be asserted that they were in any way identified with the god himself.

(d)   In an inscription relating to the Great Gods of Samothrace, we are told (if the inscription has been correctly emended): "The priest shall cut up and administer the cake, and distribute the liquor to the votaries."

(e)   Again, there is a statement in St Justin Martyr (*Apol,* I, 66) to the effect that in the mysteries of Mithras the demons have contrived a caricature of the Christian Eucharist.[1] For bread and a cup of water "are set forth in the initiatory rites with certain forms of words" (or "a form of words" or "incantation"). The water was apparently mixed with *haoma*-juice, or possibly, in the West, with wine. We are also told that at one stage in the ceremonies honey was applied to the tongue. There is, of course, a possibility that this Mithraic rite *is* an imitation of the Christian Eucharist, though, as with almost all the ritual eatings and drinkings discussed above, it seems to have formed part of the *initiatory* ceremonies, whereas the Eucharist is the often-repeated meal of those who are *already* Christians. It is interesting that the worship of Mithras was probably already common in Asia Minor before the beginning of the Christian era.

(f)   With regard to the Egyptian-Hellenistic deities, Isis and Serapis, we have an interesting papyrus in which a certain Chairemon invites someone to dinner "at the table of the Lord Serapis, in the Serapaeum, to-morrow", and we are told by Aristides that unto this god alone men share in the real communion of sacrifices inviting to the hearth and setting him forth as banqueter and host. If this refers to a mystery-worship of Serapis, it is one of the closest parallels to the Pauline presentation of the Eucharist (I *Cor* X). But there is not a trace here of an identification of Serapis with the meal that is eaten.

We have now considered the important cases of sacred eatings and drinkings in the mystery-religions, insofar as the scanty evidence will allow. On the basis of these facts a theory has been

[1] Cf. also Tertullian's reference to the Mithraic meal.

built up, which may be divided into two parts: (a) It has been suggested that some at least of these meals were "theophagic" i.e. that at least in some of them the worshipper believed himself to partake of the very substance of his god; (b) it is then argued that the Christian Eucharist owes its character of a partaking of the Body and Blood of Christ to the influence of the mystery-religions. It is asserted that such a sacrament cannot be supposed to have originated in its present form with our Lord, whose human nature expressed itself in forms congenial to his Palestinian Jewish environment, an environment to which a sacramental meal consisting of the Body and Blood of a supernatural being would be completely alien. This, however, is often made one part of a larger theory, which is concerned to explain, as a distortion of primitive Christianity by pagan influence, not merely the sacramentalism of the Church, but its Christology also.

### III

I am concerned here to deal only with that aspect of this far-reaching theory which concerns the Eucharist. And it may be pointed out, at the outset, that the Christian who believes in the divine over-ruling of the Church can confidently submit the matter to the best historical criticism, convinced that even should paganism be shown to have had any material influence on the Eucharist, such influence would not have been exerted without the permission of God. As a matter of fact, the theory lays itself open to severe criticism.

Firstly, it will be recalled that in our examination of the sacramental eatings and drinkings in the mystery-religions we could find no clear trace, early or late, of the idea of eating the god. Even the idea of life being conveyed by the Attis-meal is only to be inferred with considerable doubt from the remarks of a late Christian writer. For actual theophagy we have to turn to what can be conjectured concerning non-mystery Dionysiac cults in Greece, Crete, and the Aegean Islands, and to the barbaric or primitive ideas of Egypt and other environments remote from that of St Paul. But if we can find no trace of theophagy in the mystery-religions, their sacramental meals cannot give us much positive assistance in explaining the Christian Eucharist; for to find religious meals in the neighbourhood of early Christianity we need go no further than the Jewish sect of the Essenes; thus the idea of such a meal might well have come, not merely to the Palestinian Apostles, but to their Master himself, quite apart from the mystery-religions, while the actual nature of the food and drink, as the Body and Blood of Christ, can be paralleled by no extant analogies either among the Jews or in the mystery-religions of that age.

It must also be remembered that New Testament eucharistic thought seems to cluster around the idea of sacrifice; St Paul compares the Eucharistic Food and Drink with the sacrificial offerings at the Jewish Temple and with the animal "sacrifice to idols". And the reference to "the New Covenant in my Blood" recalls the blood of the sacrificial offerings wherewith Moses sealed the Old Covenant. But it would seem difficult to detect any sacrificial ideas associated with the ceremonial meals of the mysteries, except probably that the evidence of Aristides with regard to Serapis points in this direction, for that god's worship alone.

Again, it is a cogent argument, that, in contrast with the majority of the Gentile religions of the time, Christianity, like Judaism, was proudly and self-consciously exclusive. To become a Christian was not so much to gain a somewhat fuller insight into the nature of religion; it was to turn from idols to serve a living and a true God. Thus, quite apart from the secrecy with which the mystery-religions enveloped themselves, borrowing from them on the part of the early Church is almost inconceivable. In particular, Dr N. P. Williams has pointed out the enormous *a priori* improbability that St Paul, whose attitude towards pagan cults varies from abhorrence to contempt, "should have unsuspectingly allowed the texture of his devotion and his thought to become saturated by conceptions borrowed from those very 'Mysteries' which it was the object of his mission to destroy".[2] I am glad, also, to be able to quote Professor Percy Gardner to the effect, not only that "there is no adequate evidence for the notion that there was in the pagan Mysteries anything at all parallel to the Christian Eucharist," but also that, generally speaking, he thinks "we should be sceptical as to any direct influence of the Mysteries on Christianity".[3] Parallelism, he says, "is far more probable than derivation".

[2] Dr A. E. J. Rawlinson concurs.
[3] *Modern Churchman*, Vol. XVI, pp. 6-8.

Then, finally, if we turn to the evidence of the New Testament itself, we are struck by St Paul's assertion: "I have received of the Lord that which also I delivered unto you," with which assertion he prefaces his account of the institution of the Eucharist, including the words, "This is my Body," "This cup is the New Testament in my Blood," and "This do in remembrance of me." "I have received of the Lord" might conceivably mean "I received by direct revelation, independent of any human tradition." But the following considerations make it probable that what St Paul means is that he received this piece of instruction from the Christian or Christians who prepared him for baptism, and imparted to him the traditions of Christianity at Damascus twenty years before, and that he believes it to rest ultimately on the authority of our Lord himself in his earthly life.

(a)  Both here and in I *Cor* XV, where he is recalling the traditional teaching with regard to our Lord's death and resurrection, St Paul seems to identify his own relationship to the tradition with that of his converts; but since they obviously received it from human lips as part of the common deposit of Christian truth, it is reasonable to suppose that he did too.

(b)  Both the style and the content of the succeeding verses suggest that they are a piece of sober Christian, almost credal, instruction, and not that St Paul is relating visions of the Lord and things ineffable.

(c)  The words "This is my Body", "This is my Blood" of the New Testament are found in the Marcan account of the Last Supper. This gospel was probably written by a Christian Jew of Jerusalem, who had been a companion of St Peter, and who produced his work at Rome. The Roman Church was thriving, as we can see from the Epistle to the Romans, long before St Paul came into personal contact with it. In the circumstances, it is paradoxical to suggest that St Mark's gospel contains an account of the Last Supper which, as to its essentials (and highly controversial essentials they would surely have been), is based merely on a vision of St Paul.

(d)  There is no clear trace of any controversy in the early Church caused by this version of the Eucharist; but St Paul's opponents among the Judaizers might have been expected to seize on an innovation by him of such a kind.

Thus we are driven to the view that St Paul owes his Eucharistic teaching to tradition, and there is every probability that he received it shortly after his conversion. Now, quite apart from the fact that this is narrated in Acts before the great appeal to the Gentile world at Antioch, and that (consistently with this) St Paul was baptised by a man with the Jewish name of Ananias (and in fact would never have gone to Damascus unless there were enough *Jewish* Christians to make their extradition worthwhile), the early date and the region to which this Eucharistic teaching has thus been thrust back seem to make "mystery-religion" influence almost inconceivable.

We conclude that what we know about the mystery-religions, along with the general character and spirit of early Christianity and St Paul, and, finally the actual evidence of the New Testament itself, critically considered, constitute three great converging probabilities, leading on the whole towards the conclusion that Christian Eucharistic ideas and practice, at the stage of their development represented by St Paul and St Mark, are in all essentials free from the influence of the mystery-religions.

# One Aspect of the Christian Fact

1937

Christianity, Newman says, has been long enough in the world to justify us in dealing with it as a fact in the world's history. It is one aspect of that Christian fact that I propose to consider in the following pages. I do not propose to enunciate any novel hypotheses, but rather to emphasise something almost platitudinous which for that very reason is perhaps too little pondered by some students and interpreters of Christian origins. I shall assume nothing as regards the inspiration or inerrancy of the New Testament texts; such assumptions as are implied with regard to the historical trustworthiness of them will appear sufficiently in the course of the article. At this moment, it will suffice to remark that if these documents allow us to discover, implied and indeed almost unconsciously implied rather than asserted on their surface, an organic "idea" lying behind them, an idea on which their very existence appears to have depended and by which the form and matter of their evidence is controlled, then at least they are a very considerable corpus of evidence as to the existence and power of that implied idea. False evidence is like window-dressing: it is most convincing when most carelessly regarded; its hollowness is exposed when we penetrate below the superficial experiences; it conveys only the impression it meant to convey. Whereas the vestiges of a real object become more and more illuminating, more and more suggestive of a truth beyond themselves, the more carefully and docilely they are examined.

Everything in Christianity, at every recorded stage of its history, has pointed forwards, on to some tremendous climax and finale of human affairs; Maranatha, come Lord Jesus; *qui venturus est iudicare vivos et mortuos.* And everything also has pointed backwards. But while the dating of the future terminus has been vague, mysterious and prophetic—of that day and hour knoweth no man—the backward index is prosaically definite; "who witnessed a good confession under Pontius Pilate"—*Tiberio imperitante supplico adfectus.* Something is going to happen, none knows when; but the certainty is based on another fact: something has happened, at a known point of place and time. Can we discover something of the inner nature of Christianity by examining what did, by its own account, actually happen; what was the history it had to tell of its own origin? It is not always the best way. The inner nature of a bird or plant is not best discovered by an examination of the egg or seed. But then the bird or plant is ready enough to let bygones be bygones, and this Christianity will never do.

Indeed we have perhaps discovered here one of the characteristics that are constitutive of Christianity's nature. The Greeks were not given to supposing that universal relevance appertained to particular historical facts or institutions. They were capable enough of appreciating the importance of such facts or institutions to those who suffered or lived under them. Thucydides can tell, with magnificent Greek objectivity and a kind of Attic irony, some moving story like that of the arrival at Athens of the news of the Sicilian disaster. And when Pericles is made by him to say that the Athenians should be passionately in love with their city he is expressing a sentiment superlatively Greek. But it would have seemed absurd to require such sentiments towards Athens from a Corinthian or a Persian who had their own city or nation to love. Herodotus scoffs at the naiveté of those who attribute an absolute value to the moral and religious norms of their own society; one nation will burn and another bury their dead; each is right from its own point of view and for its own members. It is true that the Greeks were inclined to think that they had some natural superiority over the barbarians: the defence and diffusion of Hellenism seemed to them more like a crusade than an expression of mere patriotism. But when Aristotle wishes to justify such preferential regard he appeals to their alleged *natural* excellence; barbarians were sub-human, by *nature* slaves. The typically Greek explanation of the universal relevance of Hellenism would be, not that the Greeks were an ordinary people with a supernatural vocation, but that they were extraordinary people with a natural superiority. And when Greek thinkers came to philosophise about the historic process they tended to envisage it as circular, as a perpetual *Da Capo*. If you stood exactly on the equator and proceeded always due West you would come back to your starting-point and go round and round on your own tracks. Greek thinkers had an idea that the sum of things in the same way described some vast cycle—*rursus ab integro saeclorum nascitur ordo*. The most you could hope for on this showing—and it was a rather illogical intrusion of an alien scheme of thought— was that by ethically or ritually right behaviour your soul might

39

qualify to escape from the cycle of existence to some Elysium outside of time.

Now imagine Paul of Tarsus, the short, bow-legged, keen-eyed Hellenistic Jew, whose face was at times that of a man but at times shone like an angel's, trying, with his usual proclivity for being all things to all men, to explain before the inquisitive, cultured, sophisticated Epicureans and Stoics of the Areopagus, the consonance of his teaching with all that was best in Greek thought. Idols and temples were a misconception: the Stoics could understand that point of view though they had found for themselves a *modus vivendi* with the superstitions of the masses. God was an all-pervading invisible spirit, as certain also of their own poets had said; even the Epicureans must admit that this view had *droit de cité* in educated circles. But when St Paul went on to tell them that God had "appointed a day wherein he would judge the world in equity by the man whom he had appointed; giving assurance to all by raising him up from the dead;" he was breaking right into their charmed circle; for he implied that history was a straight line to a final point, and further that the material order in man's physical body had some more than passing, more than negative relevance to men's spiritual well-being.

Christianity takes what may be called a historical view of history. History is made because men think it worth making; and they think it worth making because they judge certain ends good and attainable only by action in the historical order. And Christianity maintains that its own particular current of history, from the manger-cradle of Bethlehem to the opening of the graves at the Parousia, is of supreme and normative significance for mankind as a whole. When some Catholic modernists thirty years or so ago sought to evade the assaults of the critics of Christian origins by suggesting that it did not matter how Christianity began since the important thing was what it had become, and conceded that Jesus of Nazareth might be surrendered to the critics, since the Christ of faith was an idea of independent value, they were offending an essential Christian instinct, the instinct that will have its values incarnated in fact.

There was not the same deep-seated conflict of tendency between Christianity and Judaism as between Christianity and Hellenism. The Jewish view of the world was essentially, like the Christian, dramatic. Their knowledge of God was derived not from patient and persevering intellectual effort but from God's self-disclosure or intervention in the history of Israel, whom he had chosen to be his peculiar people. He had not waited for Abraham, Moses or David to test and reject hypothesis after hypothesis till by some metaphysical *tour de force* one of them arrived at a scientific formulation of the proof of God from causality; he had "called" Abraham, had revealed himself to him, had made promises to him, had tested and praised his obedience and faith. Similarly, he had revealed his will through Moses to Israel, after the miracles of the Exodus, to the awful accompaniment of thunder-storm and theophany. And David he had anointed to his kingly office by the hand of his prophet when he was still but a shepherd-boy at Bethlehem. In all this, God figures not as the Something Beyond which experience points to but whose inner nature it leaves mysterious, but as the Lord of Creation intervening, or one might even say interfering, with the world and the men he made but has not left to their own devices.[1] And, if one particular course of history, the history of Israel, had in Jewish eyes an absolute significance such as Attic history did not have for Athenians, this was because the God of the Jews was the Creator of the world; the Jewish people had from him a supernatural vocation and not mere natural national egoism; religious faith made them see their own nation as the centre, the protagonist, in the drama of humanity. Why had God chosen Israel? You will find an answer to that question hinted at in the second half of the book of Isaias. But the ordinary Jew was perhaps not particularly preoccupied with that answer. What he did believe, if he was a devout Israelite, was that sooner or later God, who had intervened so often, was going to intervene again, in the person of a sort of super-David, an anointed vice-gerent of God, through whom Israel was to find the accomplishment of her destiny, a redemption more tremendous than that from Egypt, a vindication more final than the overthrow of Pharaoh and his host in the Red Sea, a happiness and glory under the sway of God more complete than the golden days of David and Solomon.

Not that this Messianic hope was particularly vivid in every Jew of the first century of the Christian era. How many Christians, who recite the Creed and therein express their faith in the future

---

[1] He remains numinous ("Holy, Holy, Holy") but he is a *praesens*, nay an *agens* Numen.

coming of Christ to judge the living and the dead, find their waking moments transfigured by the radiance of this expectation? How many have, towards the Parousia, the devotion of a M. Olier or of the early Church? The Jews did not go in for Creeds; but expectation of the coming intervention of God was a factor in their general religious position whose potentialities could be exploited with some confidence by St Paul. Indeed, Judaism, in contact with the great Empires, with the Persian religion and the universalising Hellenistic philosophies, had produced, under the burden of its political oppression, cultural insignificance and apparent worldly and spiritual failure, some who had expanded and deepened the prophetic outlook till their anticipations took on a cosmic grandeur, as they taught men to await the destruction of the present order and a triumphant glorification of Israel in a new heaven or a new earth. In this they were indeed faithful to both elements in the old Israelitish belief—the element of universality, always present in the Mono-Jahvism of the authentic religion, and the element of particularity in Jahveh's predilection for his chosen people. What is to be observed is the radically *historical* character of the whole of this religious position, along with the interesting fashion in which its historicity abuts, if we may so put it, on the supra-historical plane of the Age to Come in which history finds its fulfilment and meaning, and of the God whose eternity embraces past and future alike.

Nothing of all this was rejected by the New Movement whose apostles were "turning the world upside down" in the second and third quarters of the first century A.D. Nothing of all this has ever been rejected by anything that succeeded in maintaining any sort of claim to be Christian. No re-interpretation of Christianity that tears it away from these roots in alleged spatio-temporal fact, from this preoccupation with history, this dramatic interest, but will thereby destroy an essential property of Christianity, and (according to the measure of its success) Christianity itself. This affirmation of history hardly needs illustration from the pages of the new Testament. It stares at us in the opening words of the Gospel of St Matthew: *The book of the generation of Jesus Messias, son of Abraham.* The principle of selection in St Mark's Gospel is St Peter's personal observation of what actually happened from his own call to follow Jesus up to the command to the women at the empty tomb to go, tell his disciples and Peter that "he goeth before you into Galilee". St Luke proposes to give Theophilus an authentic version of the things related by original *eyewitnesses and ministers of the word, the things which Jesus began to do and to teach.* St John, having *heard, seen and handled,* bears witness of *the life eternal which was with the Father, and hath appeared to us.* St Paul is intransigent: *if Christ be not risen again, then is our preaching vain, and your faith is also vain.*

And if we penetrate into the very core of the material comprised in the first three Gospels, we shall find the same thing. The motive determining the construction of the incidents in St Mark's Gospel is not merely a desire to focus attention on a true, or even merely a true and new teaching; it is a desire to focus attention on the authority with which the Teacher is invested, on the supernatural power with which his actions are pregnant, on the awfulness of his Person. It is thus not merely an interest in what is universally true, but in what at a particular place and time happened, in a particular figure in history. *The men wondered saying: What sort of person is this, that even the winds and the sea obey him?*[2] I doubt if it be possible to penetrate within these Markan anecdotes to any more primitive core of Christian tradition in which this constitutive interest in history is no longer discoverable. And if you turn to the matter common to St Matthew and St Luke but absent from St Mark (the so-called "Q" matter), you will find the faith of the centurion, which is praised, to be not merely a faith in God, but a faith in the supernatural power emanating from Jesus. And it is not merely loyalty to his teaching but loyalty to his person that is emphasised. Here again, it would be possible indeed to extract a collection of sayings or teachings which do not superficially emphasise more than a truth independent of its historical exponent (e.g. much of St Luke's Sermon on the Plain) but there is nothing in the "Q" material itself to authorise such discrimination.[3] Historical criticism cannot authorise any reconstruction of a Christian message independent of historical fact. It may be suggested, in passing, that this point does not receive adequate emphasis in such a work as Harnack's *Wesen des Christentums,* or any presentation of Christianity that limits its essence to a purified universal ethic and a doctrine of the Fatherhood of God.

[2] *Mt* VIII 27.

[3] St Luke should rather be held, in his effort to reduce the *Jewish* reference of his material, to have at times torn away therewith also the basically Christian reference to historical happening.

And we may go further, and take a deeper view. This categorical affirmativeness in regard to history is one part of the general assertive character of Christianity. Christianity is at the opposite pole from the Kantian emphasis on "As if": "act as if your will were free, your soul immortal, and God a reality", such might be called the Kantian Gospel. Thus, in *Religion within the Limits of Reason Alone,* Kant makes his way to the *idea* of Man in his moral perfection, as eternally existent in God, God's only-begotten Son, the Word of God by which all things else are made[4]: but at the same time Kant holds that "to demand that we be certified that this Ideal has actually been manifested in history, or to require that its authority be attested by miracles, is proof of a 'moral unbelief' which does not recognise the Ideal as a sufficient motive for action".[5] Kant "presents the sacred history of Christianity as presenting under a 'mystical husk', a universally valid truth".[6] Whether Kant's attitude is right or wrong is not, be it noted, our immediate concern here. Our purpose is to contrast the primacy, for Kant, of the ethical "Ought" with the primacy for Christianity, of the factual "Is". For Kant, the historical empirical order is too coarse to form any integral part of the basis of religion; for Hegel, on the other hand, it may be said the transcendental order was identified with the historical. For Christianity, the historical order is *invaded* by a *real,* yet *abidingly transcendent,* order. And both as regards the transcendence and the invasion, Christianity is categorically assertoric. Of its insistence on historical fact something has already been said. But its emphasis on the reality of the supra-historical order is not less strong. It is epitomised in the parable of the Rich Fool, whose horizon had been voluntarily limited to temporal welfare, and who heard God say "This night they require thy soul of thee"; it is implicit in the appeal to the example of divine munificence in the indiscriminate bounty of sun and rain; it is the nerve of the teaching about the coming Reign of God, in which at last the discord between the divine will and human rebellion will be resolved.

I anticipated, a moment ago, by hinting that Christianity not only insisted on the essential, vital, significance of something that had actually, so it says, happened; but that it regards this happening as essentially the invasion of the historical order by

[4] C. C. Webb, *Kant's Philosophy of Religion,* (Oxford, 1926) pp. 117f.
[5] *Ibid.* p. 119.
[6] *Ibid.* p. 127.

the transcendent, supra-historical order. It may be well to develop this point a little. It has already been said that Judaism and Christianity are both radically dramatic, historical, in their convictions; like Judaism Christianity looks forward to a supersession of the historical order, at the end of time, by the supra-historical order, the Age to Come. What then was the essential conflict between the two religions? It lay deeper than a difference about external observances. And it was not merely that Christianity accepted, and the Jews rejected, Jesus of Nazareth as latest of the prophets. The two disciples on the road to Emmaus had hoped, once, that Jesus was the redeemer of Israel: that hope seemed shattered by his death; yet they still regarded him as a prophet. No, for Christianity, there had come upon the scene something greater than David, than Jonah, than the Temple, than the Law. The Law and the prophets were until John, but now it is implied that the curtain of history has risen on something still more tremendous. On what?

It is essential, if my meaning is to be grasped, that it be understood that the Reign of God is not, in Jewish New Testament language, a vague human ideal like the Jerusalem which Blake proposed to build in England's green and pleasant land. Man does not build, cannot found, the Reign of God: let God arise and let his enemies be scattered. The Reign of God is always something which as to time and mode of its coming, as also for its effective realisation, depends simply and solely on the wisdom, will and power of God himself. Of that time and that hour knoweth no man; the sun shall be darkened, the moon shall not give light, the stars shall fall from the sky, and the powers of the sky shall be shaken—this prelude of universal catastrophe is no more subject to man than was the deluge, and *a fortiori* the Act which it ushers in will be an Act of God and not of man.

And secondly, it is essential to realise that this Act of God is to be final and definitive; it will terminate the drama of history, it will mean the final separation of the sheep from the goats; it will mean unqualified bliss for the good, and eternal banishment from the divine presence for the wicked. So it is depicted in the Markan "Q" tradition; and all this is consonant with Judaism. All this again is accepted by St Paul for whom the future coming of Christ is an unquestioned *datum,* and has features indistinguishable from much that is found in regard to it in St Matthew's Gospel. The future to which Christianity persistently looks forward is one in which God will be All in All. Men will survive, indeed; and if we may make a conjecture based on Christianity's emphasis on the dual precept of charity, "Thou shalt love the Lord thy God with all thy heart . . . and thou shalt love thy neighbour as thyself"; if we may lay stress on the social character of one or two pictures (symbolic, surely) of the Age to Come—the wedding celebration, the reclining at the table with the Son of Man—and on the very idea of a Reign over numerous subjects; then we shall suppose that there will be something like a Kantian Kingdom of Wills, a universal harmony of the wills and hearts of the elect, close knit and for ever inseparable in the bond of the divine will and charity. And we must not think of this as a union of mere souls, for Christianity ratified the Pharisaic tenet of a Resurrection of the Body. But in all this super-organism, the life-blood of the Will of God will circulate free and unimpeded: in his Will will be our perfect peace.

So much for the future. But what has already *happened,* according to New Testament Christianity? I venture to suggest that the full tremendousness of the Christian claim be sought for in the Synoptic Gospels. And we are offered the following clue: when in the Synoptic Gospels not merely the prelude to the End of history but the actual End itself is depicted, there is regularly a figure at the centre of the picture who is identified with Jesus of Nazareth. A specially clear case of this identification is, of course, the remarkable canvas of the sheep and the goats in Chapter 25 of Matthew, where eternal sentence is passed on the nations *by the Son of Man,* a title applied only in the New Testament, and only by Jesus himself (except once by St Stephen in Acts, and twice in the Apocalypse), to Jesus. It has, of course, been pointed out before now that the fusion of the Son of Man idea with the Suffering Servant idea is a great triumph of creative religious genius; we pause here to lay stress on the fact that the homeless persecuted Son of Man remains for all that, in the New Testament, one who will hereafter come in a glory no less than that belonging, in the Book of Daniel, to the one like unto a son of Man.

We talk of the Second Coming of Christ, though it is not a New Testament phrase: for in the New Testament what we call Second Coming is simply Parousia, Coming. And we regard it as a peculiar novelty of the Christian Messianic belief as contrasted with Jewish, that it has the idea of a *double* coming of the

Messias. But what needs to be clearly realised is that it is not the *Second* Coming which is a novelty, but the *First*. Jews were prepared for a Messias who should come in glory and power to terminate the historic process; what was surprising to them was that this Coming in glory should be anticipated and fore-shadowed by a hidden coming in humiliation, ignominy and apparent failure. The Son of Man on the throne of his glory they could believe in; the Son of Man who had not where to lay his head was an enigma to them.

But this enigma suggests the solution to our problem. *Operatio sequitur esse*. The function of the Son of Man at his glorious Parousia will be to establish the glorious Kingdom of God. His function in his historical, humble first Coming, a Coming so different in quality yet substantially identical as being the Coming of the same person, was to establish the same Kingdom in historical lowliness and gradualness.

That is what is meant, it may be suggested, by the "Mysteries" of the Reign of God, and why those Mysteries are wrapped up in the parables of growth. There is no growth in the post-historic manifestation of God's Reign; process and change will cease with the Coming. But growth is characteristic of the historic order; growth and struggle, advance and setback, capture and casualty. The Reign of God is like a mustard seed, like leaven. Here is an enigma parallel to that of the Son of Man who had not where to lay his head. And it is all one enigma. For *If I by the finger of God cast out devils, then the Reign of God has come upon you;* this is manifestly untrue the Pharisees might retort; it is manifestly irreconcilable you might suppose, with Christ's own prophecies of the Parousia, nay with the prayer he taught: *Adveniat regnum tuum*. Yet it is no more irreconcilable than the First with the Second Coming of the Son of Man.

Hence it is that Jesus can say to his disciples: "many prophets and just men desired to see what you look upon, and saw it not and to hear what you hear, and heard it not". For the prophets and just men looked forward to the coming of the Reign of God; and the disciples are eye-witnesses of its mysterious inception.

Thus there is one Son of Man but two comings of the Son of Man; and there is one Reign of God but a twofold realisation thereof, one in the historic order, the other post-historic; and there is organic inter-relation of the historic with the post-historic realisation. The one can be regarded as the anticipation of the other, or the second as the prolongation or repetition of the first. Personally I am convinced that the truer view, and the one more consonant with the mode of expression in the Synoptic Gospels material, is that which regards the post-historic Reign as the Reign of God, and the historic Reign as its real anticipation. The acorn is not to be the explanation of the future oak tree, but the oak tree is the explanation of the aforetime acorn. Glory is not so much grace transformed, as grace is glory hidden.

Note then that the essence of the Christian position, if the above interpretation is correct, involves the overlapping, the intersection, of time and eternity. Eternity is brought down into time in the Christian dispensation: the believer has already passed from death to life. We are not concerned here to grapple with the philosophical obscurities that may be thought to surround such a conviction. We are concerned with what, historically regarded, Christianity *is*. And we may point out, in confirmation of this general interpretation, that for St Paul, the Resurrection, not Christ's but ours, is a *future* event, a feature of the Parousia; yet it has already taken place, in baptism whereby we were incorporated in Christ. In fact the key to the understanding of Christianity is precisely this conviction that the beatific future of redeemed humanity is already contained, though not exhausted, in its militant present. And once this key is accepted, it is found applicable at page after page of the New Testament. Thus in I *Peter* the Christians are regarded as possessed of a new life-principle which is incorruptible; they are severally living stones, and are to be built up into a spiritual house, a temple for the true worship of God through Jesus Christ. It is not difficult to discern beneath the different imagery the same conviction that the Reign of God has found its historical incarnation in the life of the Christian society, what St Paul calls the Israel of God. For the Kingdom of wills, the "heavenly Jerusalem" as we might call it in Biblical language, has its real, three-dimensional, historic, body-and-soul anticipation in the Christian society with its historical unity, its universal mission of sanctification, and its Christ-derived authority. And if Christianity is true, that society will remain, as the ark of salvation, and the embodiment of God's will for humanity, till Christ comes in glory to bring the Church out of its larval condition into the unfading glory which will disclose its true nature.

# Unification

1937

From Thales and the Hylozoists of the sixth century down to the Flight of the alone to the alone of Plotinus, the problem of unity, coupled as it was from the time of Socrates onwards with that of the unification of human life, may be said to have been basic to Greek philosophy. The observation is not without interest since the Greek tradition was essentially uninfluenced by Christianity and may therefore serve as independent confirmation of the thesis that the Catholic religion, in its claim to present men with a means of unification resting on a revelation of ultimate unity, does in fact offer to fill a lacuna, and to answer a vital need which man can discover but cannot by himself supply. If this thesis can be maintained, it would then be desirable to turn back to the origins of the Catholic religion, to seek an answer to the question whether or not this far-reaching claim, as it presents itself today, is in essence one with the claim involved in that "auctoritas" in which the original Gospel was invested. Ordinarily, in England, we tend to proceed in the reverse order, attempting to decide, by examination of the records of its origins, what line of development primitive Christianity ought to have followed, and how far anything that goes by the name of Christianity today can validly claim to be the identical living reality presupposed by the New Testament documents. However, it is not so easy to forecast the man on the basis of an analytic study of the infant as it is to establish the identity of the man with the child of thirty years ago. Moreover, if it can be shown that nothing but the Catholic religion can fill the lacuna in human experience, the question of what Christianity might have become would be relatively uninteresting unless it must have become Catholicism.

Unity is indeed a controlling and inspiring principle of human experience and activity in all its phases and at every stage. An individual may be said to begin to have experience from the time when first, from the vague totality of his consciousness, some one feature or group of features stands out as such, and, so standing, is distinguished from—set over against—the rest; it thus becomes the object of attention, while the remaining content of consciousness serves as its background and frame. The ancients defended their notion of a harmony of the spheres by the acute remark that its complete and unchanging regularity gave our attention no moment of contrast through which to grasp it. It is the contrast of one element with the rest of consciousness that makes attention possible.

Attention itself, then, is a selective act, but is not arbitrarily selective; it could not come into act unless it were solicited by the quantitative or qualitative peculiarities of that feature in the vague content of consciousness, to which in particular it addresses itself; while on the other hand these peculiarities could not stimulate attention unless they appealed in some way to some special potentiality in the needs or interests of the conscious subject. A farmer will be blind to the strategic possibilities of a tract of country whose agricultural qualities may leap to his eyes; and an artist may never read the geological lessons conveyed by that same landscape to his scientific companion.

The principle of unity is thus operative from the beginnings of conscious life: operative as the constitutive principle of the object of attention, and operative at the same time as a character of the act of attention. Indeed, it is not only operative thus in the act and the particular object; it is latent in the vague totaliy of the field of consciousness, and in the subject hidden within and behind the act. It is latent in the vague totality of consciousness; for the "pure manifold" is unthinkable and impossible; a "many" can neither be nor be affirmed unless it be in some way one. I can without effort think of three horses—for they share one specific nature. I can think at once of a horse, a house, and a hill; for they are all corporeal, and can be grouped in space. It is only with difficulty that I can think in a simple act of a dog, an act of mercy and a mathematical surd; and scarcely at all unless I regard them for instance, as all alike possible elements of a conscious experience; that is, as diverse features of a *unitary* whole. And on the other hand the totality of a consciousness is one, in the last resort, because it is the correlative of one conscious subject, the conscious "I", the hidden author of the act of attention.

To speak of an act of attention is, however, to remind ourselves that conscious life, among men, is not a state but a process; it thus becomes important to consider its direction, the law of its development and the end towards which it moves.

We mentioned above the needs and interest of the subject which alone make possible its stimulation by particular features in the field of consciousness. These needs and interests are presupposed by any particular act of attention, and their origin must therefore be sought, deeper than fully conscious experience, in the very nature of the subject himself. The particular act will be the subject's endeavour to express in conscious life the potentialities with which he finds himself naturally endowed; to express, in fact, himself; to transmute the latent unity of individuality into the articulate unity of personality—all this by means of, in union with, and yet over against, the world revealed in conscious experience.

Again, the achievement of articulate selfhood is correlative to the organisation of the vague totality of experience into an ordered world where part answers to part and each element gives and receives significance and enrichment by virtue of its inherence with the others in the whole.

For the principle of unity, whose ubiquity and importance we have been considering, is not the bare unity of arithmetic; it is not a "one" whose simplicity has been reached by subtraction. It is, more or less in all its manifestations, a "one" that dominates, organises, and makes possible a multiplicity; a "unity" achieved by inclusion and order; an ordered richness. The act of attention itself is a unity of volitional and cognitive elements with at least an undercurrent of emotion. The "simplest" object of attention (I abstract for the moment from God) reveals on inspection a duality of the "what it is" and the "that it is". There is no need to waste many words in emphasising the multiplicity within the finite subject itself—a multiplicity already visible in the union of origin, process and term in every act.

Such again, as we move up from the tentative beginnings of consciousness towards the mountain-summits of its highest achievements here below, is the unity revealed in the objects of its attention and of its devotion. A great work of art must be one not merely with the unity of the canvas on which it is expressed, but with a rich and organised unity of its own, a unity indeed dependent upon and expressing the unified artistic personality of its creator, but revealing or suggesting hidden depths of a unity beyond any individual experience. The sciences have each their unity, and within each there is organisation and interplay of unities within and against unities. And in political life, no man can serve two masters. You cannot at the same time be the complete German and the complete French patriot. You can be an excellent Pennsylvanian as well as an excellent American, but that is because these two loyalties are "hierarchised"; they stand on different planes and, ideally speaking, do not conflict. Monogamy itself is a natural expression of the control exercised by unity on all life's higher manifestations.

Hitherto we have confined our attention primarily to a single consciousness. But a man finds himself one of a society (actual or potential) of conscious individuals. There is a sense in which he has more direct knowledge of others than of himself; for human attention from the first hours of babyhood is turned outwards, away out towards the mother's breast and the bed's warmth, the mother's smile and the mother's voice; only secondarily, by a reflex act of attending to his acts, does the child by slow and painful degrees learn of himself as contrasted with the not-self. He may be said to be his parent's child, his brother's baby brother, before he is to himself, himself. He is a member in act while still only potentially a person.

We thus enter upon a whole world of fresh unities—the family and the nation, the municipality, the cultural epoch, each real and rich and important only insofar as it is one; one in nature to begin with, and one in aspiration and ideal. And out beyond and within them all is the unity of humanity.

It may be objected that there is little sense in speaking of the unity of humanity, if anything more be intended than the specific unity of human nature. But the objection may be met by the observation that the individual himself is only a unified personality in potency; his unity has to be realised by personal activity. (*dikaioi gignometha dikaia prattontes*). So too the unity of humanity is a potential unity; a unity *de jure*, a unity of ideal. A unity of the future or the beyond, it may be said; but a unity so real that it needs must colour our local and individual feeling, thinking and willing. For wherever there is potentiality and desire, the law of present progress is derived from the nature of the future goal. In particular, no solution of the ultimate problems of any individual's experience can be valid "for him" unless it is valid "for all"; there is an undertone of absoluteness—of catholicism—in even our most whimsical personal affirmations. I cannot hold as true for me what I am not prepared to assert as true for all. There is a social responsibility involved in every thought and action, in every act of self-determination. Every poet is a "vates". Every devotee is a prophet; and of every devotee we have a right to ask: "By what authority doest thou these things?"

The potential unity of humanity, and all its partial realisations, depend on some means of bridging the gulf between subject and subject; that means is the material world which is, by reason of our bodies, our common home. The body is thus no mere encumbrance of the self; it is not only the vehicle of sense-experience but is further the link between intellect and intellect, will and will. It colours and conditions our experience through and through, making us "a little lower than the angels"; making us incapable from the start of natural solitariness. Already, then, we see that the unity to which man tends is not a sheer invisible kingdom of God or of Ends, but is a historical or quasi-historical Society, in which spiritual values are incarnated in material realities and temporal events; a way of life in which not "soul helps flesh more now than flesh helps soul".

Let us revert for a moment to the individual and his quest of personal unity by a unification of his experience. We saw that the human act is a response to an object one in itself—at least as perceived—and other than the background against which it is set; and this response finds its reason in some need of the agent, a need which the object is to supply, and which is therefore a need of unity, and itself a unitary need. But any human act is the act of a subject whose needs and potentialities of development and enrichment are manifold and of very various depths and qualities. This subject lies deeper than the particular need inspiring any particular act; to him the needs go back, and he is thus the deeper reason for his acts. But this means that any particular act is one stage in the continuous process by which the subject moves in quest of a good in which he will find his own unity, the supply of the deep need which is in some sense identical in scope with his self; while any particular object will be sought as an element in our means to this ultimate unitary good.

The act, then, if it is to give full value to the agent, must be a "member" in an organised activity of the whole person such that it gives scope, expression and perfection to the single personality. A natural dialectic carries us up and out from the narrow confines of a comparatively insignificant single act into a world of organised and enriching experience, shot through and through with gleams of some ultimate unity where the real and the good in all their fullness are identified each with each. An act is now seen as a single peak jutting out from a whole mountain-system; or as a verse in a poem, drawing beauty from, and adding beauty to, the context in which it occurs. In proportion to the completeness of the individual's actuation, and to the extent to which he had developed from individuality to personality; in proportion to his "mastery" over self and situation, and to the real humanisation of his activity in all its fibres, such that each element of it is unmistakably impressed with his personal "style" and fulfils his real intentions: in that proportion, the necessity increases of regarding his whole life as one act. He is no longer distracted between conflicting or unrelated claims; no longer does he live on the surface of himself and his world, as a *eutrapelos* or even almost a "dissociated personality"; he has probed to the deep heart of reality and has found there the desideratum of the depths of his own heart—the *unum necessarium* which alone can give sense and significance to the changing features of human experience; the *summum bonum* which, itself not comparable with the lesser ends of life, is yet the only reason why they can serve as ends for human effort.

It is true that this unification of the subject is never completely achieved in our ordinary lives; but what is possible, and necessary so far as possible, is that there should at least be a unitary unifying "habit" underlying all the habits and acts of an individual's life; and since habit is subordinate to act, this means that there must be, and that there must have been contact with, an object one and all-comprehending, an object transcending the values and exceeding the reality of every particular object; an object capable of penetrating and satisfying the depths of personality; that is to say a Lover and a Beloved, unchanging, absolute, divine—not a mere vague universal, but the possible object of particular acts and the abiding sustenance of a personal habit; a Reality, then, never absent from the profundities of the self, and moreover presenting itself, at least from time to time, within the borders of the self's experience, in a concrete embodiment capable of serving as a focus for the discharge of act.

The *Republic* of Plato might serve as an elaboration of much that has been said so far. That magnificent dialogue is no mere political treatise, it is a profound study in the dialectics of human action—or, if the phrase be preferred, of the implications and the worth of moral goodness. This duality of aspect in the *Republic* authorises us to carry out the results we have attained hitherto to the social sphere. Already we have seen that, so far as concerns conscious human experience, a man may be considered to achieve social membership before he attains to individual self-possession; indeed it is precisely by the exercise of membership that he reaches himself, just as his personality may be the best and greatest of his services to society. From a more philosophical point of view, again, he needs and seeks society as a great reservoir of the real richness on which his spirit must feed; individual experiences are heightened in value and become more personal by union in a great corporate whole, in the same way as a single act is enriched by articulation in a whole organic life. And the society the human individual seeks must, at long last, be the society which is in principle and right the one incorporation of humanity; anything short of this is an impoverishing provincialism. Since, moreover, the deepest human need, as we have seen, is of God; it is inevitable that the supreme human society will be not a world-state or an ecumenical economic organisation, but a universal church; a society in which human experiences are unified, in reference to God by concrete association in historical and actual fact, and by actual events and real acts incarnated in the material order. The need of a church, of a universal church, is no more excrescence upon religion; it corresponds with the very constitution of human nature and the natural orientation of human activity; and it is implied most deeply in man's creatureliness, in his natural tendency to God. Moreover, the church's position as the supreme human unification among other human associations will correspond to God's position above other human objects; the church will be an *ou sunarithmomenon agathon;* adherence and loyalty to her will hinder no other legitimate loyalties; indeed it will involve and inspire other loyalties, since it is to be the rationale of them all. It will be a definite adherence in a particular society; but any attempt to put the claims of the church on the same plane as, and therefore in conflict with, those of other societies would at once bring the church herself down to the level of a human organisation.

It is at this point that the danger of superficial views becomes acute. The idea of a church suggests at once a visible institution, and does so rightly; but the visible institution has got to be seen as the material and (at present) anticipatory embodiment of a great spiritual reality—of the spiritual unity of humanity, a unity found precisely at the deepest levels of human experience. As such, the church becomes an imperative necessity for the wellbeing of the individual life. The fact may be illustrated especially by reference to the implicit "absoluteness" of all human affirmations. We have seen that in asserting an opinion a man is necessarily making some sort of a claim to legislate for all men—for humanity as a whole; this is because truth is one, humanity is one, and reality is one. And every human thought and word and deed—such is the spiritual continuity, actual or potential, of mankind—has incalculable repercussions through time and space. This being so, the responsibility of an unaided decision on the more fundamental issues becomes too heavy for the shoulders of a solitary individual. If we were endowed from birth with an intuitive certainty in regard to ultimate metaphysical and religious truth, the matter would be otherwise. But in actual fact these truths are above and beyond our unaided power adequately to apprehend and grasp and live by. Hence it comes about that, apart from the Church, men's opinions on the matters which most concern us all have only such stability and reasonableness, more or less, as their political creeds. Failing to reach a conclusion which he knows to be true, a man consciously or unconsciously falls back on the ideas suggested by the environment in which he finds himself, or with equal irrationality reacts against them.

Now if there exists, and if we can recognise, a classic incorporation of the spiritual life of humanity with a valid claim to present a true account of the Reality of which we stand in need, then these other presentations of religion can be judged by its norm, and we can see how much "saving truth" there is in Anglo-Catholicism or militant evangelicalism. But if there is no such norm then there is no means of discriminating and every man must fall back on his own personal judgment; it is not, he will have to contend, because Anglicanism teaches a certain set of doctrines that he holds those doctrines as each and all true; but he is an Anglican because those doctrines are severally convincing to him.

The root objection to this position is that the functions of subject and object have been reversed. We have seen how all along the actual life of man is controlled by the unities which "impose themselves" on a man's attention, which appeal to a need of unity within him, and which when reacted upon by him, do in fact progressively actualise the potential unity of his hitherto undeveloped personality. The deeper the stratum of experience concerned, the graver is the need of the reality and real priority of the unifying object of human activity. Is there not a legend of some mythical Daedalus who fell in love with his own statues? And are not those who construct their own metaphysico-religious systems his modern representatives? They are weaving, out of their own natural or acquired powers and property, a Reality which they only need precisely because they have it not already; and *nemo dat quod non habet*. Thus they have relapsed into subjectivism, and virtually proclaim with Pythagorus "A man is the measure of all things" each for himself.

Subjectivism, however, is not the end of their story. For the claim to absolute validity is one which cannot be bleached out of human affirmations. Yet each individual, apart from the "Church" whose necessity we are maintaining, is bound to recognise that his own judgment on these ultimate matters, however sincerely and painstakingly it may have been formed, is as little likely to be correct as that of the countless others who with equal opportunity have formed an equally painstaking and sincere, but very different view. And the recognition of this leads inevitably, in the long run, though not necessarily in the case of a particular individual, to agnosticism.

Now agnosticism is plainly not the position towards which man is by nature directed. The whole of our analysis of human experience and activity shows that the need for an object attained in consciousness as the specifying, unifying correlative of our potencies, already operative in the most superficial of our still scarcely human acts, only becomes more urgent at the deeper levels. It attains its maximum when we envisage human life at its deepest spiritual level and in its potential corporate unity of all individuals through all history. The spiritual capacities and history of mankind are an impossible futility, its spiritual life an incredible illusion, unless the "Church" of which we have spoken is a real possibility.

The "Church" however is not precisely the ultimate object, but rather at once the medium through which the individual is unified with his fellowmen in God (the ultimate unity), and also the preliminary actualisation of the potential unity of all humanity. In its character as such it will therefore be a divine gift to man, since otherwise man, the potentially one, would have created from himself precisely what he lacked—an impossible feat. We should expect therefore to find it claiming a divine origin, and its founder claiming at least to be the supreme and definitive divine envoy to man.

We can go still further. If religion, as we have envisaged it hitherto, is man's quest of God, it is, still more fundamentally, God's self-donation to men; and these two aspects, the human and the divine, are both aspects of one indissoluble fact. Thus by incorporation into the "Church", the unified "communion" of the human religious quest, a man is in some way incorporated with God; and God is in some way "oned" with man—with humanity as a whole.

How is that unity effected? If we retrace the history of the extant Christian Church, we shall eventually reach a period at which it existed as a historical and Christian reality only in the person of its founder, from whom, as from a source, its broadening stream has flowed in a continuous process of development and increase. In him, focused to a point, we shall seek the actuality of all that the society's growth will have by slow degrees to articulate and bring home to souls. In him we shall seek a union of divine and human of a unique and personal kind. In him, man's quest of God, man in quest of God, find their fulfilment in union with the object sought and that object's self-revelation. He will be man at the term of his potentiality, in complete and absolute self-surrender to God; and, still more deeply, he will be God assuming man into a union of identity without absorption. And all this, for the sake of the society, and with a view to the due perfection of all individuals by complete incorporation into the society—into that unity of the society which finds its focus of total integration in the person of its founder, so that he and it are one: he, the head, and it, his Body.

Thus it would appear that a definite continuity binds the moments of human development from the dawn of specifically human experience up to its highest reaches here below: the bond consists in a certain unitary capacity, itself one aspect of human nature itself in all its "creatureliness" and dependence. And the actualising of this capacity, while on the one hand quite outside the range of anything that man can do or even claim for himself, will yet on the other hand (in the given historical order) not be effected by any dispensation short of a universal religious society "visibly one", in and through which individuals can come face to face with God in a concrete focus—in short, with God Incarnate: with God as love in an ecstasy of self-donation, summoning man to a participation in that same ecstasy of love.

Can it be necessary at this stage to spend long over the theory which envisages the one society as capable of persisting in a state of disunity in fact and faith? The basic vice of any such idea is that, if the society is not actually one, with the "visible" unity that essentially belongs to a fellowship of spirits whose intercourse is by means of the material world, then it falls to the individual to find for himself—and each for himself—the *ratio* of the unity of the separate members. But in that case, it is no longer the one society which unifies humanity one and all, but the individuals who create each for himself an "ideal" of human and religious unity; it is not united humanity legislating for the individual, but the individual imposing his own ideas upon anyone who will listen. The natural order is reversed, and we are back in subjectivism, and on the road to agnosticism. Catholicism, or rather some such society as we have depicted, is the only way out from the trammels of solipsism.

In any case, there is no need to show that the essential claim of the Catholic Church corresponds to what I have argued to be the essential "need" of human nature. It would remain to show how the records of the New Testament present, in the language and thought-frame of Judaism, a society and a person whose basic claims are identical with those of the modern Church; a claim to bring to the world a revelation and a divine gift which all men need but which man is radically incapable of acquiring by his own efforts; a claim to unify men in a brotherhood transcending all contingent barriers, a brotherhood whose own unifying principle is God in Christ; a claim finally to be the introduction into human affairs of a new principle, a new creation, a life which is identically live, personal, active, concrete, unifying, a love that unifies even the two great commandments, because it is itself at once human and divine.

# Authority in the New Testament

1939

The following pages offer a quite elementary study of the notion of authority in the religion of the New Testament, insofar as that authority concerns not action but belief. In the sphere of action, the role of authority in society will hardly be questioned except by anarchists; its role in the region of belief, as a means to the perfect freedom of the divine friendship has often been held suspect.

It will be convenient to begin by distinguishing authority from ordinary "evidence" of a proposition's truth. That the whole is equal to the sum of its parts is a truth held not on authority but on its intrinsic self-evidence. That the cube root of 343 is 7 is a truth held—by me—not on its immediate self-evidence, but still on the intrinsic evidence of a process of arithmetic, at no stage of which am I dependent on anything other than self-evident truths, my own reason, and my own memory. In another sphere of thought, my views on the critical problem of the literary relations of the first three Gospels are based not on authority but on evidence. But when a doctor tells me that I have an obscure disease for which a certain kind of diet is requisite, I may have no evidence of an intrinsic kind, but accept his verdict on his authority as an honest expert.

There are truths which can be held either on authority or on intrinsic evidence. Thus I may accept the answer to a complicated sum on the authority of another who has worked it out, or I may prefer to work it out for myself and reach the same answer.

Thus we may say that the authority for a religious or other belief or opinion is the person or persons, the institution or document, whose word determines our assent to that belief or opinion.[1] And in fact, since a word is the expression of a thought, we may say that an authority for a belief is always, in the last resort, a thinker, a person, capable of establishing contact with

[1] Sometimes an authority whose credentials are not above suspicion may influence belief without being sufficient to determine it.

those who are to believe. Thus our prime authority for the historical opinion that Christianity had made great strides in Pontus by the second decade of the second century is the younger Pliny, overheard by us in his famous correspondence with Trajan. The authorities for our reconstruction of the Peloponnesian War are mainly Thucydides and Xenophon. In most such cases, the authority of the positive witness conspires, to some extent, with the tacit authority of those who were in a position to have independent knowledge of the subject and likely to protest against erroneous accounts of it. In some cases this combination of positive and tacit witness is sufficient to produce a "motive of credibility" whose certainty is "evident".[2] But it should be noticed that the intrinsic evidence in any such case, may relate only to the credibility of the authority; the truth to which the authority bears witness is then accepted merely "on the word" of the authority. In other cases, the word of the authority may be confirmed by direct evidence of the fact alleged.

The early Protestants proposed the Bible as the supreme authority for the determination of Christian doctrine. The First Vatican Council implied that such authority is possessed by the Church, and defined that this authority is wielded by the Pope when he speaks *ex cathedra.* The Liberal Protestant may be said to reject by implication all supernatural authority, and is inclined to contrast "religions of authority" with the "religion of the spirit". This is perhaps a special case of the opposition falsely alleged between authority and freedom. Freedom involves the absence of external interference with the proper self-realisation of an agent; but when that agent is, as such, a member of a social whole (man is a "political animal", says Aristotle), the *legitimate*[3] operation of social authority is not an interference with, but a requisite condition of, his self-realisation.

Meanwhile, we may observe that insofar as a man is to be considered as a single personality, it is only in a rather special sense that we can say that he submits to himself as an authority; this could only mean a reliance, in the present, on his memory of a verdict given by himself in the past. On the whole, "private judgment" may rightly be contrasted with "assent to authority".

[2] Thus, that Charles I was beheaded is a truth accepted by us on the authority of witnesses whose credibility is overwhelmingly certain.
[3] The qualification is vital.

It stands to reason, however, that it is by an act of private judgment that we decide that such or such an authority has a valid claim on our submission.

Having determined that the claim of a *soi-disant* authority is valid, we naturally accord to its determinations a credence corresponding to the certainty or probability with which they are propounded. Thus if we decide on the veracity and competence of a witness who tells us that he certainly saw a certain action performed—that he saw Caesar cross the Rubicon, or Charles I lose his head—we believe with certainty that this is true. If a witness, however, tells us only that a certain proposition is probable, we may find ourselves in possession of some other information or evidence that deprives it of its probability. It follows that a religious teacher who proclaims doctrines as certain and claims credence for them as such simply on his own authority, is implicitly claiming infallibility as a teacher of religion. Or, to put the matter another way, if religious belief is to be determined on authority, and if such belief is to be categoric and certain, the authority must be held to be infallible. If I am expected to believe with certainty, *on the authority of Church or Bible,* that Jesus of Nazareth was God Incarnate—then I am being asked to believe that Church or Bible is infallible. If, on the other hand, I hold only as probable the categoric propositions of a given authority, it is obvious that I reject the claims of that authority *qua* determining authority, though I may be giving weight to its assertions as evidence or to its authority as being probably valid. A man who said "I think that the immortality of the soul is probable because it is asserted with such unhesitating conviction by Christianity in its doctrine of the resurrection" would obviously not be accepting the determining authority of Christianity (else he would hold immortality as certain), and he would be taking the assertions made by Christianity as data to be argued from, as data of "religious experience"; he reserves his private judgment and does not submit to authority. It follows that no *soi-disant* authority can retract any of its past categoric determinations of doctrine without at the same time refuting its claim. Had its claim been valid, its past categoric propositions would have been true and it would have been incapable of retracting them at present.

The Christianity of the great tradition—of Catholicism before 1054 as of Catholicism, Eastern Orthodoxy and old-fashioned Biblical Protestantism since—has always been a religion of authority and infallibility. Even those early heretics the Gnostics sought to preserve this note of authority for their own aberrations, appealing from the public tradition of the apostolic churches to an alleged esoteric tradition of their own. The purpose of this essay is to show, on the assumption that the New Testament documents are historically trustworthy, that the note of authority is original in Christianity.

Christianity has always claimed to inherit from the Old Testament. *Novum Testamentum,* says St Augustine, *in Vetere latet; Vetus in Novo patet*: the New Testament is implicit in the Old Testament, and the Old is explained in the New. The Old Testament presents the question of authority in a vivid form in the episode in which Moses is commissioned to lead the children of Israel out of Egypt (*Exodus* III, IV):

> God said again to Moses: Go, gather together the ancients of Israel, and thou shalt say to them: the Lord God of your fathers . . . hath appeared to me saying: Visiting I have visited you, and I have said the word to bring you forth out of the affliction of Egypt.

Moses objects: "They will not believe me—but they will say: the Lord hath not appeared to thee". And to meet this objection he is given a miraculous sign to accredit him—"That they may believe", saith he, "that the Lord God of their fathers . . . hath appeared to thee". The supposition is that miracles are due to divine intervention and, if manifested in due moral connection with a claim to speak in God's name, are a divine authentication of that claim.[4] It should be noticed that a demand for a sign in case a claim to authority is not already sufficiently accredited, is not only licit but necessary in order to justify assent to the claim. It is illicit and a proof of infidelity when a sufficient motive of credibility is already present to the inquirer.

The prophets, like Moses, claimed to be spokesmen of God: "The Lord took me when I followed the flock, and the Lord said to me: go, prophesy to my people Israel. And now, hear thou the word of the Lord" (*Amos* VII 15f). "I heard the voice of the Lord. And he said: go, and thou shalt say to this people"

---

[4] This is commonsense reasoning and perfectly valid.

(*Isaias* VI 8f). "And the word of the Lord came to me, saying: go, and cry in the ears of Jerusalem, saying: Thus saith the Lord." And again their claim is accredited by miracle, by fulfilment of some one or other of their predictions, or by the agreement of their message with the type of already accepted prophetic messages; often, doubtless, the high moral character and evident sincerity of the prophet played their part in winning assent to their claim.

In fact, the religion of the Old Testament is essentially a religion of authority, because it is a religion of public revelation. "The Lord" is not inferred as the first cause of phenomena; he is the God who with an outstretched arm brought the Israelites out of Egypt—demonstrating his reality and power by personal action in history; and the Israelites are to practise justice, piety and humility not simply as obligations imposed by natural law but as the revealed will and precepts of the Lord. Such revelational religion is accepted by the believer not on its intrinsic evidence but on grounds of credibility.

This authoritarian note may be illustrated, from one of the latest books of the Old Testament, by the passage in I *Macabees* IV where we learn that the Jews, uncertain (it would seem) as to the right disposal of the stones of the altar polluted by Antiochus Epiphanes, stored them apart till a prophet should come and settle the matter:

> Judas . . . considered about the altar of holocausts that had been profaned . . . And a good counsel came into their minds, to pull it down . . . so they threw it down. And they laid up the stones in the mountain of the temple in a convenient place, till there should come a prophet, and give answer concerning them.

The spirit of prophecy was one of the seven things whose absence was felt by the Jews in the post-Canonical pre-Christian period, and it is this that constitutes the real difference between this period and that preceding it. In Old Testament times religion was still progressive, because fresh revelations were still being made: in the post-Canonical period religion was essentially static; no new revelations were forthcoming and the Scribes had to content themselves with the codification, exegesis and application of the tradition, till One should come who would speak "with authority and not as the Scribes". But throughout, religion remained authoritarian for its content was determined by appeal to the words of accredited envoys of God, Moses and the prophets.

An examination of the New Testament makes it clear that Christianity accepted all these presuppositions of the Israelite religion, adding that St John Baptist and Christ had brought fresh tidings from on high.

> God, who at sundry times and in divers manners, spoke in times past to the fathers by the prophets, last of all, in these days hath spoken to us by his son (*Hebr* I 1f).

Nothing could be clearer. If Christianity differs from Judaism, it is not that it rejects the authoritarian attitude; nor that it denies the authority to which Judaism appealed; but simply that it accepts the authority of a further envoy of God. Hence Christ is not only the high-priest of the Christian profession (*Hebr* III 1) ; he is a greater than Moses, and God is offended with those who do not "hear his voice", who "have not known his ways", who are "incredulous" (*Hebr* III 7, 10, 18).

For St Paul the Christian teaching is a "gospel" or divine message, the fulfilment of a promise made by the mouth of the prophets and enshrined in the Old Testament "scriptures" (*Rom* I 1f). It is the "gospel of Christ", the contents of which are a revelation from God (*Gal* I 7, 12, 16); these contents are therefore immutable, and St Paul anathematises any teaching inconsistent with the "gospel" (*Gal* I 8 f). Before the coming of Christ, the Gentiles, as being outside the Israelitic society, not included in the terms of God's covenant with his people, and ignorant of the promise latent in the Old Dispensation, were "without God in this world" (*Eph* II 12). It was Christ who came and preached peace to them as to the Jews (*Eph* II 17). And it was in response to St Paul's proclamation of the divine message "entrusted" to him by God that his Thessalonian converts "turned to God from the idols, to serve the living and true God" (I *Thess* II 4; I 9). This message they received as "not a human utterance, but—as in truth it is—an utterance of God" (I *Thess* II 13).

The same world of thought is disclosed to us in the First

Epistle of St Peter, who tells his readers that they have been "begotten again of incorruptible seed, through the word of the living God. The grass is withered, and its flower fallen; but the word of the Lord abideth for ever. This is the word which has been conveyed to you as a divine message" (I *Pet* I 23-25). As Christians, they are distinguished from "those who refuse submission to the divine message" (I *Pet* IV 17). Similarly St James says that God has "conceived us by the word of truth", and bids his hearers "receive with meekness the engrafted word which has power to save their souls" (*Jas* I 18, 21). And St John "announces" to his readers what he has "seen and heard", and bids them "let that abide in them which they heard at the beginning", so that they may "abide in the Son and in the Father" (I *Jn* I 3; II 24). Thus they are contrasted with those who, after belonging to the Christian fellowship, have shown, by separating themselves from it, that they were never really "of our number"; and the crux of their disagreement appears to be that they deny the truth that "Jesus is the Christ" (*Jn* II 19, 22).

"Christianity is not anything which could be discovered or invented for himself by any person, however intellectually or spiritually gifted, in independence of historical tradition. . . . He must be content (in the first instance) to derive his knowledge of it from authority, whether the authority in question be primarily that of a living teacher, or of past tradition".[5]

From the Epistles we turn back to the four Gospels and the Acts of the Apostles. In studying the Gospels an historian will distinguish between the ideas of the writers and the teaching of Christ himself. The ideas of the writer of the Fourth Gospel are clear enough; they are those of the Epistles of St John. Jesus of Nazareth was the divine Reason or Utterance, the Word of God.[6] The Word was made flesh, and as the law came through Moses, so grace and truth came through Jesus Christ: "No man hath seen God at any time; the only-begotten Son, who is in the bosom of the father, he hath disclosed him" (*John* I 18).

Our Lord in this Gospel makes the unmistakable claim to speak as the Envoy of God, and to be believed as such. He has been "sent by the living Father" (*John* VI 58, 63, 45): and the

---

[5] E. G. Selwyn, ed., *Essays Catholic and Critical* (S.P.C.K., 1926) pp. 85f.
[6] The Greek word is ambiguous, but in the Johanine order of ideas it is sufficiently clear that the notion of utterance is included.

**words which he speaks** are "spirit and life". "Every man that has heard from the Father and learnt, cometh to me" (*John* VI 58, 63, 45). So when he asks the Twelve "Will you also depart?" St Peter replies: "Lord, to whom shall we depart? Thou hast words of eternal life. And we have believed and made up our minds that thou art the Christ, the Son of the Living God" (*John* VI 69).

St Luke is fond of the idea of Christianity as a "message" or "an utterance of God". He speaks in the Preface to his Gospel of those who "were from the first eye-witnesses and ministers of the word". He speaks of the crowd pressing on Christ "to hear the word of God" (*Luke* V 1). He records Gamaliel's warning that what the Apostles stand for may be not "of men" but "of God" (*Acts* V 38f), and of the Apostles' incessant "proclaiming of Jesus Christ as a message from God" (*Acts* V 42).

So, too, St Mark in describing Christ's preaching in Galilee, adds to St Matthew's record of the teaching of Christ, the significant words "Believe the divine message". St Matthew's own view emerges not only in his insistence that Jesus was the promised Messiah, the fulfilment of prophecy and the Son of God, the "great light" manifested to them that sat in the land and shadow of death (*Matt* IV 16), but in the record he has left of Christ's own self-presentation as a Teacher with authority, whose teaching is a sure foundation for human life, and through whom alone men can know the Father (*Matt* XI 27).

It is to this teaching of Christ himself, as recorded in the Synoptic Gospels, that we now turn. The evidence of his earliest believers is unanimous—they all regard him as having brought a decisive revelation of God to man. It would be extraordinary if his own teaching disclosed a different view.

And in fact it does not. On the contrary, he is shown as imposing on his own authority ("Ye have heard how it was said to them of old: but I say unto you—") a re-reading of the Mosaic law, which he had come not indeed to "dissolve" but certainly to "fulfil" or endow with final completeness or authority. He offers his teaching, as we saw above, as a sure foundation of human life. He claims to be "sent" by God the Father, to have been given all authority in heaven and on earth (*Matt* X 40). And he bids the Eleven to teach men of all nations to "observe all things as many as I have enjoined upon you" (*Matt* XXVIII 18, 20).

Thus the claim enshrined in the New Testament documents is quite clear, however strange and unwelcome it may sound in the ears of a modern "liberal". There is no idea here of humanity left to itself to conjecture what it can of ultimate reality from the evidence of nature. There is no idea of religious truth as simply latent in experience as a whole, and educible thence on the same terms as scientific or philosophic truth. We have, indeed, the "oracular"[7] idea of a truth that is deliberately and specially conveyed to man on divine authority, a truth which man has not to discover for himself but to accept by an act or habit of intellectual obedience.

Plato was familiar with this idea of a revelation made with divine authority. In a pathetic passage of the *Phaedo,* a speaker emphasising the importance of the problem of the soul's immortality says that we must, *failing natural proof or a divine information,* find the best substitute we can by human reason, and if certainty be impossible, make this our precarious raft to carry us through the waters of life. The Platonic Socrates frequently speaks with respect of Orphic, Delphic and Egyptian traditions of such divine revelation. He is far from the rationalistic "free thought" of the modern liberal. But he stops short of the New Testament position, because he will not simply accept these alleged revelations on their own claim. He respects them, he thinks there is in all probability a great deal in them, but he uses them to fortify his own judgment; he hankers after their suggestions as an alluring "perhaps"; he does not, in the end, simply "assent" to them as decisive because in fact divine. His position—if it may be said without offence—seems like that of the modern liberal Protestant: he brings forward these ancient traditions as *evidence* not as *authority;* or as probable authority influencing belief, not certain authority determining it. But the New Testament attitude is that of the old-fashioned Protestant and of the Catholic: Lord, to whom shall we depart? Thou hast the words of eternal life.

If Plato had been reproached with his attitude of reserve towards the alleged Orphic and other revelations, he would pre-

[7] Not "oracular" indeed, if the word suggests any human power to compel a "revelation".

69

sumably have replied: Attractive as the content of these "revelations" often is, and venerable as are the traditions in which they are enshrined, I have yet to find satisfying credentials of their divine origin and authenticity: if it is abominable self-opiniatedness to reject a credible authority, it is yet wrongful credulity to accept such "revelations" on insufficient evidence of their claim to such acceptance.[8] I am convinced that there is truth lurking in the religious traditions of mankind, but press me to accept some delimitation or definition of that truth, an articulation of it in a series of propositions, and I cannot follow you; I can only fall back on my private judgment as my ultimate criterion and that means that philosophy has the last word.

The New Testament is far removed from this reverent and honourable agnosticism. It makes a clearcut distinction between the Judaeo-Christian traditions and the other religious traditions of the world. The Gentiles worship "idols" or "devils". It is vehement in its denunciation of the Jews who have refused the faith of Christ, and urgent in its warning against any compromise with their position (*Gal* V 2) while those who, in modern terminology, would be called "heretics" it calls "antichrists" (I *Jn* II 22). So that we are driven to ask what credentials are offered for this exclusive and overwhelming claim? Granted that the New Testament Christians presented their religion as an authoritative revelation, granted that Christ did likewise, what reasons are we offered for accepting this claim? What are its "grounds of credibility"?

We may distinguish two periods. After the resurrection of Christ the ground mainly insisted on in Christian preaching was that fact itself. As St Paul said to the Athenians: God had fixed a day to judge the world in justice, by a Man by whom he had determined to do so, "giving assurance to all by raising him from the dead" (*Acts* XVII 31). So St Peter, when it was a question of filling the place of Judas Iscariot in the apostolic college, says that one of those who had consorted with them throughout Christ's ministry must "become with them a witness of his resurrection" (*Acts* II 22).

Before the resurrection, though Christ could and did prophesy its occurrence, he obviously could not offer it as a present ground

[8] *Laws* 887 c, sqq.

70

of credibility. But he could and did appeal to the miracles that accompanied his teaching. Doubtless there was also an implicit appeal to the intrinsic credibility of his teaching, of its authoritative tone, and of his character: "Never man spoke as this man". Men were amazed at his teaching "for he taught as one having authority, and not as the Scribes". The poignancy of the alternative *"Aut Deus aut non homo bonus"* did not need to be expressed in so many words in order to be felt. "Which of you convinceth me of sin?" And doubtless there is in this set of facts a miracle of the moral order sufficient by itself, in given circumstances, to give adequate rational basis for faith in Christ's claims. But in fact, hand in hand with this claim, this teaching, this note of authority, this moral character, there went the evidence of the miracles—so abundant apparently as to make one think of that famous record of St Bernard's miracles, made by the personal witness of the named individuals who accompanied him on his journey in Germany.

And when it grew late, when the sun had set, they brought to him all those that were ill and the possessed. And the whole city was gathered to the door (of St Peter's home apparently). And he healed many sick with divers diseases, and cast out many demons (*Mk* I 32-34).

And when they had disembarked, straightway recognising him, they ran round all that district and began to carry about on beds the sick, where they heard that he was. And wherever he entered into villages, towns or countryside, they put the sick in the market places, and begged him that they might touch even the fringe of his garment. And as many as touched him were made whole (*Mk* VI 53-56).

That Christ was fully aware of the inference to be drawn from these miracles is clear from the tremendous passage: "Woe unto thee Corozain, woe unto thee Bethsaida, for if in Tyre and Sidon had happened the miracles that have happened among you, they would long ago have repented in sackcloth and ashes. And thou, Capharnaum, that are exalted to heaven, unto Hades shalt thou be brought down. For if in Sodom had happened the miracles that have happened in thee, it would have remained till this day" (*Matt* XI 21-23).

And again, he rejects with scathing condemnation the

Pharisees' suggestion that he cast out devils by the prince of devils: "but if I cast out devils by the spirit of God, then the kingdom of God has come upon you".[9]

We may note in passing the formidable difficulties which the New Testament presents to the modern unbeliever. Can the good faith of the early Christians be doubted? Can their conviction of the fact of Christ's resurrection be doubted? Can their conviction of the miracles of St Peter and St Paul be doubted? Can St Paul's own conviction that miracle was a common accompaniment of the new faith be questioned? Can the honesty and fidelity of the records both of an abundance of miracles in general performed by Christ, and of numerous particular miracles of which details are given, be doubted? Can *all* these miracles be reasonably held to result from merely natural causes? And behind all this, can the astounding nature of Christ's claim to authority from on high, the organic sublimity of his moral and religious teaching, or the integrity of his character, be called in question? And yet, if each one of these questions must receive the answer "No", how is it possible, within the borders of reasonable commonsense, to withhold assent from the basic Christian claim, that God gave to mankind, through the lips of Christ, an authoritative message from on high?

The main purpose, however, of these pages is to understand something of the note of "authority" that is inherent in the Christian religion. We now pass on to our final problem. If the message from on high was a message not merely for those who could "know Christ after the flesh" but for others also, for "all nations" and for all time "till the consummation of the age", how was its integrity to be preserved and ensured for those who could learn it only through intermediaries? (*Matt* XXV 32; XXVIII 19f).

This was a problem whose urgency was perhaps not immediately apparent. Christ had preached publicly, and many of those who were at length converted by the apostolic witness to his resurrection had doubtless heard him preaching, knew something of his message already. But at least in the latter part of his ministry there was, if not contrast between an esoteric and an exo-

---

[9] *Matt* XII 28. If Christ refuses to produce "signs" to order, this is because he will be the Master of his own actions; the Pharisees could find sufficient grounds of credibility if they would humbly look for them.

teric doctrine[10]; yet more *explicitness* in the teaching to the inner circle[11]; and it was the inner circle which might be supposed to be in possession of the *total* doctrine of Christ (*Jn* XVIII 20; *Matt* XIII 11). Still, at first it could hardly be that one was prepared to accept the apostles' story of the resurrection of Christ and yet would dispute their account of his message.

But it is well known that dispute did soon break out, a dispute on a very fundamental issue, and one as to which we still find it hard to discover a decision in Christ's own recorded words: Was the observance of the *matter* of the Mosaic Law still universally obligatory?

St Paul's reaction to this dispute is characteristic and interesting. He asserts by implication that his own version of the "Gospel" is correct, and he affirms vehemently that anyone, even an angel, who teaches otherwise is to be anathema (*Gal* I 8). But then, this is—again by implication—to maintain, or it must lead him on to maintain, that what he said was true because the apostles had authority, from God or Christ, to teach in Christ's name. And he does in fact go on to affirm that he received his Gospel directly by divine revelation, and in the next chapter points out that his divine commission to evangelise the Gentiles was recognised by (apparently) Saints Peter, James and John. Now the whole of St Paul's line of reasoning must break down—indeed the whole scheme of Christianity as a religion of authority must collapse—unless the apostolic commission carries with it a divine guarantee of the apostolic message.

We are thus led on to the idea of the authority of the accredited Christian teachers, as a derivative from the idea of the universal authority of Christ. And to find this idea we need look no further than the words of Christ himself: "He who receives you receives me; and he who receives me receives him who sent me". "All authority has been given to me in heaven and on earth. Going therefore, make disciples of all nations, teaching them to observe whatever I have enjoined on you. And

---

[10] "I spoke openly to the world, always I taught in the synagogue and in the temple, where the Jews always congregate, and in secret I spoke nothing."

[11] "To you it is given to know the mysteries of the kingdom of heaven, but to them (to the crowds) it is not given."

lo, I am with you all the days until the consummation of the age".[12]

Now it must be obvious that the need of such authoritative exposition and explanation of the Christian religion would not cease with the death of the last of the original apostles. Plato, to revert to the great standard-bearer of pre-Christian philosophy, distinguishes between the "utterance" that is committed to books, in which it is incapable of answering for itself, and the "utterance" that is enshrined in the living mind of a pupil, where it partakes of his vitality, and can explain itself to the questioner. Although the Christian religion did not have to wait long for an inspired literature of its own, nevertheless the books of the New Testament do not purport, either singly or together, to be an exhaustive analysis and formulation of Christian doctrine. Christianity has shown itself in history to resemble the leaven and the mustard seed of Christ's parables. It has been a dynamic, active, vital, self-developing force; and this developing quality has been exhibited not only in its ritual, its law and its policy but in its thought, in the Christian "idea".

It follows that, since for each age Christianity is necessarily contemporary Christianity, there is an abiding need for a contemporary authority, derived doubtless through the original apostles from Christ, the divine Apostle of God the Father. This contemporary doctrinal authority, in a society which, like the Church, has doctrine as the constitutive principle of its own social character as such, will naturally be found there, where the general authority of the society is found; it will appertain to the organ of sovereignty in the society, so that the society itself as an institution will be an embodiment, an incorporation of authoritative doctrine.[13] The society will present itself, as the Church is represented in the New Testament, as the "pillar and ground of the truth" (I *Tim* III 15).

[12] The need would not exist in the same way, if it were possible for everyone to reach certainty, by a study of historical evidence, as to the full content of the Christian revelation. But in fact this is proved impossible by experience; one may refer to the dissensions among "Bible Protestants".

[13] It must be remembered that the apparent "externality" of doctrine, thus viewed, is more and more transcended in the mystical life of the soul, under the operation of the gifts of the Holy Spirit, especially the gifts of wisdom and understanding. Even at the lowest degree of the life of faith, faith's object is not the *enuntiabile* (the authoritative formula), but the *res enuntiata*, of which the highest is God self-revealed.

Such, indeed, is the Church's claim, as understood by the churchmen of the Patristic period. As an interesting illustration we may refer to the letter entrusted by Bishop Capreolus of Carthage to his deacon Bessula for the Council of Ephesus (A.D. 431). He there warns the assembled bishops not to contradict previous doctrinal formulations: "If anyone should allow things already decided to be called in question over again, he will be thought to be doing nothing else than himself doubting about the faith that has hitherto prevailed". And he points out that any other attitude towards the past would undermine any purpose of their own to bequeath a permanently valid formulation to posterity. The implication is that the Church's official teaching is true, and that it is found in her official formulations, past, present, and to come. This is the doctrine of infallibility without the name.

To complete this elementary exposition of the place of authority in the New Testament "idea" of Christianity, it should be observed that, as credentials were necessary in order that Christ's own claim to authority might be justified, so also the Church's authority needs credentials. These are to be found on the one hand in Christ's recorded commission to his apostles and in his promise to be with them till the consummation of the age, and on the other hand in the miracles that mark the Church's course in history. Analogous to the miracle of the moral order accrediting Christ's claim is the moral miracle of the Church herself, the certitude with which she professes to fill a role so unique and yet so harmonious with man's highest conceivable aspirations, the consistency and elevation of her teaching, the holiness that springs up in her path, her unity combined with catholicity, her permanent vigour, her perennial youth, and the wonderful propagation of the Christian religion. And alongside of this moral miracle, the Church—like Christ from whom she derives her authority—can point to physical miracles such as those of St Bernard referred to above, those of St John Bosco, or the cures connected with the miraculous grotto of Lourdes. Antecedently to the verification of any of these alleged miracles, it is a distinct argument in favour of Catholicism that the Catholic Church recognises the need of some such grounds of credibility, that she is not afraid to affirm that they exist, and that such affirmations of frequent and established miracles can be maintained in the broad daylight of critical enlightment.

# The Priority of St Matthew's Gospel

1947

It may be suspected that the total victory, in non-Catholic scholarly circles, of the theory that St Mark's is the earliest Gospel and that it was copied by St Matthew and St Luke, has ended by causing interest in the Synoptic Problem at Oxford and Cambridge to decline. The dominance of this theory will come one day to seem comparable to the sway of the Ptolemaic astronomy in the Middle Ages; in the meantime the pioneers who dare to question it must expect to meet, at the hands of academic inquisitors, with the supposed fate of Galileo. The theory has been sterile of constructive results in the study of the Christian documents,[1] but it has produced a grotesque brood of subsidiary hypotheses and subjective reconstructions of the evolution of primitive Christianity.

A faithful attendant upon the Marcan hypothesis is the "Q" conjecture, the theory, that is to say, that the passages in the first and third Gospels which are parallel with one another but have no parallel in St Mark are derived from a supposed lost document (to which for convenience scholars refer as "Q"), mainly consisting of sayings and discourses of our Lord. This document would have been written in Greek (or translated into Greek from a Semitic original, Hebrew or more probably Aramaic, the spoken language of Palestine in our Lord's time), and conservative scholars may toy with the idea that it was written by St Matthew; you will hardly find a "Marcan priorist" who believes that the first Gospel was written by an apostle.

Then the late Professor Streeter supposed a third source for parts of the first Gospel not derived from St Mark or from "Q", and a fourth source for some of the peculiar material of the

---

[1] "It is surprising, and a little mortifying to scholarship, to have to admit that this fundamental conclusion is the only assured result of the vast amount of incessant labour which has been expended on the so-called Synoptic Problem in the whole of the past hundred years and more." (J. H. Ropes, *The Synoptic Gospels*, Harvard University Press, 1934). Professor Ropes was an eminent American Biblical scholar, whose work on the text of Acts in *The Beginnings of Christianity* (Vol. III) is well known in this country. It is the fundamental conclusion of course, that is wrong. Error, as Newman pointed out of heretical theology, lacks the principle of organic growth.

third Gospel. He further supposed that the third Gospel is a second and enlarged edition of an earlier conjectural work, to which he gives for convenience the title "Proto-Luke". A "collection of proof texts" has also been conjectured, not to speak of an "oral tradition" in the church of the city of Rome or elsewhere. Thus, in one way or another, a great deal of oral and literary evolution is held to have gone on between the original Gospel facts and our extant documents; and these documents are relegated to the second quarter-century after the Resurrection (Bishop Rawlinson dates St Mark's Gospel, the earliest of the three in his opinion, about 67 A.D., a third of a century or more after the Resurrection). Naturally, you can suppose a good many metamorphoses in the tradition before these dates, though St Paul's Epistles (dating from about 50 to about 65 A.D.) will impose some check upon you. But the opportunities for Liberal Protestants and antisupernaturalists are enormous.

Two noteworthy attempts have been made in the last thirty years to destroy the foundation of all these theories by showing that in fact St Mark's Gospel, far from being a source of St Matthew's Gospel is itself dependent on it.[2] But so far the prejudice has been too deeply rooted for these attempts to be given a fair hearing.

I do not propose here to enter into full technical details, but it is not difficult to show up one faulty piece of reasoning put forward by adherents of the theory of Marcan priority. The late Professor B. H. Streeter's brilliant work, *The Four Gospels, A Study of Origins* (Macmillan, 1924) is still probably the best introduction to its subject among those that have emanated from the great English Universities. In it he points out that where all three Synoptists relate the same incident we usually find a large measure of agreement in the actual words used, and constantly, where one differs, either St Matthew or St Luke agrees with St Mark; while St Matthew and St Luke never (except either accidentally, or in apparent cases which he thinks can be explained away) support each other against St Mark. And he proceeds

---

[2] H. G. Jameson, *The Origin of the Synoptic Gospels,* (Blackwell, 1922); Dom John Chapman, *Matthew, Mark and Luke,* (Longmans 1937). The "Q" hypothesis has been criticised in *How Luke was Written,* by E. W. Lummis (Cambridge University Press, 1915) and by the present writer in "St Luke's Debt to St Matthew", *The Harvard Theological Review,* October 1939. Mr Lummis writes that "Q" is an unnecessary hypothesis: "not only so; it is excluded". With this judgment I agree.

(p.161): "This is clear evidence of the greater originality of the Marcan version".

Professors of Logic may amuse themselves by asking their pupils to detect the fallacy in this piece of reasoning. The reader may have seen it for himself already, but I will not apologise for pointing it out since—to take one example that happens to come easily to hand—Bishop Rawlinson, in the stimulating introduction to his commentary on St Mark (Methuen, 1925), after recalling the same facts, says (p.XXXV): "It is obvious that these facts are most simply explained by the hypothesis that St Matthew and St Luke each independently used St Mark's Gospel as a source."

One can only hope that, if either Professor Streeter or Bishop Rawlinson ever taught in a school or marked examination papers, he did not have the unpleasant duty of investigating cases of what is known as "cribbing". Let us suppose that Bishop Rawlinson has received essays on the origins of the Synoptic Gospels from three pupils, Brown, Jones and Smith. His trained critical faculty quickly convinces him that copying has been at work. Practically everything in Jones's essay, including a large proportion of his very words, is found in the essays of either Brown or Smith, and a great deal of it is in both. But he finds that Brown and Smith never coincide in content, wording or order except when both also coincide with Jones. Two of the young gentlemen are guilty, but which two?

Bishop Rawlinson is sure that they are Brown and Smith, who are consequently "reported" to an overworked headmaster and incontinently punished. Is this justice? It may be, by accident, but there are two chances to one that one or other of these two victims is innocent. It is *equally probable* that Brown and Jones are the guilty parties, or that Brown is innocent and Jones and Smith are guilty.

Bishop Rawlinson assumes that Jones wrote his essay first, and that it fell into the hands of Brown and Smith (separately) who used it as a labour-saving device. This is quite possible. But it is equally likely that Brown wrote first, that Jones copied his essay, and that Smith copied Jones'. And it is equally likely that Smith wrote first, that Jones copied him and was copied by Brown. Any one of these hypotheses will, equally with the others, explain the given facts that the essays are in part all identical, and that Brown's and Smith's essays sometimes respectively support Jones' against the third essay, but that they never support each other against Jones.[3]

If the reader does not yet agree—and not infrequently, I think, a student will agree that all three hypotheses are possible, but will continue to think that Bishop Rawlinson's is the most probable—I beg him to re-read the two preceding paragraphs, and in any case not to read on further till he is convinced. For it is vital to realise that the three hypotheses are all equally probable.

But the evidence adduced does justify one inference of maximum importance for the solution of the Synoptic Problem. The non-agreement of St Matthew and St Luke against St Mark makes it certain that the link between St Matthew and St Luke in these passages is St Mark's Gospel or something indistinguishable therefrom.[4] St Mark, in other words, is the intermediary document, and our choice of a solution is at once reduced from nine contending hypotheses to three, all equally probable.

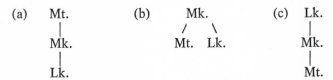

And, incidentally, this evidence excludes for practical purposes the supposition that the connection between the first three Gospels is purely oral. In the past it has been suggested that the similarities between the Synoptic Gospels may be due to their being each independently of the others based upon the oral tradition of our Lord's life and teaching preserved in the primitive Church; and a great deal of amusing work can be done in investigating the memory feats of primitive tribes—though the

---

[3] On looking up Mr Jameson's treatment of the school-boy illustration I note that it was actually used by Dr E. A. Abbott (*Diatessarica* II 47) to prove the innocence of the "intermediary"! And Dr Abbott was a headmaster!

[4] For simplicity of exposition I have here omitted certain minor considerations that have led some scholars, mistakenly as I think to suggest that there were two editions of St Mark, and that the real intermediary was not our extant edition but another not preserved.

companions and disciples of St Paul were not exactly primitives. The basic objection to this theory is the relative failure of St Matthew and St Luke to support each other against St Mark where all three are parallel. If the three evangelists stood all in the same relation to an oral tradition, and were each independent of the others, we might expect agreements of all three, and agreements of each pair against the third; but in fact we find that agreements of *one* pair (St Matthew and St Luke) against the third are conspicuous by their relative absence (in passages where all three are parallel). Reflection shows that, this being so, the oral tradition tapped by all three—if the oral theory is accepted—must have been practically identical with what we actually find in St Mark's Gospel. That is to say St Mark would have preserved the oral tradition practically verbatim and the other two would have diverged from the oral tradition exactly as the Marcan priorists maintain that they diverged from their written source, St Mark's Gospel. Whether an oral theory is worth having on these terms its supporters may judge. But, as it is critically identical with the theory of Marcan priority, it will be liable to the same objections as that theory, and they are insuperable.

For completeness it may here be remarked that if the oral tradition be supposed practically identical with St Matthew's or St Luke's Gospel, instead of with St Mark's, then the absence of agreements between St Matthew and St Luke against St Mark dictates the inference that St Mark's Gospel is also based on the oral tradition or on the Gospel, whether St Matthew's or St Luke's supposed to be practically identical with it, while the remaining Gospel of the three *must be based on St Mark's Gospel itself*. This is at most a mixed oral and literary theory, and as critically worthless as that discussed above.

It is no small gain to have established, for critical purposes, the positions that the connection between St Mark's Gospel and the other two is not merely oral but literary, and that St Mark's is the intermediary Gospel. But it is a blemish on the history of critical scholarship that evidence which validly establishes these two positions should have been used illegitimately (though of course in good faith) to exclude the hypothesis of the priority of St Matthew's or indeed of St Luke's Gospel. Very few scholars indeed—and I am not one of them—wish to maintain the priority of St Luke's Gospel. But the case for St Matthew's priority deserves to be given a fair hearing; it is in fact convincing, and this despite the evidence, very justifiably adduced by the Marcan priorists, that St Mark's Gospel is written in a crude and conversational style, as compared with the other two.

The chief internal reason for accepting the priority of St Matthew is derived from a careful comparative study of the bits of discourse in St Mark's Gospel, and various small sayings in it, corresponding to the great sermons and discourses of St Matthew's or to parts of them. Such a study shows clearly that St Mark was excerpting from or telescoping a Greek source indistinguishable from these sermons and discourses in St Matthew's Gospel. The evidence is objective and scientific—like finger-prints—and cannot be subverted. It is "hanging evidence" against St Mark.

I will give one instance, sufficiently intelligible without reference to the original Greek. If the reader will turn to St Matthew XXII 41-6 and St Mark XII 35-7 he will see that these are parallel accounts of our Lord's question about the Davidic sonship of Christ. They are followed, in each Gospel, by strictures upon the scribes (and Pharisees in St Matthew). After this, St Mark has a short incident (the Widow's Mite) which is not found in St Matthew, and then both Gospels come together again for the prophecy of the destruction of the Temple (*St Matthew* XXIV 1-3 *St Mark* XIII 1-4).

But whereas St Matthew's strictures extend to thirty-nine verses (or one less if, with the stronger manuscript tradition, we omit verse 14—but I suspect that it is genuine), St Mark's are only three verses long. St Mark's three verses are parallel to the second half of St Matthew's verse 5, verse 6, the first half of verse 7 and verse 14 (perhaps not genuine). The question is: Has St Matthew built up his long discourse round this bit from St Mark, or has St Mark extracted these few lines from St Matthew's long discourse?

There can be no doubt about the answer, provided that the matter is not prejudged by a previous decision, on other grounds, that St Mark is prior to St Matthew. Compare St Matthew's "They make their phylacteries broad and enlarge their fringes" with St Mark's "Who love to walk in long robes" (literally "wishing to walk in robes"). If you look up a commentary, you will discover that a phylactery was a purse containing extracts from the Mosaic Law, worn upon the forehead by Pharisees; and the specially long "fringes" of their garments are thought, on the basis of this passage, to have been special insignia of their Pharisaic profession. But St Mark's largely Gentile readers (or— see below—St Peter's hearers) could not be expected to know this, nor to have handy commentaries to explain it. He has therefore hastily substituted his own rather odd phrase, thus rather spoiling the point; for St Matthew's text pillories religious ostentation, whereas St Mark's only suggests childish vanity. It is unbelievable that St Matthew, writing in Greek, could create his own version out of St Mark's; the opposite hypothesis is both natural and easy.

Furthermore these lines in St Matthew cohere both in content and in their literary structure with what immediately precedes or follows them. They are in fact the opening lines of the first example given by Dr C. F. Burney, in his book on *The Poetry of our Lord,* of a kind of Semitic quasi-poetic literary form which he calls Synthetic Parallelism. (Dr Burney accepted the priority of St Mark.)

And, finally, St Mark confesses that he is making an excerpt by his introductory words (v.38): "And he said to them in his doctrine" (cf *St Mark* IV 2, where he uses the same form before similarly excerpting from *St Matthew* XIII).

The reader may well ask: How is it that these facts have not been realised by the Marcan priorists? The answer is probably that they have already answered the question as to St Mark's priority before getting down to this comparative criticism of the documents—partly through their false inference, pointed out above, and partly because of the impression of greater primitivity that St Mark's Gospel undoubtedly conveys. Yet, to take only this one example, how delighted they would be to be able to point out similar demonstrative evidence of St Matthew's dependence on St Mark!

It remains to add a word about our poor mythical friend "Q". In a full-length study on the Synoptic Problem I should be inclined to dispose of "Q" before directly examining the relations between St Matthew and St Mark. But "Q" 's real claim to existence was as a shadow (with very vague outlines) cast by the supposed priority of St Mark. For if St Matthew's Gospel, like St

Luke's, was based on St Mark's it is true that its author could be shown to have made various additions to the substance of Marcan incidents and discourses, additions that are often identical, or almost so, with passages in non-Marcan contexts of St Luke's Gospel. (Occasionally, as in the Temptation of our Lord, St Luke's additions are in the same Marcan context as their Matthaean parallels). Whence did St Matthew obtain these additions? Not, as we admit with the Marcan priorists, from St Luke's Gospel. It was an obvious suggestion that St Matthew and St Luke both obtained them from some second source—hence "Q".

But as St Mark's Gospel was in fact based on St Matthew's these "additions" in St Matthew are not additions at all, and require no other source than the rest of the Gospel, including those parts copied by St Mark. And, as regards St Luke, it can be proved that he copied his "Q" passages direct from discourses and sayings that he found in a source indistinguishable from St Matthew's Gospel. So, to sum up, St Matthew's Gospel was written (in Aramaic, first, and then translated into Greek; but this is a point requiring separate proof); St Mark's Gospel is dependent on St Matthew's; and St Luke is dependent directly on St Matthew's as well as on St Mark's Gospel.

I may add, as a personal opinion, that I believe that between St Mark and his source there has intervened, to some extent, the oral teachings of St Peter, based on such parts of St Matthew's Gospel as he could corroborate by his own eye-witness recollections of what actually occurred. St Peter's rough-and-ready conversational style has played havoc with the lucid, careful Greek of St Matthew's Gospel, and is reflected in St Mark's. St Luke has re-written what he borrows from St Mark, imposing on it the veneer that pervades his writings.

We may now revert to the question of the dates of composition of the three Gospels. All that we could prove about the date of St Luke's Gospel by establishing the positions outlined above is that it was written subsequently to the other two. But if on other grounds we hold that it was written about 60 A.D., this will, of course, give us a useful *terminus ante quem* for his sources. If St Mark's Gospel is based on the Greek St Matthew it is obvious that the latter existed before it; and if St

Peter's oral teaching intervened between St Mark and his source, then the Greek St Matthew existed before St Peter's death. If St Matthew's Gospel was originally in Aramaic, then this gets us still further back.

Only when the above positions have won *droit de cité* in the world of scholarship is due justice likely to be done to two pieces of acute criticism that can carry us still further with the problem of the date of composition of St Matthew's Gospel. They are contained in articles by Dom John Chapman and Dom Bernard Orchard.[5] In 1912 Dom Chapman argued that St Paul's Epistle to the Galatians shows clear traces of dependence on the "Thou are Peter" passage as found in our Greek St Matthew; this article was written at a time when its author apparently still held the theory of Marcan priority. More recently, Dom Bernard Orchard made a careful study of St Paul's Epistles to the Thessalonians and presented a cogent case for the view that they presuppose chapters 24 and 25 of St Matthew's Gospel (in Greek). There are good grounds for thinking that the Epistles to the Thessalonians were written about 51-2 A.D. The Epistles to the Galatians may date from about 48 or about 55 A.D. Archdeacon Allen, a Marcan priorist, wrote in his commentary on St Matthew[6]: "On all these grounds . . . the relation of its evangelist to the law, its limitation of the ecclesia to Jews and proselytes, its primitive organisation, its eschatological teaching, the earlier the Gospel can be placed the better. What is there to prevent our dating it about the year 50?" It would seem, if the arguments of Dom Chapman and Dom Orchard carry weight, that 50 A.D. would be rather too late a date for our Greek St Matthew; its Aramaic original will be still earlier. The Crucifixion is assigned to various dates by different scholars—say, between 29 and 33 A.D. inclusive.

If the points indicated above can be established, it will be seen that St Matthew's Gospel is remarkable in early literature, Christian and pagan alike, for the amount and kind of attestation it receives in authors writing very soon after its first appearance in its present Greek dress. It appears to have been used by St Mark, even by St Peter himself. It was used by the author of the third Gospel, whom we have good reason for identifying with

---

[5] Revue Benedictine, 1912; *Biblica*, 1938.
[6] Second edition, pp. 328f.

Luke, the companion of St Paul. It was used by St Paul himself. And if it was not directly used by the fourth evangelist, it has from him indirect attestation in the fact that he used St Mark's Gospel and St Luke's.

This external attestation is probably to be carried forward by reference to such knowledge as we possess of the lost work of Papias, second century Bishop of Hierapolis. This name takes us into another area of scholarly controversy, but I think Dom Chapman's thesis is probably substantially true, that the "John" of Papias was St John the Apostle, and that his reference to works composed by Matthew and Mark are to our first and second Gospels. It looks as though the result of the best critical scholarship, when it is sifted out, will prove to be a remarkable vindication of traditional views. In particular, there seems some hope of getting away from the modern passion for "cycles of tradition" and back to the primitive Christian interest in known and accredited personal witness and authority.[7]

Not that the honest-hearted reader has to wait upon the decisions of scholarship. There is a sense in which the Gospels— and some of St Paul's Epistles—can be said to be self-evidencing. An unprejudiced enquirer, who wishes to discover the truth, will generally decide, if he reads and re-reads the Synoptic Gospels as whole books, that the authors were themselves honest men, setting down what they sincerely believed to be true. He will then realise that they could not have believed these things to be true unless the historical facts were, substantially, such as they represent them to have been. And further, he will see, forced upon his attention through the medium of their written word, glimpses of the personality of One who "spoke with authority and not as the scribes", whom no one "convicted of sin", who made claims that would have been preposterous if they were not true, who performed wonders of preternatural power such as to render inexcusable the townships that hardened their hearts against him, who died as he had foretold and was buried; and, as he had foretold, rose again the third day from the dead.

---

[7] For a later, and more carefully qualified, statement of the author's views on the synoptic problem, cf. B. C. Butler, "The Synoptic Problem", in *A New Catholic Commentary on Holy Scripture*, Nelson, 1969, pp. 815 ff., particularly the conclusion—p. 821.

# The Duality of History

1950

What is the value, for a Christian, of art and literature, science and humane culture, all the good things of this life, all that, for the unbeliever, sums up the possible good for man?

The Christian is taught that he has, in the providential ordering of things, only one goal to aim at: the beatific vision of the Holy Trinity in the life to come. And he is taught that not the excellence of human making, but the moral goodness of human behaviour, is the means to the attainment of this goal—the action of grace being of course presumed. He is taught, as in an impressive passage of Newman, that nothing can justify any, even venial, sin—not the saving of his own life, nor the happiness of those he loves, not the safety of his country or the preservation of all human culture; and, providing we understand aright what we mean by sin, this is true, not to say a truism.

Does not all this mean that, in the only scheme of "values" admitted by Christianity, all cultural achievement is simply worthless? It is the old question that has haunted Christians since the day the Church emerged from the Catacombs, a theoretical question, indeed, but one that has been agonisingly personal to many a good Christian. It is St Jerome's question, and that of the Christian humanists. It was raised again by Friedrich von Hügel in his *Mystical Element of Religion*.

This question is being re-examined today, and Père L. Malevez S.J. has distinguished (in *Bijdragen*, 1949, part 3) two divergent answers, that of "eschatological theology" and that of the "theology of Incarnation". Those who favour the former solution stress the fact that our final end, the Reign of God, is beyond our power to produce; it is something discontinuous with profane history; only by dying can our civilisations make way for it. For "the whole world is in the power of the evil one" (I *John* V 19). The Gospel sets man against man. Human institutions will destroy each other, then the powers of heaven will be shaken and the end will come. "I have not come to send peace but a sword". It is not promised that all humanity will be converted, Christianised, but only that the Gospel will be everywhere pro-

86

claimed. In this world we are strangers and pilgrims; our fatherland, the Reign of God, is not realisable here below. We must
renounce all things, and wait humbly for the Reign of God. The
Incarnation is a remedy for human ills, but a terrible remedy,
since it spells the Cross. It sows life in the world, but life beyond
death; a life, therefore, which urges this world to die. The Spirit
of God is given to enable us not to embellish the world, but to
confront its hostility. Our eternal destiny is born in a hard travail,
and we pass from our divided world to God by a *salto mortale*.
What we construct here below is an interior good, not any exterior
achievements.

The theology of Incarnation, on the other hand, asserts that
human action in all its forms, provided that it does not abuse
created realities, prepares the coming of God's Reign. Christian
action, in particular, is enriched by the presence of the Holy
Spirit and a share in the attributes of the incarnate Word; thus
it has an interior quality which disposes it gradually through the
ages for receiving the good things of the Reign of God, which
will be the gift of free grace and yet will consummate, not simply
conclude our long story. Time is the flower, eternity the fruit, and
Christian action has a certain "condignity" with eternal life. The
whole man is regenerated by baptism; his body is Christ's member
(I *Cor* VI 15). Adamic grace shows that of its nature grace
tends to transform the body itself and its *milieu*. Jesus was the
perfect man in his human nature; the normal repercussion of the
Incarnation had to be restrained so that his Body might be
passible, but once the redemption was accomplished grace transfigured it. And since then history shows an amelioration; man
has become more the master of his environment, especially in the
West where Christianity has been most effective. The Church
saved for man the values of ancient Rome; and Christianity
will not be perfect if its recipients are and remain barbarians.
To all this may be added evolutionary considerations, tending to
show that Christianity is a higher stage in a long process culmi-
nating, before it, in *homo sapiens* (English readers will bethink
them of the late Dr Temple's *Christus Veritas*). Christianity does
not teach us to desert the world but that human effort is our duty.
Thus the layman's tasks in the world are not incapable of
sanctification. Even technical progress, it is argued, favours the
mystical life.

It may be desirable to scrutinise a little more closely the New

Testament bases of these two conflicting tendencies. The New Testament is not only a first precipitate of the Gospel revelation; it is an inspired deposit of tradition. The whole Christian doctrine is a development of the original teaching substantially recorded in its pages, and its contents are therefore normative for theology. Hence it is all to the good that this great debate should be argued first on the New Testament ground. But theology is a science, and Scripture does not speak scientifically, but rather "prophetically". It does not purport to give us a ready-made system of thought, although it is pregnant with such a system. It does not teach scholastically; it preaches. There is a danger of distorting the Scripture message if we treat it as we do the Code of Canon Law or the *Summa Theologica* of St Thomas Aquinas. Thus, when our Lord tells us to "turn the other cheek", we must not treat this as a precept on the same level with the obligation to hear Mass on holy days; it is at once more and less than that. The Sermon on the Mount is not a treatise on moral theology; it is more like a poem; it is, in fact, a sermon. We are faced here with a question of interpretation like that which Maritain has examined in connexion with St John of the Cross. St John of the Cross is profoundly Thomist. Yet you could draw up a list of his sayings, especially on the worthlessness and anti-spiritual character of creatures, that would seem to be in stark contradiction with St Thomas' teaching on the intrinsic goodness of all things and on grace as perfecting and "crowning" nature. Much of the hostility to the spiritual teaching of St John of the Cross rests on such misinterpretation.

There is also a particular consideration to be borne in mind in interpreting the New Testament. The New Testament writings are in large measure the deposit from a vast explosion of spiritual force, a sort of volcanic eruption, the accompaniment, part cause and part effect, of the supreme event in human history, involving a transformation in the religious element of that history. There had taken place a new birth, a "generatio" in the fullest sense, involving a "corruptio" of the previous form of religion. And the travail, the shocks and reactions of this tremendous event have left their mark on the New Testament literature, on its modes of expression, on its rhetoric. We must allow for this in assessing the New Testament teaching, especially when we are concerned to state with measured accuracy the relations between the Gospel and the world. In the initial stages of the new religion it was more conscious of, more anxious to assert and to emphasise, the

infinite gulf of difference and discontinuity between it and its
environment than to dwell with complacency on the homo-
geneities, the interconnexions, the mutual dependence that were,
we may suppose, really there and really operative all the time.
Perhaps the extreme limit of this emphasis on discontinuity was
reached in Marcion's teaching that the Gospel had literally no
historical human antecedents; that the Old Testament did not
record any revelation from the divine Father of Jesus Christ; and
that Christ himself appeared suddenly from heaven, a grown man
without human ancestry, to proclaim an utterly new religion. The
Church, guided by the Holy Spirit, rejected this extreme position
in favour of the Catholic standpoint of St Paul and St Irenaeus.
This rejection should be borne in mind when we attempt to deal
with the great questions raised by Père Malevez.

In his article, Père Malevez has conveniently labelled the two
contrary tendencies in the Christian "philosophy of history" as
respectively eschatological and incarnational. But the convenience
of this nomenclature must not blind us to the real *differentia* of
the Christian Gospel. In fact, Christian eschatology and Christian
incarnationalism are not mutually exclusive. Eschatology without
Incarnation is not Christian at all, but Jewish. Incarnation without
eschatology is—I know not what; Buddhism, perhaps, or
Platonism. Born within the Jewish tradition and of Jewish spiritual
stock, Christianity has been eschatological from the beginning,
from before the beginning, we might almost say. But its novelty
was, not that it simply lodged the idea of incarnation within an
eschatological framework, but that it proclaimed a real "mystical"
or "sacramental" anticipation of the Last Things as the unique
new gift that God was bestowing on Man in the Gospel. And of
this real anticipation the Incarnation is the epitome and the
fountain-head. In other words, the Incarnation is itself an
eschatological fact and can only be understood as such. We have
not to choose between an eschatological and an incarnational
outlook. Incarnation for us, is eschatological, and eschatology is
incarnated.

Hence Christianity holds fast to its central differentiating
proclamation of the *two* comings of Christ. The novelty is not
the second coming, which corresponds with the expectations of
Jewish eschatology, but the first coming. Yet the first coming is a
coming of the Son of Man who is still to come. And as he will
come, in his second coming, to perform the great post-historic

Act of God, to inaugurate the perfect Reign of God, so in his first coming he came to anticipate that final Act and to inaugurate not a shadow or semblance, but a real historical unique anticipation of that Reign. As the end of every movement is implicit in its beginning and in all its stages, so the post-historic Reign of God is implicit in the history of the "Christian fact" from its beginnings. And already in these beginnings this anticipation is an act of God, it is prevenient grace; yet always, as grace always is, it is a grace that assumes nature to itself and habilitates it for a goal that is at once the goal of nature and of grace.

And if the Incarnation is, in the sense outlined above, an eschatological fact, it is also true that Christian incarnationalism must profoundly modify Christian eschatology. The post-historic Reign of God is no longer for us what it might have been without the Incarnation, in sheer discontinuity with history. It will be the ratification and glorification of something that has become part of the texture of history; it will show history for what it really is, and will not abolish but transfigure historical values. The post-historic harvest is homogeneous with the historical seed, and in its growth that seed exercises its mysterious biological alchemy upon the inanimate matter upon which it feeds.

It seems to me that only such an interpretation of the Christian proclamation can give full meaning to many striking New Testament passages, and indeed to the New Testament as a whole. St Paul is strictly unintelligible on any other view. When he tells us, for instance, that we are dead and buried with Christ and with him are risen to a new life, and yet affirms that we are redeemed *in hope,* warns us against relapsing, and himself desires to be dissolved and to be with Christ, he is implying the view of Christianity as a "sacrament" of the world to come, an efficacious symbol of it, really pregnant with it, and yet studiously respectful of our historical conditioning and of the *posse peccare* that belongs to our state of probation.

When we turn back to the Gospels, we note that our Lord's message is summarised by St Matthew in the words: "Repent, the Kingdom of heaven is at hand." If we remember those to whom our Lord was speaking, and the thought-world in which they lived, we can hardly avoid the conclusion that the "kingdom of heaven" (that is the Reign of God) is the divine Act which terminates our mundane history. But was this Act "at hand" when our Lord spoke? As we measure the 1900 years that have elapsed, the obvious answer is in the negative, but it is one that no Christian can tolerate, since it makes Christ into a false prophet. Nor can I think it adequate to point out that in one sense this final Act is always imminent, always "just round the corner", on the grounds that man's temporal experience is forever a passing moment lodged in the framework of eternity. For in that sense the Reign of God was no more imminent when Jesus began his mission than in the days of the "many prophets and just men" who "desired to see" what the disciples of Jesus saw "and saw it not". It seems to me that the Reign of God was "at hand" in an entirely novel sense in the mission of Jesus, and yet mysteriously so: it was its anticipatory, "sacramental" advent that was imminent, and was indeed effected by his mission. This sacramental advent was, I suggest, the core of those "mysteries of the Reign of God" to understand which was the privilege of the disciples of Christ.

This real but mysterious advent of the Reign of God, as the result and meaning of Christ's mission, explains why St John Baptist was "greater than the prophets". The prophets had announced the advent of God's Reign from afar, but St John Baptist's work was, in order of public revelation (as our Lady's vocation was in a more profoundly ontological order) the penultimate disposition for that advent; so that a greater than he was not to be found in the past public history of institutional religion, though he that is least in the new order of the sacramental Reign of God is greater than the Forerunner. The ultimate disposition for God's Reign was and is the mission of Jesus himself, continued in the mission of his "little flock". And an ultimate disposition is at once the cause and the *effect* of the reality with which it is pregnant.

Hence our Lord could claim that "if he by the Spirit of God cast out demons" the Reign of God had supervened upon those who were witnesses of his work. It had supervened obviously not in its post-historic perfection but in a real sacramental anticipation. And in this sacramental form, by a paradox that was "to the Jews a scandal", the Reign of God was even to be subject to the vicissitudes of history, though always triumphant over them. It is the object of violent struggle, and the prize of those who are prepared to pay the price of strenuous effort on its behalf. It is the pearl of great price and the hidden treasure, to be purchased by its Lord, and thereafter by his followers, at the cost of every other value. And yet we must suppose, since it really is God's Reign, that it contains within itself, reintegrates and establishes on an eternal basis, every other value through the whole range of all that is desirable. For the Jewish-Christian tradition differs from Zoroastrianism, Manichaeism and all other ultimate dualisms by refusing any form of spiritualism that maintains itself at the expense of matter, any form of supernature that destroys nature.

It is perfectly true that expressions of apparent dualism can be culled from the New Testament. "We know that we are of God, and the whole world lies in (the power of) evil." "The world is crucified to me, and I am crucified to the world." "He who loses his life for my sake shall find it." But in order to understand such expressions and the profound truth that lies behind them we have to remember two things. To begin with, as we have already reminded ourselves, the advent of a new form has its inevitable *negative moment*—it involves the *corruptio prioris*; yet all that is of positive value in that which is superseded may yet be taken up into the new substance, and such is the very nature of growth and evolution as contrasted with mere change and substitution. Secondly, in the particular case with which we are dealing, the consequences of sin and the Fall have to be taken into account. These consequences, as Père Bouyer (quoted by Père Malevez in the article above referred to) reminds us, are no mere superficial disfigurements of the world, but a "deep-seated cancer". They plunge right down to the roots of human nature, though never corrupting its ontological goodness. And man in the historical order is fallen man. The advent of the Reign of God must therefore spell "death" to historical man, precisely because it brings "resurrection" to ontological man.

It is just here that, as it seems to me, a fatal exaggeration is possible; an exaggeration whereby cultural values are surrendered to man as fallen, not only in their empirical actuality but in the ontological potentialities which they actualise. It is quite true that cultural achievements are, except as flowing from a principle of grace, commonly the products of man as sinful, and that in that sense they are embellishments not of the City of God but of Babylon. But the potentialities which they thus not only actualise but deform are potentialities of ontological man, and as such may participate in the "resurrection" of grace. They and their products are therefore susceptible of supernaturalisation and can be made to subserve the Reign of God, in which indeed they will be glorified. "Created nature has been condemned to frustration . . . with a hope to look forward to; namely, that nature in its turn will be set free from the tyranny of corruption, to share in the glorious freedom of God's sons. The whole of nature, as we know, groans in a common travail all the while" (*Rom* VIII, 20-2). Now it is a fact that, as St Paul in this section of the Epistle to the Romans points out, the redemption of nature, like our own redemption, is an object of hope, and is therefore a post-historic consummation. But it would also seem to be true that, like our own future redemption, it is mysteriously anticipated in the "eschatological sacrament" of Christianity. We do not enjoy a few stray "advances" upon our eventual inheritance. It is the *whole* of that future inheritance that is mysteriously anticipated in grace. And it might seem to follow that every human achievement, at every level of human interest, that is done or pursued "in grace" will find its apotheosis in the post-historic Reign of God. There shall never be one good lost; what was, shall be over again, not its semblance but itself. In the beatific vision we shall see not only God "in himself" but God in creatures and creatures in God. We cannot afford, if we value the beatific vision, to depreciate anything that is capable of this apotheosis, for every such thing will enhance heaven for us and enhance God's glory in our happiness.

In this connection it may be pointed out that the metaphor of the Christian "way" to the heavenly "fatherland" is in one respect misleading. It is derived from Judaism, that is from a religion in which "eschatology" had not yet been "incarnated". It may erroneously suggest that our purpose in this life is to pass through it, get it over, and arrive, without luggage but personally safe, at the end of the journey. The Christian, however, has a different calling. He has to take with him all that he acquires on the road, and what he has to declare at the final customs house will determine for ever his enjoyment of the fatherland. It will be *in* the experience that he has stored up while on earth, in that experience eternalised and transfigured, that he will see God. If it is true that even on earth our "subconscious memory" forgets nothing, this is at least an analogy, and perhaps something more, of the fully actuated condition of the blessed.

It is not irrelevant, it is in the highest degree apposite, to refer here to the teachings of mystical theology. The spiritual life starts from a first conversion and proceeds by successive conversions, each of them under the sign of St John of the Cross's *Nada, nada, nada*. But it proceeds towards the unitive way and the spiritual marriage, in which (in principle) the transitional disharmony and conflict between (fallen) nature and grace have been transcended. It may indeed be argued, since it is only in the final stages of mystical progress that this harmony is achieved, that therefore for all souls during most stages of the progress, and for the overwhelming majority of souls till death, the disharmony persists and creatures must be rejected. But in the first place it should be observed that this is a question of practical ascetics and does not affect the truth of what we may deduce from the characteristics of the unitive way, namely that creatures are fully "supernaturalisable" and are not in any more than accidental, transitional opposition to the Reign of God. Secondly, the complete "abstraction" that is taught by St John of the Cross is abstraction from creatures precisely insofar as they present themselves as competitors with God; insofar as they are viewed in their true nature and redeemed status. Finally, it may be said that the life of prayer, the spiritual life, of a soul in grace is homogeneous in all its stages; its end is implicit in its beginning.

Perhaps we may now turn back to examine some of the assertions of the historians of the "eschatological" school. (1) The Reign of God is "beyond our power to produce". This is of course utterly true. But the Reign of God will consist for each of us in the beatific vision; and this vision, though produced in us by God and entirely beyond our own unaided powers of attainment, will yet be a "seeing" in which we are raised to the summit of our activity and actuality—we shall "see him as he is". And on earth efficacious grace is not a substitute for human action but an actuating influence upon it. The anticipated Reign of God is thus all God's doing, yet summons forth in us, and is manifested in, our own activity. (2) The Reign of God is "discontinuous with profane history". This again is true. But this discontinuity is analogous with that which divides life from inanimate matter, although life evolves in matter, animates what was before inanimate, and actuates potentialities in matter. (3) "Only by dying can our civilisations make way for it." There is a dangerous equivocation here. Considered as effects of man insofar as he is fallen and sinful, our civilisations are of course doomed to death and destruction. But this is an abstract view and they were never merely such. They flow from a nature that is ontologically good, and none of them is entirely graceless. As St Augustine saw, we cannot make an empirical distinction between a stream of history that is all Babylon and another stream that is all the City of God. We have to make a practical judgment every time we are called upon to act, but only God can effect the ultimate discrimination. (4) Our "fatherland" is unrealisable here below. This seems to me very much like a negation of the differentiating Christian truth that the Reign of God is mysteriously anticipated through the missions of the Second and Third Persons of the Holy Trinity. (5) The Incarnation is a crucifying remedy. This again is a truth that can be misunderstood. The mystical "death" whereby grace "heals" nature is the death of nature considered as fallen; it is at the same time the resurrection of nature as God created it, of nature in its fullness. (6) What we construct here below is an interior good, not any exterior achievement. This seems to me to involve an impossible Kantian psychology of the good act. An act is formally good, no doubt, by virtue of its interior qualities; but no act is possible without an object apprehended as good, and all behaving is with a view to "making", whether of our souls or of some exterior thing. As creatures of flesh and blood we cannot dispense with exterior action nor with the making of things exterior to ourselves—things which we cannot make without judging them to be good.

In general, I should argue that the "eschatological" attitude and mood are an exaggeration to which minds are specially prone in a time of secular calamity, breakdown and foreboding. They constitute a temptation for Christians at such times as insidious as the comfortable "bourgeois" optimism that makes its appeal in periods of stable prosperity. Our task is, surely, to preach hope in a time of public despair, and to emphasize the Gospel warnings in times of complacency. Mr Christopher Dawson's second series of Gifford Lectures on religion and the rise of European culture seems to me to be useful reading at a time like the present; and it is hard to believe that the positive cultural influence of Christianity in the formative centuries of the Middle Ages was a total misdirection of the forces of religion.

I have fewer criticisms to offer of the "incarnational" school. I should myself say that human action is not only preparatory of God's Reign, but when informed by grace, is an effect of the anticipated Reign of God. And I should make a similar observation with regard to the "parable" of Père Congar, in which I gather Père Malevez finds the sort of position which he would himself adopt.

A master puts a pupil to work on a set of very difficult problems. The pupil will not find the right answer, though he will get more or less close to it and tries over and over again. His master will tell him the answer, but only when, by dint of his own efforts, he has developed his mind and his powers in a way which he would never have dreamed of if the answer had been given him at the start. The pupil will have in some way raised himself to the level of the solution; he will only really receive it because, in his effort to discover it for himself, he will have as it were expanded himself so as to be capable of it.

Few parables are completely adequate allegories, and this one is deficient insofar as it suggests that our mundane efforts are not themselves, as preparatory of the Reign of God, the effects of grace and therefore of the anticipated Reign of God; or that they do not survive, in their transfigured fruits, in the post-historic Reign of God.

There is one question which may still be asked. Are *all* human achievements, done in grace, capable of apotheosis in the post-historic Reign of God? Do we not ordinarily distinguish between ends, that is objects willed for their own sake, and means, that is objects and courses of action that are chosen only for the sake of some ulterior end? Are "means" capable of "apotheosis"?

This distinction of ends and means seems to me, for our present purposes, unsatisfactory, if only because so many of our objects and modes of activity are at once, though under different aspects, ends and means. It may be more helpful to remind ourselves of the hierarchy of human faculties, and the consequent hierarchy of values. What sets man apart in the animal kingdom is his possession of intelligence, and the intellect is his highest faculty. We can distinguish two elements in intellectual activity, the ratiocinative and the contemplative, and of these the former is "with a view" to the latter. In contemplative activity we are in touch with the real and are united with it, and there is nothing beyond union with the real. By virtue of memory these moments of union are incorporated into the abiding stuff of our soul, so that it is when we contemplate, insofar as we contemplate and insofar as we contemplate the most worthy objects, that this world becomes for us a "valley of soul-making" and is at the same time taken up into our own immortal being. I therefore suggest that our activity in this life is capable of being "eternalised" insofar as it is contemplative.

It should be added that in this suggestion there is no implication of an exaggerated intellectualism. In contemplation we hold commerce not with concepts but with realities, and especially with personalities. We contemplate those whom we love, and love those whom we contemplate, above all the Holy Trinity. And I would further add that contemplation, as I use the word here, is an element in all human action and experience, though occurring in very various degrees of depth and significance. Its focus and *raison d'être* are found in the liturgy, where with Christ, through him and in him, mankind comes into the right cognitive and affective relation with *Ens a se,* and therefore with all that, in any sense, is.

# The Unity of the Church

1950

This paper requires a word of introduction. It was written over twenty years ago, when Catholic participation in the ecumenical movement in England was embryonic and tentative. I should not write in the same style today. The basic thrust of the paper's argument I still endorse. But it requires completion on at least two points. (1) The paper makes no acknowledgement of the status of Christian communions other than that of the Catholic Church. I now believe that we cannot overlook the fact that these communions have a response to divine revelation at the roots of their actual existence, and that, as the second Vatican Council puts it in its Decree on Ecumenism, they are "by no means without significance and importance in the mystery of salvation". That Decree's distinction between imperfect and complete "communion" is a valuable tool for the deeper understanding of the mystery of the Church. (2) The paper advocates a "movement of approach" towards Catholic doctrine on the part of the other Christian communions. It ought also to have urged that the Catholic Church has much to learn (even if only about half-forgotten parts of its own heritage) from the other churches, and that unity should mean a mutual enrichment, as is indeed implied by the paper's reference to the inclusion of "all that is positive in the positions of the reuniting bodies". I have written more recently about ecumenical matters in my book *The Theology of Vatican II,* Darton, Longman and Todd, 1967.

B.C.B.

There is a homesickness for visible unity in the Christian world today. The crisis of our civilization, the growth of secularism, the menace of conscious, deliberate, organized anti-Christian forces have no doubt in part occasioned this heightened sense that Christians must unite in face of common perils. And again, the serious disadvantages (to use no stronger language) that attend upon Christian missionary effort, both at home and abroad, through the mutual contradictions and competition of the various Christian communions, are perhaps more vividly realised at present than at most times in the past three hundred years. But surely the driving force of what I may call the reunion movement is something deeper, more native to Christianity as such, than even these grave practical considerations. Surely the dynamism of the movement, or movements, comes from a growing conviction that disunity can be justified only by a virtual denial of something that is of the very essence of Christianity, that it would mean contradicting the intention of God Incarnate. Did he not himself remind us that a kingdom or a house divided against itself *cannot stand*? And have we not his assurance that the Church which he would raise up *would* stand triumphant against the worst assaults of its enemies until the end of the world?

St Paul saw Christ and the dispensation inaugurated by him, a dispensation which was itself a historical phenomenon operating in the world of real history, as the great unifier of Jew and Gentile, breaking down the middle-wall of partition between them. He saw that unity in Christ was deeper than our racial and cultural differences—in him there is neither Greek nor barbarian, slave nor free, but all are one person in Christ. In its at-one-ment with God in Christ mankind was to find its at-one-ment with itself.

Now here I wish to lay down a principle which I hope may be acceptable, and which will underlie all I have to say. It is the principle that visible Christian unity, however it is attained and maintained, must be basically a unity of doctrine. Spiritual sympathy, however real and deep, is not adequate as a foundation of visible unity. I may have warm and deep spiritual sympathy with an orthodox Jew, Moslem or Buddhist. But since he does not agree with me in what I hold to be essential religious beliefs, he and I cannot unite or even co-operate in practical religious matters, except within a most restricted field and at a very superficial level. Why? Because our religious practice, his and mine, must flow from our religious beliefs. That is the nature of deliberate human action—it is the practical consequence of knowledge or belief. It flows from the evaluation of an historical situation; and such evaluation requires a criterion, a yard-stick, a standard of values, which can be provided only by our intellectual convictions. My own religious efforts, as a Christian, must be to bring men to find in God Incarnate their saviour, their support and their hope; but for the orthodox Jew the very notion that Jesus is the Lord God must be a frightful blasphemy. How can

he unite with me, or I with him? No, religious unity, and therefore Christian unity, presupposes agreement as to the essentials
of religious faith.

How far does such agreement at present extend? Well, on
this particular issue of unity there is today at least a widespread
agreement among Christians that visible Christian unity is a
consummation much to be desired, with perhaps a disposition
to agree that unity of some kind was not only hoped for by
Christ but established by him and destined to endure throughout
history. It is not my purpose today to dwell at length on the
interior unity of the Church, a unity which will be fully realised
in heaven and which is in the last resort a participation, here by
grace and hereafter in glory, of the absolute unity of the life of
the triune God. My own subject is the much more humble one
of the visible unity of the Church as an historical phenomenon.
We may remind ourselves that there is a twofold unity in every
individual human being—a unity of body and a unity of soul.
The latter is more important than the former, as the soul is
higher than the body. But the unity of the body is *necessary;*
and it is in the visible unity of the body that our several members
retain their connexion with our soul. Similarly, to anticipate
what will be said later on, the Catholic position as regards the
Church's unity is that visible unity of the Church as an historical
entity is necessary, and that local churches as corporate parts
of the whole retain their connexion with the life of the Church,
a life deriving from the Holy Spirit, by remaining within that
visible unity. Most Christians, as I have said, probably tend to
agree that unity of some kind is characteristic of God's Church.
But Catholics add that unity is a characteristic *mark* of the
Church, enabling the enquirer to identify her and to distinguish
her from other bodies. They therefore affirm that unity is both
inward and outward, both future and present. This affirmation is
not made in any full sense by our separated brethren in those
communions that owe their independent existence to the religious
upheavals of the sixteenth century. Thus a recent Lambeth
pronouncement clearly implied that the Church is something
wider than the Anglican or any other single communion. The
same assumption breathes, if I am not mistaken, through the
pages of the report on Catholicity recently presented to the
Archbishop of Canterbury by a committee of scholars and
theologians mainly of the Anglo-Catholic communion. Thus for
many of our Anglican brethren, and I think for a growing

number of Christians in non-conformist bodies, visible unity is not indeed of the *esse* of the Church; but it is of its *bene esse,* an end to be hoped for, prayed for, striven for.

Nearly everyone would agree that in heaven the unity of the Church will be complete; a Kingdom of Wills, to use Kant's classic expression, a complete harmony of thought and love of which the glorified Christ will be the centre, the focus, the directive Head. And it is well to remind ourselves that the Kingdom of God, of which on earth the Church is the divinely established instrument, is essentially a post-historic reality. Our true home, says St Paul (*Phil.* III 20), is in heaven; it is to heaven that we look expectantly for the coming of our Lord Jesus Christ to save us. And our Lord himself points to his future coming in divine majesty to judge mankind, when he will say to the saved: "Enter into the kingdom prepared for you from the foundation of the world." The full manifestation of what we hope for is therefore reserved to the post-historic kingdom; and many who are not Roman Catholics would no doubt argue that the Catholic belief in visible unity as an essential property of the Church on earth is an illicit transference to the conditions of history of a consummation that is guaranteed only for the life to come.

But the expectation of a post-historic kingdom, though essential to Christianity, is not the *differentia* of our religion. Many Jews subscribed to this expectation before the coming of Christ. What distinguishes Christianity from Judaism is its faith that this post-historic kingdom has its real historical anticipation in the Incarnation and its effects. It is not the second coming of Christ which is the Christian novelty; it is his first coming. Not the advent on the clouds of heaven, not the throne of post-historic judgment, but the advent in the stable of Bethlehem and the throne of the Cross. This is the scandal and the folly of Christianity: the obscure and humiliated Messiah establishing a "contemptible" little kingdom subject to the vicissitudes of history; a kingdom to be propagated by a Church that would be persecuted and betrayed, and that would suffer from apostasies, from the competition of false prophets and pseudo-Christs and from the cooling-off of the charity of its own members. Men had called the Master of the house Beelzebub; they would not be less ready to give the same title to his servants. Yet this his household, this Church as he calls it in the famous passage in

Matthew XVI, is the little flock to whom it is the Father's good pleasure to give the kingdom. We shall never understand Christianity unless we hold fast to the fact that it is a religion on two planes, a post-historic and a historical plane, and that the historical plane is a symbol containing "sacramentally" the reality of the post-historic plane—it is what we may call an eschatological sacrament.

What, then, is this Church which our Lord said he would establish, and which we see in existence before our eyes in the New Testament? It is, quite simply, an historical society; though it is also something more than an ordinary human society. It is a society whose members have accepted as true the Gospel proclaimed first by Christ, and after him by those who have received his commission. It is a society that is entered into by the reception of baptism; and baptism is accorded only to those who make a confession of faith: he who *believes* and is baptised will be saved. It functions as a society. It has its officials, for example the apostles, who exercise authority in it and have the power, which they are prepared on occasion to exercise, to deprive a member of his active membership: "My judgment is to hand over (the evil-doer) to Satan to the destruction of the flesh that the spirit may be saved in the day of the Lord." Professor Dodd has recently argued that we have here the exercise of the power of ex-communication referred to in Chapter XVIII of St Matthew's Gospel: "Count him all one with the heathen and the publican; all that you bind on earth shall be bound in heaven, and all that you loose on earth shall be loosed in heaven." As a society, and under the leadership of the apostles, the Church legislates (*Acts* XV). It is conscious of itself as a society distinguishable from its non-Christian background: "Give no offence," says St Paul, "to Jew or to Greek, or to God's Church" (1 *Cor*. X 32). And to this Church Christ promised indefectibility: built upon a rock, the gates of Hell would not prevail against it. We must infer that if this society should cease to exist on earth Christ's promises would be proved untrustworthy. This society takes the place in the new dispensation of the Jewish people in the old. Its rulers the apostles teach infallibly—such is the inference we may draw from Professor Cullman's study of tradition in the New Testament—and it is itself the pillar and the ground of truth, the Temple of God, God's building, the inheritor of the kingdom.

Two writers in the S.P.C.K. one-volume Commentary, Dr Sparrow Simpson and Bishop E. Graham, may be referred to here. The former tells us that the primitive Christian community at Jerusalem contained in germ three elements fundamental to the Catholic interpretation of Christianity: Dogma, Hierarchy and Sacrament. The original leaders of the Church did not derive their authority from the community but from Christ. In great and vital questions the decision did not rest with the local church but with the central and original society. And the decision is unthinkable without the apostles as directing and presiding. He tells us that when St Paul speaks of the Church as the Body of Christ he means not the local church but the world-wide Church, not an invisible entity but that Church in which God has set the apostles. According to St Paul, as interpreted by this same scholar, an individual is brought into relation with Christ through incorporation into the world-wide Church. The distinction between those that are within and those that are without the constitution of the Church is fundamental. The Church is the object of Christ's love. It is the corporate institution that is redeemed (this is the principle later summed up in the epigram: *extra ecclesiam nulla salus*).

Bishop Graham says that for the author of the Epistle to the Ephesians redemption implies membership in a corporate society of divine origin, the Church of Christ, a visible society which is also an organic unity, the organ of Christ's self-expression, the instrument whereby he works. Without the Church he would even be incomplete as the Incarnate Saviour of mankind. The report on Catholicity, referred to above, has a valuable chapter on this primitive Christian society and its unity.

As in the New Testament, so we see this society in the patristic age. St Justin Martyr sees the Christians as forming an *ethnos,* a people, distinct from Jews and Gentiles. Before him St Ignatius of Antioch speaks of the Catholic (that is to say the universal as contrasted with the particular, local) Church. Heretics leave the Church, or are expelled from it, but it survives these losses, substantially unchanged; it survives, as Christ promised that it should survive, with its traditions, its hierarchy, its doctrines and its laws. It is, we are told, the ark of salvation and the house of God; you cannot have God for your Father, says St Cyprian, unless you have the Church for your mother. And this Church is a recognizable historical entity and visibly one, one in fact as it is one in Christ's intention, the seamless robe that cannot be divided. Bodies more or less Christian split off from the Church and pursue for a time each a life of its own. But the central body continues, and continues to claim to be alone the Church founded by Christ. From this central body of patristic times all modern Christianity derives.

It seems to me of overwhelming importance to realise that the Church is an historical society and not a pious aspiration or an exclusively heavenly reality. It is as historical, as concrete, as the human nature of Christ was historical, a thing of flesh and blood. Among the earliest heresies was Docetism, which denied the full historical concreteness of Christ's human nature. It has been taken as the typical heresy; and indeed it strikes at the roots of the Christian doctrine of salvation, which rests upon the conviction that God has really assumed humanity into himself in the person of Jesus of Nazareth, and through him, proportions being observed, in us. Docetism in effect denies the precise truth which differentiates Christianity from Judaism: that God has really visited and redeemed his people, that the post-historic kingdom is already mysteriously present through the mission of Christ and of those commissioned by him. The theory of a Church essentially invisible, a Church of the elect, a Church that is a pattern laid up in heaven of which the best earthly approximations are mere human and contingent copies—such a theory is the deutero-Docetism of our modern times. Such is not the Church of the New Testament, the ancient Creeds, and the first millennium of Christian history. Nor can such an impalpable society (a contradiction in terms?) perform the functions of a Church in the spiritual life of mankind or of individual men.

Man is essentially social, as, after so many generations of exaggerated individualism, we are beginning now to realise again —sometimes with a fresh exaggeration in the opposite direction. He needs society as the medium of his human life and personal development. He needs the checks and disciplines, as well as the opportunities and enlargements, afforded by society. In social life he finds not enslavement but emancipation. If you offer man, in whom this social need is innate, not society but the idea of society (even the Platonic idea of society) the hungry sheep look up but are not fed. This, which is true of our natural life, is true also in the supernatural order—for grace crowns nature. The *idea* of a Church may titillate man's mind, but it cannot satisfy his spirit. His spirit needs the "beloved community" itself, the actual historical fact of the Catholic Church, its authority in faith and morals, its actual discipline, its forbidding as well as its attractive aspect—a reality more complete than he is himself, a reality in which his own selfhood is made more real, is stabilised and enhanced, because in the mystical body of Christ, the fullness of us all, the new humanity in which our old humanity is regenerated and transfigured. No society less than a Church which is *de jure* universal can fulfil this function for man's spirit; for any society less than that is an incorporation not of the whole but of some part of humanity; it is of necessity provincial. *Homo sum et nil humanum alienum a me puto.* The Catholic Church of the New Testament is central, classical, because it extends its sway of right over all mankind and is intended to be the super-naturalising leaven of every aspect of human life—it is Catholic both extensively and intensively.

As the men of our contemporary world are waking up to man's social nature and needs, so they increasingly appreciate the social character of the religion of Christ, and they repeat with more sense of its importance the phrase in the Creed about the holy Catholic church. But many of them have yet, so it seems to us, to realise that there is a world of difference between the *idea* of a Church and the *fact* of *the* Church.

There is one other point in regard to the Church about which there would be a very general agreement among Western Christians nowadays. Few in the West would deny that the Church is not an organ or appendix of civil society or the state; deriving as it does from a higher source than civil society, it derives from that source its independence and sovereign status. It is what the philosophers call a perfect, but what I prefer to call a *complete,* society; which means that it is not hierarchically subordinated to any more inclusive or more authoritative human association. There is no appeal on earth from its decisions within its own field of mission; and Christ tells us that its decisions are ratified in heaven. Obviously, as a sovereign and independent society it must have its own constitution, organization and government, and this government must derive its authority from the Founder of the Christian religion.

Now I wish to emphasise what is the heart of the matter for us Catholics when we are thinking about the problem of the reunion of Christendom. Yet it is a point which to us is so obvious as to be almost incapable of proof by reasoning; it appears to us to be something that one just sees, and we find it hard to understand how others fail to see it. It is that the Church of Christ is one historical society, not many such. It may indeed have subordinate groupings within it, as the church of Birmingham, the church of Paris, the church of New York, the church of Chungkin or the Maronite church of Antioch. But none of these is or claims to be a complete society by itself; each is only a local realisation, as was the church of Corinth in the days of St Paul, of a universal reality. Each is a subordinate part of the whole Church, deriving its life from actual contemporary inherence in the whole Church as a limb derives its life from inherence in the living body. Once, however, you posit a Christian communion that is detached from the universal whole, that has renounced the authority of the whole, that has determined either to live its own independent life or to subordinate itself to an authority other than that of the *Catholica,* then that dissident communion is plainly no longer a part of the real historical society from which it has seceded. And this fact—that it is no longer a part—is true, however the blame is to be apportioned for the act of separation. That act may have been initiated from either side; either the parent or the seceding body may, in your judgement, be morally responsible for the rupture. The fact remains that after the break we are dealing not with one but with more than one society. And for a Christian it can therefore require no argument that one and one only of the resultant societies is the society established by Christ and commissioned to represent him on earth.

I know that a movement named after the University of Oxford, a movement of high chivalry and Christian graciousness, at one time sponsored—or many of its adherents sponsored—a theory which affirmed that the one Catholic Church lives on in three separate branches out of communion with each other, in no inclusive subordination to a common contemporary life and a common contemporary authority. But I think it is quite clear that such a theory is impossible. You might with equal plausibility maintain that the United States of America, having seceded from the English Crown in the eighteenth century—whether justifiably or not is not the point—nevertheless remain today one society, one state, with England. True, they share—or shared—a common racial origin, they have with this country a common cultural tradition, they inherited her legal system, social structure—what you will. But they are organised under an independent sovereignty; and from the moment that this independence was a fact England and the U.S.A. were no longer one political society but two. A national church which should secede from Catholic unity, rejecting the authority henceforward of the body from which it seceded, and managing its own affairs under the supreme governance, if so be, of the national sovereign, is obviously no longer the same society as the Roman Catholic Church.

What we see, then, as we look out with unprejudiced eyes, as of a Martian paying his first visit to earth, upon the contemporary Christian world, is a number of Christian societies independent of each other, though some of them have formed federations among themselves. There is a useful distinction in political science between the *Bundstaat* and the *Staatsbund,* the federal state and the federation of states. The U.S.A. is a federal state, because the ultimate sovereignty over the whole Union resides in the central government. The United Nations are a *Staatsbund,* a federation of states, because none of the constituent members of this union has so far consented to surrender its independent sovereignty. The Roman Catholic communion is analogous to the U.S.A. inasmuch as its constituent local churches, while each possessing a measure of autonomy, recognise a sovereignty beyond themselves in Council and Pope, or in the Pope alone; but this communion differs from the U.S.A. in the mode of its origin, since it was not constituted originally by the coming together of a number of previously existing independent entities—though since its origin it has occasionally taken into its unity already existing Christian groups. But the Christian bodies as a whole form neither a *Bundstaat* nor a *Staatsbund.*

The Catholic position with regard to the unity of the Church is simple—which is not to say that it is not profound. I am speaking for the moment of unity, not of the reunion of Christendom. It is, that Christ founded a Church which was essentially a society; that he promised indefectibility to this society and that (quite apart from a particular text in St Matthew's Gospel) it is clear from the New Testament that the Christian revelation involves the indefectibility of the Church; and that in consequence unless one (one only) of the extant Christian societies is the society established by Christ, then the claim of Christianity to be a true revelation from God collapses. The matter is really as simple as that and we cannot see any answer to the Catholic position.

Perhaps it will be as well, at this point, to refer to what I conceive to be a common cause of confusion in this matter. It is stated, and truly, that baptism is the rite by which a man becomes a member of Christ's Church. It is then observed that many extant Christian societies are composed of baptised persons. And it is inferred that a society of those who have been made members of the church must be itself, as a society, a part of the Church. But the error in this inference is surely palpable. If ten thousand English families sail away from England, settle in some sparsely inhabited region of the non-British world, and establish a new sovereign authority which they henceforth obey, the fact that they were English families and that their members were English citizens does not make this new state a part of the state of England. If its citizens can be said to remain in any sense English citizens, it is not by virtue of their membership of the new state, but by reason of their former allegiance to the English Crown. Similarly, if the Catholic hierarchy of Chile renounced its allegiance to the authority of the Roman Catholic communion—*quod Deus avertat*—and set up shop on its own account, the resulting national church of Chile would plainly not be a part of the Roman Catholic society. Christ founded not simply a new *race* consisting of baptised persons, but a new society; and though baptism of its own nature makes a man a member of that society, he can frustrate this consequence of baptism by refusing to accept the implications of such membership. Yet this fact, that baptism makes a man, normally, a member of the Catholic Church has one most consoling consequence: it means that the Church regards all baptised persons as her own children and longs to see her family reunited in the one home. They are our separated brethren.

What then is the Catholic attitude to the problem of the reunion of Christendom? It is, to put it shortly, that reunion must be sought on the basis, not of the Highest Common Factor of the several Christian communions, but on that of the Lowest Common Multiple. The principle of the H.C.F. is that the doctrine of the resultant single Christian body should consist of those doctrines already held by all the separated bodies. I need not pause to point out in detail that the result would be a somewhat jejune creed. The notion of reunion on this basis has been satirised by Ronald Knox (in his Anglican days) in *Reunion All Round* and I need hardly add anything more about it now. The principle of the L.C.M. is that a basis of reunion should be sought in a form of Christianity which includes all that is positive in the positions of the reuniting bodies. I say all that is positive; and I venture to suggest that some of the reformers' doctrines which expressed positive opinions irreconcilable with Catholic truth have ceased to command the actual belief of the adherents of the Protestant Reformation. For instance, does anybody today hold the opinion of justification by faith alone in such a way as to be irreconcilable with the doctrine on justification of the Council of Trent? (Curiously enough, it is perhaps in the case of the churches most close to the Catholic position, those I mean of the separated East, that there would be the greatest difficulty in applying the L.C.M. principle—if it is true that these churches really hold that the so-called Orthodox communion is the one true church of Christ.)

As a matter of historical fact, and apart from any judgment on the implications of that fact, the Roman Catholic communion is and has been since before the origin of any other extant Christian communion the central stream of Christian history. Of the extant Christian bodies, none can claim historical continuity with Christian origins except by derivation from that central stream. Suppose our Martian, not content with a survey of contemporary Christendom, were to hire a time-machine from H. G. Wells, set the engine in reverse and so travel back through the Christian centuries. What would he see, as he went backwards from 1950 towards the first century A.D.? He would see Christian reunion taking place before his eyes. He would see the non-Catholic Christian bodies being absorbed, one by one, into the Catholic centre. As he passed the year 1925, or thereabouts, he would notice that the Czech National Church slid back into unity with the Holy See. Reaching the year 1870 he would see the same thing happening to the Old Catholic communion. Then in the 18th century Wesleyanism would reunite with the Church of England, and in 1560 and again in the 1530's the Church of England itself would be reunited to the Catholic Church. The same would happen to continental Protestant and Reformed churches in the same 16th century, and in the 11th century the Eastern so-called orthodox separated churches would have the same experience. Finally in the 5th century the Monophysite and Nestorian communions would revert to Catholic unity, so that when our Martian reached about the year 430 A.D. none of those separated societies which now stand outside the Catholic unity would remain; we all spring, as I have said before, from the Catholic Church of 30 to 430 A.D.

Yes, you may say, but what right have you to maintain that the Catholic Church of 430 is identical with the Catholic Church today? Well, in the first place, if Christianity is a true religion, the Catholic Church of 430 A.D. must be identical with *one or other* of the Christian bodies which surround us at the present time; and we ask with some confidence, which of these contemporary bodies can make any plausible claim to this exclusive identity except the Catholic Church? There is only one Church which has been able to maintain, in the face of the ordinary judgment of mankind, the *title* "Catholic"; it is true for Roman Catholics today, as it was for Roman Catholics in the days of St Cyril of Jerusalem, that the way to find their meeting-place in a strange town is to enquire "not simply where the Lord's house is, but where is the *Catholic* Church". Again, the Catholic Church today, like the Catholic Church of 430 A.D., is a body claiming Christ's authority to dispense the sacraments and to teach infallibly to all mankind the traditional faith, claiming too that, objectively speaking, it is the duty of all men to belong to her. Again, in the Catholic Church today as in the Church of the fourth and early fifth centuries, there is one local church and See, the Roman, that claims to be the organ and necessary centre of this obligatory unity. St Ambrose, before the end of the fourth century, speaks of Rome as the church whence the laws of unity derive. St Jerome, also before 400 A.D., writes to the Pope of that time: "I address myself to the successor of the fisherman and to the disciple of the cross. Making none my leader save Christ I am united in communion to your beatitude, that is to the See of Peter; on that rock I know the Church to have been built. He who eats the Paschal Lamb outside this abode is profane. If a man is not in Noe's Ark he will be submerged by the flood." It cannot be plausibly maintained, if the Church of Christ has survived at all, that it is to be identified with any other body than that in which the Roman See still makes the claims that are implied or affirmed in these quotations from Catholic doctors of the fourth century.

A scheme of Christian reunion that left out the Roman Catholic communion would hardly be regarded as other than a very imperfect realisation of the impulse to unity. But on what terms could reunion *include* that communion? I am not now speaking dogmatically as a Catholic, but soberly as a man of ordinary commonsense. And I ask, could the Roman Catholic communion meet the non-Catholic bodies halfway? If we are thinking of such things as a vernacular liturgy, a married clergy, a patriarchate of Canterbury—then I say, of course, yes. But if we are referring to the sphere of defined doctrine, then we are faced with an obvious and insurmountable difficulty. The whole Catholic dogmatic system, including our belief in the Godhead and perfect manhood of Christ, is based on what we believe to be a divine guarantee given to the Church's teaching: the Church is the pillar and the ground of truth. The whole structure of Catholic doctrine, and every component of it, is thus accepted for the same reason, namely that it is true with the truth of an utterance of God himself, and that it carries his guarantee. To ask the Catholic Church to retract any of its dogmas, even to ask it to admit that any such dogma is an open question, would be to suggest the suicide of Catholicism, not only as Catholic, but as Christian. The dogma of the Church's infallibility, which is implicit in every other Catholic dogma, makes it impossible for the Church to retrace her steps in this dogmatic sphere.

But this dogma of infallibility is itself linked up with the assertion that the Roman Catholic communion is not just a part, but the whole of the teaching Church established by Christ. It is not simply that we *will* not compromise here; it is that we cannot. If we could yield an inch, the whole Catholic position with regard to defined doctrine would be destroyed at once. We saw the instinctive Catholic reaction to such a threat forty years ago, when Modernism made precisely this suggestion—that dogma was not final but contingent. The suggestion was violently and totally rejected; and indeed nothing resembling historical Christianity could survive the disappearance of dogma. The epoch-making controversy of the fourth century, with regard to the word *consubstantial,* can have no meaning, must have been a huge and disastrous mistake, unless Christianity is a dogmatic religion.

It may of course be asked what grounds there are for supposing that, if the Catholic Church cannot withdraw from its doctrinal positions, other Christian bodies should find it easier to change their formularies. But it will at once be perceived that a society that makes no claim to infallibility is in a very different situation, in this matter, from one which does. If a society has said in the past that the Catholic doctrine of sacrifices of masses is a dangerous deceit, but has never claimed to be infallible in making such an assertion—then it can withdraw the proposition on the principle of an appeal from Philip excited to Philip calm.

It therefore appears to us that, desirable as reunion is, it could only come about not by the jettisoning of Catholic doctrine, but by a movement of approach to that doctrine on the part of the non-Catholic communions or their members. Meanwhile, and at all times, the Catholic Church persists in its affirmation that, objectively speaking, every man is called to share in Christ's redemption by personal submission to the "Catholic claims".

We have always to remember that God foresaw what has been the actual outcome of the mission of Jesus Christ. The actual outcome has been the Church. Apart from some rather vague references in Jewish and pagan literature, all that we know of Christ and his teaching, all that he has meant and means to men, including the New Testament itself, is derived from the Church.

The separated Christian bodies themselves can claim no tradition except what is derived from this source. We see, looking backwards as God saw looking forwards, not only that this was to be so; but we see, as he saw, how the Church was to develop— its features, its structures, as it declared itself ever more clearly in history; a society that was to be persistently, incurably doctrinal, sacramental, hierarchical, authoritarian, infallibilist. At no point, so far as we can see, were these features introduced by a revolutionary change of direction, but always in the process whereby the Church has been becoming ever more characteristically and manifestly what she always had it in her to become.

The question which we submit with all humility and in all charity to our non-Catholic friends is this: This development, the central and typical outcome of Christ's historical mission, this society from which all other Christian societies and movements in the long run derive—has it been willed by God, or has it only been permitted by him as error and sin are permitted? For ourselves, we have answered that question. We could not have known Christ apart from the Church. We see in the Church that sublime purity of moral ideal and of spiritual teaching, that transcendent claim, that power for good in the measure in which her teaching is accepted and obeyed, that miraculous victory in apparent failure, which she has taught us to venerate in Christ himself. And by faith we see yet more. We see in her the ever new, ever contemporary, yet ever traditional re-presentation of

Christ himself, who was dead and behold he is alive for evermore, yesterday and today, and the same for ever. And then, looking back, we see that Christ, who is God, intended to establish a Church, establish it unshakably upon a rock. Are we to be blamed for holding that the Church with which history presents us, the Church which still speaks to us as she spoke to Origen and Augustine and Bernard, to Dominic and Francis, to Thomas of Aquinum and Francis of Sales, to Thomas More and to Newman, is the fulfilment of that promise—since other fulfilment there is none? For us, then, the question can have but a single answer. And seeing in that answer the key to the problems, the supply of the spiritual needs of mankind, we long to transmit the vision of it to our separated brethren and to a whole world which can come, in the final issue, to God only through Christ, and can come to Christ, in the final issue, only through the Church.

I will conclude by emphasising that in all this, if I seem to sit in judgment on non-Catholic forms of Christianity, I wish to pass no sort of moral judgment on non-Catholic Christians. It is no part of my task to apportion guilt to the originators of Christian disunion. As regards those who have grown up in such separated bodies after they had long been in existence, I am confident, and indeed bound in charity to believe, that the vast majority of those among them who practise their religion are, as we say, "in good faith". Being in good faith, so long as they remain in good faith, they are capable of divine grace and I do not doubt that they receive it. God's mercy is unbounded; and if I understand our Lord's teaching aright, there may well be excuse for failure to recognise explicitly either God in Jesus of Nazareth or Christ in his Church. But there could be no excuse for a Catholic who deliberately "spoke a word against" what his conscience tells him is a manifestation of the Holy Spirit. Nor on the other hand will that man attain salvation who has in his conscience recognised the divine authority in the Church so long as he pertinaciously (to use a technical term of the canonists) refuses her his visible allegiance.

# The Catholic Faith and the Bible

1957

One effect of the breakdown of the medieval synthesis and the long subsequent dominance of the Protestant tradition in our culture is that, consciously or not, many people take it for granted that a man's religion is his private concern, that belief and religious practice are in essence entirely and exclusively his own affair. No creature, it is held, may "come between my soul and God". The religious witness and experience of others may indeed help to direct my mind towards God; but in the act of religion I am a solitary individual, responsible immediately and solely to God himself. Religion is "what a man does with his solitariness", no one's business but his own, something into which no other man has any right to intrude.

The very term "catholic faith" expresses the difference between this idea of religion and the teaching of the Catholic Church. The word *catholic* means *universal,* and the Catholic faith is the faith not originally of individual Catholics but of the whole body to which they belong and from which they learn it. It is something that existed and was believed before the individual believed it. It is the common faith of a whole society, which the individual accepts and assimilates and makes his own. Though thus assimilated by individuals, it does not cease to be a common faith, but becomes a spiritual bond uniting all the Church's members in a common mind, the "mind of the Church". It is something distinct, not only in its object but in its nature, from my literary tastes, my aesthetic preferences, or my political opinions. My faith is the Catholic faith only if I accept it in its pre-existent wholeness, precisely because in its totality and in each of its items it is the faith of the whole body, and not precisely because each item of it has commended itself separately to my private judgment.

The Church teaches that God has revealed himself not simply here and there to separate individuals, but in a public revelation, given and entrusted to a society, the Church herself, whose function is to convey and transmit the revelation to all mankind. The climax of this public self-disclosure of God was in the earthly life and resurrection of Jesus Christ, whose perfect manhood subsists in the very personality of God the Son. But

114

this climax was led up to, and prepared for, by an agelong process of partial and developing revelation, which the Church traces back through the wise men of Israel, the priests and the prophets, to Moses and beyond. God had not left mankind without witness in those long centuries preceding the Incarnation. His creative activity "in the beginning" had been matched by his gradual and progressive self-manifestation till at last the stage was set and men's minds were prepared for a manifestation which was also a complete self-giving. The whole process may be regarded as a divine education of man, in which each succeeding stage builds upon the enlightenment previously given.

The education of an individual man depends upon his memory, in which past lessons are stored up and made available as the basis for subsequent more advanced lessons. Without memory we should be uneducable, at least if we include under the general heading of memory our capacity of acquiring bodily skills.

What corresponds in society to memory in the individual is tradition. Tradition makes available to one generation the fruits of the education and experience of men in preceding generations. Tradition can stifle activity, just as memory of one's own past can inhibit initiative; but without tradition cultural progress is impossible. Philosophy, science and the arts all have their traditions; so have schools and villages, cities, countrysides and nations. The best modern astronomer, sociologist or architect will be the first to admit his debt to those who have pioneered the trail for him and have thus enabled him to push on one stage further and to transmit the legacy of the past enriched by his own, relatively tiny, contribution. Even the rebel from tradition is usually far more indebted than he is aware of to the past. Descartes is hardly to be understood with any completeness without some knowledge of the scholastic tradition which it was his ambition to supersede. A loss of tradition is for a culture, for mankind in general, what amnesia is for the individual. Insofar as it occurs, to that extent man has to begin at the beginning again.

Tradition is stored up and transmitted in a variety of ways. The artefacts of one generation convey a lesson of skill upon which the next generation may improve. Language itself is a crystallisation of experience, a tradition, and an immensely valuable one. Rites and ceremonies, manners, and the customs of the tribe are all parts of tradition, all fulfil a function of education. And along

115

with all these goes oral tradition in song and lore and legend, binding each generation to its past, teaching it the wisdom of the ages, giving direction to the new contribution which it itself will make to the future. It is important to realise that written records are a comparatively late vehicle of tradition, and that even after the invention and exploitation of writing the other vehicles are not absorbed by it, but continue to play their part, perhaps a somewhat reduced part, in the education of succeeding generations.

One of the main functions of writing, especially in early times, is to give fixity and relative permanence to oral tradition. The unwritten poetry of early bards and minstrels did something of the same sort, the rhythmic patterns of song serving to discourage extensive alterations of its content. Writing, though still imperfectly, does this with greater efficacy. Normally, however, the written tradition is less extensive than the sum total of traditional material.

For the historian Christianity comes to birth as the faith and religious practice of a new human fellowship that took shape in the womb of first century Judaism, under the impact of the life and teaching, the crucifixion and resurrection, of Jesus of Nazareth. We are told of only one occasion when Jesus wrote, and then he did so in the dust on the ground. Thus the tradition of Christianity was originally unwritten, and such for some time and to some extent it remained. When St Paul speaks of "the traditions you have been taught" (II *Thess* II 15) he is probably thinking primarily of the oral instruction given to catechumens and neophytes. St Mark's Gospel was written perhaps a quarter of a century (many scholars would say, thirty-five years or so) after Jesus' death, and it reads in many parts like a record of the oral teaching of someone who had been an eyewitness of Christ's public life—perhaps St Peter. The Fourth Gospel may have been in large measure preached or taught orally before it was committed to writing. St Luke in his opening sentence says that several before him have undertaken to draw up (doubtless written) records of the Gospel story, and a critical study of his Gospel makes it very probable—practically certain—that he utilised written records, among them St Mark's Gospel; but St Luke probably supplemented these sources with information derived orally from eyewitnesses. It is possible that St Matthew's Gospel is in substance earlier than all these, and that it is substantially the composition of an eyewitness compiled in part from notes almost contemporaneous with the events and teaching it records.

We are fortunate to possess, in the New Testament writings, a fairly extensive collection of written documents of primitive Christianity. But we should do well to remember that the primitive tradition will have been far richer and more extensive than these writings are, and that however early were the beginnings of a Greek formulation of the tradition—all our extant documents are in Greek—these writings themselves disclose to the scrutiny of scholars a substratum of Aramaic thought and language. Under divine Providence it looks as though a good deal of the evidence contained in the New Testament has been almost accidentally preserved. Thus, with the possible exception of St Matthew's Gospel, St Paul's epistles afford our earliest evidence for the Christian Eucharist and its institution by Christ. But St Paul's mention of its institution is prompted, so far as we can see, not by a purpose of systematic doctrinal or sacramental teaching, but by his concern about some disorders which had apparently crept into the meetings of the Corinthian church in which the Eucharist was celebrated. And just as some of our evidence is in this sense accidental, so we have to realise that a great deal that we might have wished to know is irretrievably lost: *There is much else besides that Jesus did; if all of it were put in writing, I do not think that the world itself would contain the books which would have to be written.* The New Testament tells us that Christ appointed and empowered twelve apostles; but of half of this number it tells us practically nothing after about 50 A.D. And there are all sorts of gaps in what we are told about Jesus himself, and plenty of obscurities and difficulties in the information that we do possess.

Meanwhile it must not be forgotten that the transmission of the tradition of Christian origins was not confined to the New Testament writings. For a time, oral tradition will have gone on and played its legitimate part alongside the written materials. Papias of Hierapolis, writing about A.D. 130–140, told how as a young man (perhaps about A.D. 100) he had eagerly gleaned such information as he could from those who had seen Jesus, or else from their immediate disciples. More permanent were the usages and sacramental rites of the Church. The rites of baptism and the Eucharist were not originally derived from the New Testament documents, but preceded them. And rites have a very tough life and survival-value. Perhaps hardly less important, but less calculable, was the impression left on the original disciples, and passed on by them in a thousand indefinable ways of communication available in the common life of a society, of the Founder of this new form of belief and practice which was yet an old form.

For while to the historian Christianity is the faith of a new society of which the apostles were the first officers, to the theologian it is the legitimate continuation, development and completion, of the faith and practice of ancient Israel. And the new society itself, *the Church of God,* is, for theology and faith, the old People of God transformed as a larva is transformed into a butterfly, or as inorganic matter is transformed by the advent of life. The Church has resolutely refused to disown its debt to the old Israel. The debt, indeed, could not be disowned without disloyalty to Christ himself, who claimed implicitly to be the expected divine envoy or Messiah who should establish in Israel that reign of God to which Old Testament prophecy had pointed forwards.

As the New Testament books are a record of the traditions of the primitive Christian Church, so those of the Old Testament are documents illustrating the developing religious tradition of pre-Christian Israel. They include books which are usually classified as historical, and along with them collections of prophecies, psalms, and books of proverbial or traditional wisdom. To the Jews of the period immediately preceding the Christian era the most important part of this collection was, as it remains for Judaism to-day, the Pentateuch or *Law of Moses* as it was named. This Law, or revelation, viewed as a guide to right living, had by the beginning of our era become the governing basis of the Jewish faith and practice.

Broadly speaking, the Old Testament books disclose to the discernment of critical scholarship the story of the early and protracted struggles and eventual triumph in Israel of faith in Jahveh, the Lord, as the one holy creator God who, it was believed, had chosen Israel as his peculiar people, had made his *covenant* with them, and who would one day intervene to establish among them, and through them over all mankind, his perfect reign or kingdom. They also show, in their latest strata, an interest in the life after death, whose quality would, it was held, be determined by the moral and religious quality of the life lived on earth.

The Old Testament is probably regarded with some embarrassment, as a sort of *damnosa hereditas* by a good many people who would prefer to see Christianity unencumbered by this record of often very primitive morality, not to say immorality, with its dosage of creation "mythology", its apparent historical inaccuracies, its seeming irrelevance to any of our modern problems or needs. We shall have to consider some of these difficulties presently. For the moment, it seems important to emphasise the fact that the Old Testament and the faith of ancient Israel did in fact provide the context in which occurred the revelation in Jesus Christ. And an event, not least if that event is a revelation, depends in large measure on its context for its meaning. The Gospel is both a reaction from some aspects, and a reaffirmation of other aspects, of that context. It was not only new wine, not to be poured into old bottles; it claimed also not to destroy but to fulfil. Even from the limited point of view of understanding the Christian message it is important to preserve and to study the record of that pre-Christian tradition within which Christianity came to birth.

So far we have been considering the books of the Bible as they appear to a scholar, without reference to the Church's own teaching about them. We have not presupposed any absolute value in the tradition they enshrine as compared with those of the other historical religions or faiths. We have seen them as the partial crystallisation of one element in the threefold unity; public revelation, religious society, tradition. But once we give our assent to the Church's claim to be the guardian and exponent of the final revelation of God to mankind we have to combine with our scholarly attitude to the Bible the attitude and the belief about it which the Church enjoins upon her members.

The Church's teaching on this subject is briefly summed up in the statement that the books of the Bible are canonical and inspired.

We need not spend much time here over the attribute of canonicity. To say that these books are canonical is simply to say that they have been taken and are promulgated by the Church as the official and inspired documents of the revelation which she proclaims, of the tradition which she endorses. There were other Jewish writings besides those of the canonical Old Testament. There may have been other Christian writings of the first generation besides those (of the first and perhaps the second generation) included in the New Testament. There were certainly, a little later, various apocryphal "Gospels" and "Acts". But none of these counts as part of the official sacred literature of the Judaeo-Christian revelation. They are formally distinguished from this literature because they are not *canonical*, and have never been officially adopted as inspired by the Church.

Much more important is the question of inspiration. The Church calls these books "inspired by God", and the First Vatican Council explains this as implying that "they have God as their author", although at the same time each of the books has its own human author or authors.

This teaching requires some explanation. In what sense can a book of Scripture be said to have two authors, a human one and God? Many works of literature have two authors, but they provide no analogy for the conception of a dual, human and divine, authorship as applied to Scripture. The Church does not teach that part of the contents of a canonical book comes from the human author, while another part comes from God; nor need we hold that the human author and God have so to speak thought the book out together by interchange of ideas. She may be held to teach that the whole of the contents comes from the human author and also, in a higher sense and on a different plane of reality, from the divine authorship. The book in its totality is an utterance, a word, at once of a man and, at another level, of God.

A good analogy of this notion of dual authorship is provided by the philosophic doctrine of dual causality. Philosophy has to maintain that when I perform an act—such, for instance as the writing of a sentence—the effect proceeds at once from me and (in its totality as an effect) from God who is the source of all being and all motion in the physical and the spiritual orders alike. I am truly the cause of my own acts, but God is no less truly, no less but more fully their cause. I am their *second cause*, but God is their *first cause*. Indeed the free acts of intellectual creatures, and above all the free self-oblation to God the Father of the Incarnate Son, are the highest manifestations known to us of divine causality *ad extra.*

We have here an analogy of the doctrine of inspiration, at least if we follow one explanation of that doctrine. It is a useful analogy, since it may warn us that it is probably fruitless to try to find observable traces of inspiration in the psychology of the human authors of the inspired books. It seems probable that the psychological mechanism of human authorship is in no way altered by inspiration, and that there is nothing in the actual experience of such authorship to suggest to the writer that he is the subject of inspiration. But the analogy is only an analogy. God is of course the first cause of the books of Scripture, just as he is the first cause of all other human productions—of the works of Shakespeare, for instance. Yet we do not ordinarily describe God as the *author* of Shakespeare's plays or of the History of Thucydides. Why not? Because a human utterance, whether it be a spoken or a written word, is not only a human act but the expression, in meaningful symbols, of a human affirmation, or of some other human spiritual act. If the human word involves an affirmation, God no doubt causes the affirmation but he does not necessarily, in so doing, make a divine affirmation; he does not necessarily make the human affirmation his own *affirmation.* If he did, he would be not only the first cause but the *first author* of the word. And this, it seems, is what the Church teaches about Scripture, when she proclaims that Scripture is inspired by God the Holy Spirit. The books of Scripture disclose the mind of God not only in the way in which the facts of nature, the acts of Julius Caesar, and the works of Sophocles disclose his mind; they are a disclosure of the meaning of God, a meaning which subsumes into itself the meaning of the human authors of the books.

To speak with great precision and circumspection, and at the same time to limit somewhat the problem of inspiration, the inference from the doctrine of inspiration commonly drawn by theologians and indeed by the *magisterium* of the Church is that, as God is its author, what Scripture affirms or asserts is true, since it is the word to us not only of the human authors of these books but of their divine author—and God cannot lie.

This inference at once brings us up against formidable difficulties. At first sight Scripture seems to be full of statements which are untrue. To take an obvious and banal example: if we reconstruct the age of humanity from the apparent indications of Scripture we find that man has existed on the earth for about six thousand years only; whereas scientific archaeology makes it practically certain that he has so existed for at least a million years. The problem of the "inerrancy of Scripture" was recognised in antiquity. St Augustine, fifteen hundred years ago, wrote an ingenious treatise, *De Consensu Evangelistarium,* in which he tried to explain or explain away apparent contradictions between the Gospels. The "days" of creation, in Genesis I, are a famous traditional *crux interpretum,* to which also St Augustine directed his attention. There is a passage in his *Confessions* in which he speaks of the effect of the preaching of St Ambrose upon his own still unconverted mind:

> The Catholic faith, in defence of which I thought nothing could be answered to the Manichee's arguments, I now concluded with myself, might well be maintained without absurdity: especially after I had heard one or two hard places of the Old Testament resolved now and then; which when I understood literally, I was slain. Many places therefore of those books having been spiritually expounded, I blamed mine own desperate conceit, whereby I had believed that the Law and the Prophets could no way be upheld against those that hated and scorned them.[1]

But however difficult the problem was to educated Catholics of those early days, modern science and historical literary criticism have enlarged it considerably.

There are certain general considerations which may help to reduce the magnitude of the problem, such as it appears at first sight. To begin with, there is the obvious but sometimes neglected fact that a proposition does not always assert what grammatically it says. Thus, I read in the morning paper: "Sun rises, 7.32 a.m.", but I do not conclude from this that the editor is lending his support to the geocentric hypothesis; nor do I think that he offers "7.32 a.m." as an exact timing of the event in question. The announcement conforms to a convention of speech and to a convention of approximate accuracy. I do not question

[1] *Confessions of St Augustine,* trans. W. Watts (London: Heinemann, 1912), V.

its truth, because I understand these conventions. Such considerations, though they may appear ridiculously obvious and trivial, go a long way in diminishing the area of apparent error in the Scriptures. For example, it may be doubted whether the first chapter of Genesis asserts anything more than that our universe and all it contains were created by God, that God is the fount of all goodness as of all being, and that man is, in a higher sense than subhuman creatures, a reflection of the nature of God. The human author may have believed that the earth was shaped like a flat loaf, with the sky poised above it like the lid of a tureen; and that creation took place in a period of six days of twenty-four hours—but he need not be taken as asserting this cosmology any more than the editor of *The Times* is taken as contradicting Copernicus. There is a difference in the two cases, because obviously the editor of *The Times* does not believe what he appears to say, while the author of Genesis presumably did believe in his cosmology. Yet it may be argued that as the editor uses but does not assert an obsolete belief for the purposes of his assertion, so the author of Genesis uses a belief of his own for the purpose of making assertions which are distinguishable from that belief.

There is a further, less obvious, fact to be borne in mind. It may be doubted how far even a modern scientific historian should be taken as categorically asserting everything that his propositions, taken at face value, appear to commit him to. Often he will be merely repeating, in his own words, an accepted view which he has not seen reason to examine critically and to which he does not really intend to add the weight of his own authority. Often he may state in categorical form something which he only means to offer as a reasonable conjecture. In neither case, I suggest, should he be held to have asserted error, even if subsequently the facts are proved to have been other than he supposed.

But if such be the case with a modern scientific historian, the heir to standards of accuracy and prosaic caution that have been developed through generations of historical criticism, it is even more true of an ancient writer, especially if he lived outside the orbit of critical historiography represented by a Thucydides. He must not be judged by the criterion of factual precision that may rightly be applied to a Trevelyan or even a Bryant. We shall say that frequently ancient writers did not mean to assert what grammatically they say. It used to be a favourite essay question whether history is a science or an art. In ancient times its artistic aspect may be taken to have been a larger factor than it is to-day. We do not judge El Greco adversely because his human figures are distorted and do not correspond with "facts".

Large areas of the Bible, it must further be observed, are not primarily factual at all; they belong, if we are to apply modern distinctions, to the sphere of poetry rather than of historical prose as we understand it. What place has assertion in poetry? What does Shakespeare *assert* when he writes:

Full fathom five thy father lies
Of his bones are corals made . . . ?

The Psalms are religious poems. If, read grammatically, they speak of God slaying the monster of the great deep and giving it as food to the people of Ethiopia, they yet need not be held to assert the truth of this piece of mythology any more than the Creed asserts the truth of a "three-storeyed universe" when it says that the Son of God "came down from heaven". Similarly, the Book of Job has affinities with the tragedies of Aeschylus rather than with Caesar's Commentaries. And it is possible to hold that the Books of Jonah and Tobias are religious fiction; we do not ask whether the events of Pilgrim's Progress really happened.

We have been led on, in our study of the limits of assertion, to the theme of "literary types". The truth intended by a literary composition has to be determined by the conventions of the type or class of literature to which the book belongs. The composer of epitaphs, said Johnson, is not to be held to be giving evidence under oath. To turn for a moment from the Old to the New Testament, the Acts of the Apostles seems to claim for itself, by implication, a place among the historical works of the Hellenistic period. If (as may be doubted) it was a literary convention at that time for a historian to adorn his narrative with fictitious speeches put into the mouths of his "characters", St Luke could have done the same thing without sacrificing veracity. As a matter of fact, however, there is a tendency to-day to regard the speeches of the early chapters of Acts as good evidence for the earliest, pre-Pauline Christian preaching.

124

It might seem that we have been drastically whittling down the amount of truth to be looked for in the Bible, and it may be asked: What then in the books of Scripture can be taken as deliberately asserted by their human authors and by God? At the level of investigation which we have been adopting, the answer to this question will emerge only by slow degrees, and at various levels of probability, through the continual application of critical scholarship and historical criticism to the books themselves and to their historical setting and context. There is little finality in such critical work, and we shall presumably always be left with a central core of "assured results", surrounded by areas of diminishing assurance which shade off into complete uncertainty.

But it is time to remind ourselves that the doctrine of inspiration, from which theology has inferred the negative corollary of inerrancy, is in itself a positive doctrine. It means that Scripture is in a true sense the "word" of God, the utterance of the Holy Spirit. Scripture is therefore a phenomenon at once human and spiritual. As a human production it lies open to our rational appraisal, but St Paul reminds us that the things of the spirit are discerned not naturally but spiritually:

No one else can know God's thoughts, but the Spirit of God. And what we have received is no spirit of wordly wisdom; it is the Spirit that comes from God, to make us understand God's gifts to us. . . . Mere man with his natural gifts cannot take in the thoughts of God's Spirit; they seem mere folly to him, and he cannot grasp them, because they demand a scrutiny which is spiritual (I *Cor* II 11-14).

Hence the divine meaning of scripture will disclose itself, after human criticism has done its best, to the spiritual understanding that goes with a believing and devout reading. Just as the significance of the Word Incarnate was *hidden from the wise and prudent* and *revealed* by God *to little ones,* while the unbelievers saw him with their bodily eyes and could construe the outward meaning of his words but could never penetrate beneath these appearances, so also Scripture, considered as the word of God, as inspired by the Holy Spirit, will always be a closed book to those who approach it in any frame of mind less spiritual than that of humble faith. The books of the Bible may convey to the unbeliever a world of interesting information about the cultural history of antiquity and the "natural history" of the Judaeo-Christian religion. But they will not disclose to him the wisdom and the power of God.

Who then is the faithful and devout reader to whom the Bible, as the inspired word of God, is addressed? The answer to this question, which takes us back to the opening paragraphs of this essay, is of fundamental importance. The Bible, thus considered, is not addressed primarily and directly to the individual Christian's private judgment, but to the mind of the Church. For it is primarily upon the Church that the Pentecostal gift of the Holy Spirit has been conferred. And, as we have seen, it is only by the indwelling of the Holy Spirit that the inspired word can be understood as such. The Scriptures are not *of private interpretation.*[2] It is ultimately for the Church to discern, and to declare with authority, the spiritual meaning of Scripture, its meaning for faith—to determine, for instance, that *This is my body* is not a mere rhetorical figure but a statement of true, though mysterious, fact. Individual members of the Church share in the Church's mind and in her indwelling by the Holy Spirit, and their own reading and understanding of Scripture may be valid insofar as they do not contradict the Church's interpretation.

If, with these considerations before us, we ask what the message of Scripture is, what is the content of this word of God, the Church's answer is summed up in the one word: Christ. The whole of the Old Testament prepares the way for, looks forward to and, in a sense prefigures, Christ. The whole of the New Testament expounds Christ—the *totus Christus,* the "whole Christ", of St Augustine's famous phrase, Christ in his Church, and the Church as Christ's embodiment.

The broad truth of this basic affirmation is, for the Christian believer, obvious enough. The faith and Godward practice of pre-Christian Israel stands out against its background of contemporary religion, magic and philosophy as something practically unique. It has indeed been argued that man's most primitive faith was a perhaps naive but genuine monotheism. But long before the date of Moses this had receded before a proliferation of animism, fetishism, polytheistic cults, mythology and

[2] II *Peter* I 20. The meaning of this phrase is, however, disputed.

magic. There were reactions against this state of things in the more advanced cultures of Persia and Greece in the last millennium before Christ. Zoroastrianism seems to have been a noble, though not very successful, effort to substitute if not monotheism, at least a lofty ethical dualism for the traditional polytheistic religion. And Greek rationalism and philosophy made a similar, though less intransigent, attempt to offer to an élite a purer and truer world-outlook than that of popular paganism. But neither of these attempts succeeded in imposing itself on a whole society or nation, to become its traditional religion. And the earlier attempt by Ikhnaton to establish strict solar monotheism in Egypt lasted less than a generation before a violent reaction restored the *status quo*. In Israel, however, as a result mainly of the work of Moses and the prophets, a pure and exalted ethical monotheism had become, before the time of Christ, the faith of a whole nation, with its centre in Jerusalem and Palestine, but with outposts throughout the Near East and the Mediterranean world at least as far as Rome.

The faith of Israel never purported to be the fruit of hard critical and philosophic thinking; it presented itself as the self-revelation of God to his Chosen People through saving deeds and divinely inspired representatives. Yet ethical monotheism, which with the idea of the Covenant People forms the core of this faith, is the highest achievement of the most sincere and exigent philosophic reflection, though it had to wait till the thirteenth century after Christ for its first adequate philosophic presentation. If there is any validity in the concept of *moral miracle,* the faith and practice of Israel may surely lay claim to be an example of such. Certainly anyone who thinks that ethical monotheism is a true answer to man's deepest questionings, and who wonders whether God has ever stretched out a hand or uttered a summons to mankind from behind the veil of creatures, cannot fail to find his attention drawn irresistibly to this people and to the literature in which their religious traditions are embodied.

One of the highest points in this literature is reached in some chapters in the latter part of the book of Isaiah, in which the vocation of the Chosen People is seen not simply as for the benefit of Israel alone, but as involving a mission of enlightenment to mankind at large. This notion appears to be closely related to that of the Suffering Servant of the Lord in these same chapters, a figure in which Christianity has from the first seen an adumbration of Christ. And it is a fact that, broadly speaking, Israel's missionary work to the world in general has, since the beginning of the Christian era, been carried into effect mainly by the Church which Christ founded and by the other Christian bodies which, at various times since the end of the fourth century, have broken away from that Church. For the historian there is a true sense in which the Old Testament finds its continuation in the New, its continuation and its universal application.

All this is summed up for faith in the affirmation that Christ is God's Word to man, God's self-manifestation and his summons. But, as we have seen, Scripture itself is, according to the Church's teaching, God's word, the record of his revelation in Christ and (before him) through those *prophets and wise men who desired to see the things* which the disciples saw, and saw them not except in anticipation and prefigurement. It is obvious that Christ is the focus-point and the meaning of the New Testament. And if Christ, his Gospel and his Church, are the divinely intended consummation of the revelation and the promises to the Old Testament People of God, it follows that he is also the goal and the meaning of the Old Testament Scriptures. As St Augustine said in a famous epigram: The New Testament lies hidden within the Old, and the Old Testament is disclosed in the New.

While this is broadly speaking true and intelligible, it may be difficult to apply in detail to the various contents of the Old Testament. The late King George V is alleged to have remarked that the Bible is a wonderful book but contains some very queer things. What are we to make of the apparently unhistorical genealogies of the Book of Genesis, of the Biblical version of the myth of the Deluge, of the Semitic legislation handed down under the name of Moses, of the wars of the book of Judges and the strange story of Samson, not to speak of the imprecatory Psalms, the massacre of the pre-Israelite inhabitants of Canaan, and a hundred and one other things that are superficially offensive to modern critical ears?

This is not the place for a consideration of each several detail requiring explanation or apology. But certain principles of explanation may be offered. Of these perhaps the most important is that of development. The Old Testament, as has already been suggested, is a record of the gradual and agelong education of the Israelite people in the nature and claims of the God of righteousness. It was not an education *in vacuo,* nor were the Israelites a *tabula rasa* with no religious or ethical preconceptions to be corrected, purified and elevated. They were a group of Semitic clans, exposed through long periods of their history to the influences of the splendid and seductive nature-worship of their Canaanite neighbours, and later to those of the great world-empires. Their own faith and practice, as they were gradually elaborated, were at once a protest against, and in some respects a transposition of, surrounding beliefs and practices. The story of the intended sacrifice of Isaac by his father Abraham may be taken in illustration of this. The sacrifice of children to the local Baal was a feature at once tremendous and terrible of Canaanite religion, at least in one of its forms. It was ethically horrible. But our repugnance to it must not blind us to the sublime notion underlying it, that nothing is too good to be sacrificed to God, that God in fact is the supreme value, to which all else must be subordinated and if need be surrendered. Abraham, the man of God par excellence, conceives that it is God's will that this great principle should be carried out into practice in his own case by the sacrifice of Isaac; and this despite the fact that Isaac is the child of promise, through whom were to be transmitted the divine promises to Abraham's seed. So like St Paul at his conversion, Abraham obeys what he takes to be a divine intimation and proves in act that he is willing even to make this sacrifice for God's sake and in his honour. But at the crucial moment God intervenes and substitutes an animal victim for the child. Thus was Israel taught that God's claims are indeed illimitable and yet not inconsistent with his attribute of mercy or with the moral instincts of humanity. Nor can the Christian fail to reflect that the notion of the sacrifice of what is most precious, the sacrifice indeed not only of the first-born, but of the true seed of Abraham, was to find in the divine purposes an unforeseeable and wonderful realisation in the death of Christ. Isaac, as the Christian fathers would have said, is a "type" of Christ himself.

There is one feature of this epic story which may cause some residual difficulty. As in some other cases where a projected action is mentioned that is repugnant to our moral ideas, the proposed sacrific of Isaac is made the subject of a divine command: "Take thy only begotten son Isaac, whom thou lovest, and go into the land of vision: and there thou shalt offer him for an holocaust upon one of the mountains which I will show thee" (*Genesis* XXII 2). How could God possibly command something which is intrinsically wrong, in this case a ritual murder? This brings us to the radical truth about all revelation of God to man, namely that it is a divine self-disclosure within human experience. Here the philosophical axiom holds good, that "whatever is received or known is received or known according to the measure of capacity of the receiver or knower". The pure light of God has to be translated into human terms before it can be apprehended by man; it is only, though truly, known as *translated,* and the nature and adequacy of the translation will vary with the nature and the spiritual enlightenment of the recipient of the revelation. If it is a revelation directed to action, it will take shape in the conscience of the recipient and will be to some extent limited by his moral stature: *I have still much to say to you, but it is beyond your reach as yet (John* XVI 12). The verdict of conscience is always the voice of God and is always to be followed without hesitation as such. This is true despite the fact that conscience often dictates a course of action which is objectively deficient. In such cases, the command of conscience is truly the voice of God for the subject here and now, though not for others more enlightened, nor for the subject himself when he has made further intellectual and moral progress.

In other words, there is an element of relativity in the Old Testament revelation, considered apart from that of the New, as St Augustine realised and maintained. The absolute revelation needed for its apprehension and transmission the perfect human nature and complete moral integrity of Christ himself within the company of the new Israel in the shape of his band of disciples.

The other principle to bear in mind in studying the Old Testament as an anticipation of the revelation in Christ is that the Old Testament faith and practice were the divinely provided environment of the earthly life of Christ himself. In the Incarnation the Word of God did not merely assume a human nature; he entered into a human environment and accepted a particular human conditioning. As the Child Jesus advanced in wisdom it was on the faith and piety of ancient Israel that his human mind was nourished. It was in the pages of the Old Testament that, as a man, he read his own vocation, and it was in Old Testament forms and figures that he clothed it for others and for himself. As has already been pointed out, we cannot understand Christ apart from this historical context in which he humanly came to understand himself. It was a context consisting in a social and revelational religion, with institutional, mystical and (in a sense other than the Hellenistic sense) intellectual elements. Its characteristic embodiments—the Mosaic Law, the worship of the Temple with its sacrifice and psalmody, the wisdom of its doctors, the insight of its prophets, and the Messianic ideas which had grown up round the notions of an ideal Davidic King, of the Suffering Servant of the Lord, and of the Danielic *one like unto a son of man*—all this not only fed and gave form to the personal piety of him who is for Christians the model of devotion; it was, in substance, both endorsed by him as valid for its own epoch and transcended in the religious system established by him, somewhat as life accepts and transmutes inorganic matter. In him the pre-Christian tradition of Israel and the Christian tradition find their unity, each gaining its meaning through juxtaposition with the other. All Christian theology must continually go back to the Bible, because dogmatic theology is simply the never-ending attempt to express in scientific human thought and language, and to relate to other branches of knowledge the contents of the revelation of which tradition oral and written, is the deposit. Scripture and unwritten tradition are thus the living sources, the well-heads, the *fons et origo* upon which theology draws, sources living in and by the life of the Holy Spirit in the Church. In this connection it may be mentioned that New Testament study in the last thirty years has been immensely invigorated precisely by reason of a renewed and sustained effort to deepen our understanding of the New Testament writings and the Church of the Apostolic age in the light of their Old Testament presuppositions.

The study of the Bible, whether we mean by this the critical historical and exegetical work of the scholar and historian, or the prayerful meditation of the individual Christian under the guidance of the Holy Spirit and in harmony with the mind of the Church, is never completed and never will be completed. And it can hardly ever, by itself, give entirely certain results. Certainty belongs to the articles of the faith as defined by the Church, and to the conclusions which reason necessarily draws from these articles in dogmatic theology. All Bible study, if it is not to go astray, must in the end conform to the limits of interpretation laid down by these two connected sources of certainly. But it is perhaps not entirely irrelevant to urge that dogmatic theologians should be very careful not to impose on Bible study conclusions which fall short of certainty. It is of the essence of the critical method that it proceeds by trial and error, by hypothesis and revision of hypotheses. If it is not allowed to make its mistakes it will not, in the long run, be able to supply, for the fecundation of dogmatic theology, its positive results and new and enriching insights.

# Newman and Development

1959

Christianity is a catholic thing; that is to say, Christianity claims to have a universal relevance. The claim appears with special clarity in St Paul's doctrine of Christ as the Second Adam. For Jewish thought, Adam, as we know, was the progenitor of the human race, just as Abraham was the progenitor of the Hebrews, Jacob of the Israelites. But, for Jews, Adam was something more than the man who came first in the order of time. He also summed up, typified, was pregnant with, the totality of his descendants and their history. The Jews were not philosophers like Plato. Plato would have seen in the man who lived on earth the shadowy embodiments of the Idea of Man, and for him that Idea would have contained all that is valuable in human actuality. For the Jews, the embodiment of all human values was Adam; he was the personification of all mankind, and unlike the Platonic Idea of Man he was not an immaterial form but had been an actual flesh-and-blood individual. We modern Westerns may find some difficulty in conceiving how the fall of Adam involved us all in the tragedy of sin. But for St Paul, with his Jewish outlook, this would not have constituted a problem. Of Adam's fall, he could have said what Shakespeare's Antony says of the assassination of Caesar: "Oh, what a fall was there, my countrymen. Then you and I and all of us fell down".

When therefore St Paul proclaimed that Christ was the second Adam, he was claiming implicitly that Christ stood to redeemed humanity in the same relation as Adam stood to humanity before redemption. The history of Christ precontained the whole of the history of those he came to redeem; and, as St Paul tells us elsewhere, God was in Christ reconciling the world to himself.

This conception of Christianity as a new human beginning with implications for all mankind did not triumph in the primitive Church without a struggle. It was, perhaps, the real stake in the great controversy over circumcision. It is very proper that we should celebrate the centenaries of the great Church Councils like Chalcedon and Ephesus, but perhaps no Council better deserves commemoration than the Council of Jerusalem, which in fact decided that Christianity was not to be, as the traditionalists wished, one version of the Jewish national religion, but to be the faith of mankind as a whole.

Christianity is called to be catholic not only in extent but in depth. It claims not only to bring every man beneath the sweet yoke of Christ, but to bring every thought, every heart-beat, every aspect of human culture and civilisation, under that same subjection which is perfect freedom. The content of the Christian Good News was the kingdom, or as we might more significantly translate the word, the empire of God; and God's empire is as total in range and depth as creation.

The catholic quality of Christianity can be brought out by contrast if we examine one of its Eastern rivals—and it is going to be increasingly urgent for us to take the great oriental faiths and philosophies seriously. In his Pelican book, *Buddhism,* Mr Christmas Humphreys, an intelligent, and apparently a committed Buddhist, can write: "The West will never be Buddhist, and only the most unthinking zealot would strive to make it so" (p.230). The modesty of this position is in harmony with the fact that Buddhism is extremely tolerant of other faiths. The reason why Christianity can be neither so modest nor so tolerant is that the Church is conscious of a divine mission that is universal in the double sense already indicated.

This sense of a universal mission is expressed in the last chapter of St Matthew's Gospel in the command: "You must go out, making disciples of all nations, and baptising them in the name of the Father, and of the Son, and of the Holy Ghost, teaching them to observe all the commandments which I have given you". It is thus the task of the Church to *present* the Gospel to every human being, and to present it as relevant to the totality of human needs and aspirations.

The task of presentation involves in practice what I will call the task of translation—translation, in the first instance, in the most literal sense of the word. The Christian missionary in a new linguistic environment finds it easier and better to learn the language of the converts he hopes to make, than to induce them to learn his own language. The New Testament is a monument of such translation, and scholars delight to discern beneath the surface of its Greek expression the Aramaic clothing of the earliest Christian tradition.

But the task of translation means more than a word-for-word rendering into a new linguistic medium. The Church in its missionary work is brought face to face with diverse human cultures and diverse intellectual traditions, and it is forced to ask itself what its own essential message means in terms of these new environments, and to discriminate between the essence of the message and its contingent modes of presentation. The original Gospel was framed in the context of Jewish apocalyptic imagery and thinking. To convey the Gospel to the wider Graeco-Roman world with this framework unmodified might mean not only to fail to recommend it to those for whom it is intended, but actually to distort in various ways, in their apprehension of it, the meaning which the Church sought to convey. If the vivid eschatological hope of the first Christian generation seems to us to have become strangely faded in the second century of our era, this was not simply the decline of a theological virtue; it was, at least in part, a missionary necessity, a result of the need to show the relevance of Christianity in a world whose thought-forms were quite other than those of the authors of the Jewish apocalyptic literature. In recent centuries, the lives of the two great Jesuit missionaries, Ricci in China and Nobili in India, will serve as an illustration of the problems which are always recurring in the Church's age-long career.

The age of the great Fathers, as exemplified by Gregory of Nyssa in the Greek-speaking Church and by Augustine of Hippo in the West, was the period in which Christianity clothed itself in the garb of the predominantly Platonist thought of late Graeco-Roman antiquity and was immensely enriched in the process. It was followed, after a long age of set-back and incubation, by the adaptation of Christian thought to the Aristotelian legacy which had been transmitted to the West largely through the hands of great Islamic thinkers. Christianity, as it presents itself in the great architectonic thought of St Thomas Aquinas, has moved a long way from the stage represented by the Apocalypse of St John.

The form taken by the great religious and cultural upheaval of the Reformation was such as to throw the Church back upon the defensive and to intensify that conservative bias which is always congenial to an institution finding its credentials in tradition. She was not indeed unmindful of the missionary challenge presented by the opening up of the Far East and the discovery of America. But in Europe she became the beleaguered city. If the creation of a great liturgy had characterised the early centuries, and the construction of a daring philosophical synthesis the Middle Ages, the post-Reformation period disclosed its genius in the set pattern of formal meditation of which the great new Jesuit Society became the champion. The Benedictine age had first given place to the age of the Friars; and now these in turn made way for the advent of the Jesuit centuries. If conservation of its own identity is Christianity's first duty, we owe an incalculable debt to the Society of Jesus and the Counter-Reformation.

Meanwhile, outside the guarded walls of the Catholic citadel, men had not ceased to think and to experiment. The century of Newman was the century in which three relatively novel elements began to dominate the intellectual and social life of the West. These three elements were the experimental natural sciences, scientific historical criticism, and the industrial revolution. Each of these contained a threat to Christianity. The industrial revolution, occurring at a period when Christian vitality was low, produced new centres of population for which there was no adequate provision of churches and schools and clergy, and a working-class population that was de-Christianised. The natural sciences were sketching out a picture of external reality that seemed to many almost irreconcilably different from that which, they had grown up to think, was presupposed by the Christian Gospel. The threat from historical criticism was perhaps the most insidious of all, casting doubt at once upon the identity of contemporary Christianity with its own origins, and upon the factuality of those origins as recorded in the pages of the Bible. Christianity seemed in danger of being relegated to the domain of legend and of myth.

Meanwhile after the long torpor of the eighteenth century, the Church had given signs of awaking as if from sleep, thus illustrating the penultimate paragraph of Newman's *Essay on Development*:

It is true, there have been seasons when, from the operation of external or internal causes, the Church has been thrown into what was almost a state of *deliquium;* but her wonderful revivals, while the world was triumphing over her, are further evidence of the absence of corruption in the system of doctrine and worship into which she has developed. If corruption be an incipient disorganisation, surely an abrupt and absolute recurrence to the former state of vigour, after an interval, is even less conceivable than a corruption that is permanent. Now this is the case with the revivals I speak of. After violent exertion men are exhausted and fall asleep; they awake the same as before, refreshed by the temporary cessation of their activity; and such has been the slumber and such the restoration of the Church. She pauses in her course, and almost suspends her functions; she rises again, and she is herself once more; all things are in their place and ready for action. Doctrine is where it was, and usage, and precedence, and principle, and policy; there may be changes, but they are consolidations or adaptations; all is unequivocal and determinate, with an identity which there is no disputing. Indeed, it is one of the most popular charges against the Catholic Church at this very time, that she is "incorrigible"; change she cannot, if we listen to St Athanasius or St Leo; change she never will, if we believe the controversialist or alarmist of the present day.

The problems of adaptation to a new environment with which this modern resurgence of the Church has been faced are perhaps the greatest of their kind since those early days when she moved out from her Jewish origins to become the faith of the late Roman Empire. What has been the contribution of Newman to the solution of these problems?

I think it can be said that he never seriously addressed his mind to the particular issues raised by the industrial revolution. Of bourgeois stock, he spent his formative years at a university which was remote from these issues, and by the time that he came to make his home at Birmingham the pattern of his vocation was already set. Among English Catholics the challenge of the new urban proletariat and the de-Christianised masses was met on the one hand by the heroic army of pastoral clergy, and on the other hand especially by Cardinal Manning.

Of the questions raised by the impact of modern science he was not unconscious, and in particular his *Grammar of Assent* dealt with the problem of certainty or certitude. The traditional theology of the virtue and act of faith presupposed the possibility of certitude, and the trend of modern science was towards the supersession of certitude by shifting probability. To the extent that it undermined certitude, science was a natural ally of that "liberalism in religion" which, according to Newman in his *biglietto* speech, he had, to the best of his powers, resisted for "thirty, forty, fifty years". But the speech itself is evidence enough that Newman's resistance took shape rather in the field of theological controversy than as an attempt to "reconcile" science and religion. Still, the curious student might doubtless gather from Newman's writings many fruitful suggestions towards such an attempt, and I was interested to find that Professor Coulson, a distinguished mathematician and a devout Methodist, finds occasion to quote from the *Grammar of Assent* in his *Science and Christian Belief*.

It is possible that on the longest view of all the *Grammar of Assent* is Newman's greatest single contribution to the task of adapting Christianity to the progress of human thought. If so, I must leave it to others or to another occasion to bring out its significance. My own purpose here is to try to suggest the importance of Newman's theory of development in the situation created by the rise of modern historical criticism.

The theory was not, it would appear, in its first adumbration an attempt to answer any such general problem as that of meeting scientific history's challenge to Christianity. It took shape within the context of the more special concerns of the tractarian movement. Very broadly, the movement in its first phase may be said to have been an attempt to reassert the Catholic element in Anglicanism against contemporary Protestantism. It proclaimed a high view of the sacraments; it derived the authority of the clergy not from the State but from apostolical succession; and it pointed men back to the primitive Christian centuries as to the norm of Christian orthodoxy. Protestant critics of the movement would not be slow to accuse it of seeking to upset the Reformation settlement, and of playing into the hands of Romanism. It was to forestall such criticism that Newman, in his lectures on the Prophetical Office of the Church, had expounded his view of Anglicanism as pursuing a Middle Way between the errors of Rome and the negations of Protestantism; and the justification of the Middle Way was precisely the appeal to a Christian antiquity which was, Newman would argue, certainly not Romanist, but as certainly not Protestant.

However, while on the one hand the Middle Way was a hope for the future of Anglicanism rather than as an existing institutionalised fact, it was plainly not possible simply to reproduce the Church of Athanasius and Augustine in nineteenth-century England. History had not stood still since the Council of Chalcedon, and there is no retracing of her footsteps.

But a more serious difficulty shortly presented itself to Newman and very soon succeeded in destroying all his confidence in the notion of the Via Media. He came to realise, not by abstract speculation but by a study first of the Monophysite controversy and then of the struggle against Arianism in the fourth century, that the Via Media was in essence a compromise position, and that the Church of the Fathers had borne clear witness against compromise and in favour of positions which it so happened (and could it be an accident?) had been the positions maintained by the See of Rome. The long story of Newman's death-agony as an Anglican can be read in the *Apologia*, and also in the volume which collects his correspondence of the crucial years 1839-45.

The collapse of the theory on which he had sought to base his Anglican allegiance did not immediately lead to Newman's conversion to the Catholic Church. There remained the errors or corruptions of Rome—less, perhaps, the Papacy than the Roman cultus of our Lady and the saints. How could these features of the Roman system be acceptable to one who knew that there was no room in Christianity for any theory of expanding revelation, and who knew antiquity as he, the great lover of the Fathers, had come to know it?

Such may have been the existential situation which impelled Newman to turn his attention to the place of the notion of development in Christian theological thinking. But it must have been almost immediately that he saw that the principle of development had a far wider applicability and met a difficulty which was, if possible, even more profound than that of the contrast between contemporary Catholicism and the religion of the Fathers. Thus it was possible for him, without any sense of disloyalty, to make the pulpit of the University Church at Oxford the platform from which he propounded his first sketch of the theory of development in religious doctrine (*Oxford University Sermons* XV, February 1843). The problem is as follows:

Some writers . . . aver that, when they look into the documents and literature of Christianity in times past, they find its doctrines so variously represented and so inconsistently maintained by its professors, that, however natural it be *a priori,* it is useless in fact to seek in history the matter of that Revelation which has been vouchsafed to mankind *(Essay on Development* p. 9).

And again:

I concede to the opponents of historical Christianity that there are to be found, during the 1800 years through which it has lasted, certain apparent inconsistencies and alterations in its doctrine and its worship, such as irresistibly attract the attention of all who enquire into it (p.9).

What is Newman's solution of the problem? Having first affirmed that the variations in question "manifest themselves on a law, not abruptly, but by a visible growth which has persevered up to this time without any sign of its coming to an end" he puts forward, as "an hypothesis to account for a difficulty", the suggestion

that the increase and expansion of the Christian Creed and Ritual, and the variations which have attended the process in the case of individual writers and Churches, are the necessary attendants on any philosophy or polity which takes possession of the intellect and heart, and has had any wide or extended dominion; that from the nature of the human mind, time is necessary for the full comprehension and perfection of great ideas; and that the highest and most wonderful truths, though communicated to the world once for all by inspired teachers, could not be comprehended all at once by the recipients, but, as being received and transmitted by minds not inspired and through media which were human, have required only the longer time and deeper thought for their elucidation (pp. 29f).

In other words, he argues that the variations alleged may be not the proof that contemporary Christianity is refuted by its own origins and past, but rather the result at once of the magnitude of the original *datum* and of the very gradual elucidation by the human mind of the nature and implications of that datum.

If Christianity is the gift from God to man of an object of belief and worship, it is antecedently to be expected that the external history of Christianity will be a story of growth or development. The biological analogy is all the more interesting since the *Essay on Development* preceded by more than a decade the *Origin of Species.*

The importance of Newman's theory in the present age of the Church emerges when we realise, first, that it does not only allow Christians to withstand the hostile attack of critical history; it encourages them to embrace and apply the methods and aims of historical criticism, as the speculation of the great Fathers of the Church, and later of St Thomas Aquinas, enabled the Church both to defend herself against the objections of the philosophers and to become the great patron of philosophical thinking.

Secondly, while Newman applied his theory principally to the history of post-biblical Christian thought and practice, the last hundred and fifty years have witnessed a large-scale application of the principles of criticism to the Bible itself. It is no longer possible, in the degree in which it was once customary, to regard every text of the Old and New Testament as of equal probative value in reference to Christian doctrine. It is imperative, and Newman has shown us the way, to see in the Bible also the record of religious development, and that not only in the Old but in the New Testament. Indeed, the years between the first Christian Pentecost and the end of the first century of our era were a period of immensely rapid growth. No one, with the evidence of human life before him, will wish to maintain that growth and the variations it entails are incompatible with the continuing identity of the subject of growth. But it is the theory of development which enables us to investigate the evidences of this early Christian growth not with pained reluctance but with the exhilaration of discovering the tremendous vitality of the gift of God.

The theory of development, however, as Newman clearly saw, requires, if we are to remain assured that Christianity has not lost and will not lose its primitive identity by reason of successive adaptations, that there should be within the Christian totality a balancing principle of guaranteed doctrinal authority. Newman's theory is a perilous one except for those who recognise in the judgments of the contemporary Church a divinely given control of the centrifugal tendencies of individual human minds. It is Catholics who can gladly recognise a summary of the Church's story in the following great passage from the *Essay*:

It is sometimes said that the stream is clearest near the spring. Whatever use may fairly be made of this image, it does not apply to the history of a philosophy or belief, which on the contrary is more equable, and purer, and stronger, when its bed has become deep, and broad, and full. It necessarily rises out of an existing state of things, and for a time savours of the soil. Its vital element needs disengaging from what is foreign and temporary, and is employed in efforts after freedom which become more vigorous and hopeful as its years increase. Its beginnings are no measure of its capabilities nor of its scope. At first no one knows what it is, or what it is worth. It remains perhaps for a time quiescent; it tries, as it were, its limbs, and proves the ground under it, and feels its way. From time to time it makes essays which fail, and are in consequence abandoned. It seems in suspense which way to go; it wavers, and at length strikes out in one definite direction. In time it enters upon strange territory; points of controversy alter their bearing; parties rise and fall around it; dangers and hopes appear in new relations; and old principles reappear under new forms. It changes with them in order to remain the same. In a higher world it is otherwise, but here below to live is to change, and to be perfect is to have changed often.

# The Absurd and John Chapman

1959

Only one "spiritual" book stands to the credit of Dom John Chapman: the posthumously published *Spiritual Letters*. I hope to show that, despite the paucity of published material, he deserves a place among English masters of spiritual doctrine.[1]

Born in April 1865, the youngest child of the Archdeacon of Sudbury, he might be described as a product of Barchester—Victorian, well-to-do, Conservative, English of the English, despite his unusual familiarity with the French tongue. Health precluded him from a public school education (he would otherwise have gone to Eton), but not from Oxford (Christ Church, of course), or a First in Greats, or the moderately High Church theological college of Cuddesdon. What could have checked this brilliant and profound young ordinand in a meteoric career to the heights of Bishopthorpe or Lambeth? *Dieu dispose.* After an intellectual and spiritual struggle of great acuteness ("my difficulties are a real terror and agony. I am in a great strait. People talk lightly about 'secession' as the 'easy path'. If only they knew what it feels like! And I have known it for six months almost unbearably.") he was received into the Catholic Church in December 1890. He tried his vocation with the Society of Jesus but failed, and was ordained priest and solemnly professed at the Beuronese Benedictine Priory of Erdington in 1895. In 1913 he became temporary superior of the newly converted community of Caldey Island (now Prinknash Abbey), and in 1915 an army chaplain. The Erdington foundation was a casualty of the 1914 war and Dom Chapman was allowed to transfer his stability to Downside, whither he was recalled from his work on the Vulgate Commission at Rome to become Prior under Abbot Ramsay in 1922. On Ramsay's death in 1929 Prior Chapman was elected to succeed him, and himself died in office in November 1933.

## I

One of the most obvious things to say about Chapman is that

[1] Dom John Chapman, *Spiritual Letters* ed. G. R. Hudleston (London: Sheed, 1954). In what follows, unassigned quotations are from this volume. The abbreviation "BC" refers to his article "M. Bremond and P. Cavallera" in the *Downside Review*, January 1930, pp. 4ff.

he was a very great New Testament and Patristic scholar. Here, as in the ascetico-mystical field, his published books represent him quite inadequately though *John the Presbyter,* now largely forgotten, is a striking example of poised, acute, original scholarship, taking its own line in serene independence of the greatest names of the pre-1914 learned world, and never refuted. He was, I think, the first to pioneer the road to a true solution of the vexed question of the "Primacy Text" in Chapter Four of St Cyprian's *De unitate,* but for his work on this subject, as for so much else (e.g. his explanation of the "brethren of the Lord"), you have to search the pages of the learned reviews of the years 1895-1930. *Saint Benedict and the Sixth Century* was not only a work of Benedictine *pietas* (by which I do not mean "piety") but an audaciously brilliant attempt to "see" the work and place of St Benedict in the sixth-century Church and Empire, as no one before Chapman (and perhaps no one since) has seen it. The posthumous *Matthew, Mark and Luke* is a sort of tragedy. Chapman, like all the best critics of his generation, had come to regard *Mark* as the earliest of the four Gospels, and as a source used independently by the authors of *Matthew* and *Luke.* The Biblical Commission appeared to favour a different view, and on Salisbury Plain, during the war, Chapman began to re-examine the question for himself. The result was revolutionary. He thought he saw clear evidence that *Mark* was dependent on a source indistinguishable from *Matthew.* Material for a book began to accumulate, and had reached impressive proportions by about 1931, when he showed the manuscript to me. But the cares of an uncongenial office and the onset of a fatal disease prevented the completion of the work and the devoted editing of Mgr Barton could not turn the text into anything that could hope to win the sympathetic attention of non-Roman Catholic critics. The book was published just before the 1939 war, and has hardly been heard of during the past fifteen years. Yet anyone who, with competence and an open mind, will read and re-read it, and then read it again, will agree—whether or not it proves to him that *Mark* depends on *Matthew*—that it has shattered his belief in the dominant solution of the Synoptic Problem.

But such scholarship was only a part of Chapman's multifarious intellectual activity. A connoisseur of painting and music, he was an accomplished pianist, and once (disastrously) undertook to teach the resident community at Downside how Plainchant ought to be rendered. More importantly, he had enjoyed his philosophical studies at Oxford, and as a Catholic he could not keep his mind or his pen off dogmatic theology. I am not sufficiently in sympathy with him on this speculative side of his interests to be a fair judge of his philosophical and theological insights. I always thought that to have read the *Summa Theologica* at the rate of seventeen columns an hour did not necessarily qualify him as a master of Thomism. But he was not lacking in natural self-confidence, and there is a Downside story that he once undertook to teach to some young monks the treatise *De Trinitate,* with the remark that he was the only man who "understood the Trinity".

That story should be taken along with the warning, specially necessary for readers of the *Spiritual Letters,* that Chapman's humour was chronically irrepressible, fantastic, Carrollian, verging on the realm of pure nonsense, and often tumbling over into wild, straight-faced, absurdity. Once a visitor to the abbey, after a fascinating half-hour with the Abbot, was alleged to have reported that, charming as those monks were, they really did live in an odd world of their own; why, their Abbot had spent half an hour proving to him that the world was flat! He once excused the awkward gait of a young aspirant from the Antipodes, with the kind comment that of course he could hardly be expected to have learnt, so soon, to walk the right way up. Years before, he had got into trouble with his Jesuit preceptors because it was discovered that he had spent the time, during a noviciate walk, in proving to a companion that Napoleon never existed; this was thought to tend to undermine a proper faith in historical evidence.

A second warning may also be not out of place. Few spiritual writers have been so lacking in "unction" as Chapman was. He had a thoroughly masculine intellect, was a great realist, and by nature and habit was extremely reserved about his innermost feelings which in any case he regarded as profoundly unimportant. There is a letter of 1912, to a nun whom, I suspect, Chapman did not yet know well, in which a paragraph of not very convincing "unction" is followed without warning by a sudden outbreak of the real, scandalising, but intensely serious, Chapman:

> I must enclose a line to you, to wish you and all the Community all Christmas blessings and graces. May we learn to become very little with our Lord, if he is to do great things

145

in us, as we wish. If his love has drawn him down from heaven so low, that he may make himself like us, how much he must long to lift us up, and make us like him. It is a cruel road that he has chosen, taking our miseries and our sufferings, in order to be able to give us his joy and his glory. He makes our road very easy by comparison, though we complain, and think he is very cruel to us. I always feel the Crib so sad, as well as so sweet. It is not like Easter, which is nothing but rejoicing.

I have come to the conclusion that one can remain united to God even when one goes to sleep in time of prayer. Don't laugh! (pp. 116f).

Yet occasionally the veil is lifted, as in a letter to a young Jesuit whose spiritual experience and intellectual difficulties had plainly stirred Chapman to his depths.

The ordinary person—and you yourself when not in a state of prayer—finds God far off—unimaginable, cold—a bare desert of perfection.

He prefers—with Omar Khayyám—a glass of wine, which is here and now, and warming; and love means something nearer, and lower, and hotter to him.

And God has answered.

He has translated himself into human language—he has come —*in propria venit.*

"Thou'rt come, dear heart; this third night—nay, this dawn—Thou'rt come—but in one day starv'd love grows old."

(Don't be shocked—for the Saints use human language. Why shouldn't I use Theocritus?) (p. 229)!

Who but Chapman would have found two lines from a love-poem of Theocritus to express the yearning of his whole nature (below the "apex" of the soul) for the Word made flesh and the rising "on the third day"?

It is possible to spend a lifetime on the study of Christian origins and in theological speculation without constructing a theology of the spiritual life or becoming a master of the theory and practice of prayer. But Chapman was something more than a scholar and a thinker. His published writing give us little that is autobiographical, but there is a passage in the letter quoted above which may be important:

> At 12 (or 13) years old I felt that religion ought to be transcendent, infinite, necessary. I suppose the vague, unexpressed notion that was in my head was "The One" of Parmenides, and the idea that the ultimate explanation of everything must be "The One". Of course I knew nothing of philosophy, and very little of Christianity (p. 206).

It is probable enough that the thirteen-year-old son of the Archdeacon of Sudbury had not read much philosophy, though it is also probable that he knew more of Christianity than most children of that age. But however much or little he knew by human tradition, I think the passage suggests that, like de Condren and Newman, Chapman had from boyhood a recognition of what I can only call the godhead of God; and the quest of this divine reality became the ruling passion of his life. It was, we are told (p. 4, from the Memoir by G. R. Hudleston), at Cuddesdon that he "began that inner life, with its habits of prayer and regularity, which, humanly speaking, led him to the cloister, and made him essentially a contemplative". That he became a fervent religious goes without saying. But it is also clear that after twenty years as a Benedictine he was still groping for light in his spiritual path.

It was inevitable that one so enamoured of God, and at the same time so intellectually alive and curious, should feel the need of a spiritual theory that would "work". This was at last achieved, when he was already in his forty-eighth year. He writes in April 1913:

> I really had no theory worked out until last November; and the reason I am writing now is because I believe I can be much more useful to others now I have thought things out more definitely, with the help of two or three "contemplatives" who, of course, know much more experimentally than I do, though they are younger, and have not directed people, or very little (p. 118).

147

This passage comes from a letter written to a canoness regular of the Lateran. Chapman gave retreats to a number of communities of religious; and it is probably not far from the truth to say that it was personal contact with those who, like the English canonesses of Bruges, were leading the contemplative life and carrying on the practical tradition of prayer which came down ultimately from the great days of the Flemish mystics, that drove him with renewed concern to his questionings, and perhaps suggested the basic answer. And it was in 1913 that he was sent to take temporary charge of the newly converted, formerly Anglican, community of men on Caldey Island (now Prinknash Abbey, Caldey Abbey itself having since been taken over by the Cistercians). Here he closely questioned members of the community who seemed to him to be experienced in prayer, and so was able to check his theory against their practice.

## II

The "theory" (it is really an *ars* rather than a *scientia*) supposes that the devout Christian will "meditate" on the truths of revelation. To meditate is to occupy one's mind with a subject, where one understands by the mind the reasoning reason and/or the imagination. Chapman had no doubt that meditation was indispensable:

> We must not forget that meditation is *necessary for all.* We must all *taste* the truths of the faith, assimilate them. For priests there is the study of theology, *theologia mentis et cordis* and the preparation of sermons; for the laity there is devout reading and the hearing of sermons; monks and nuns have the divine office, and so in a way have priests. But more than this—for all of us it may be necessary and possible, even if we are saints, upon occasion to use the lower faculties, to picture hell and heaven, to make present by fancy the sacred humanity of our Saviour: sometimes a glance will be enough; but there is surely no rule, for dispositions and facility vary so greatly (BC, p. 15n).

In the modern centuries, however, two developments had taken place. It had become part of the rule or constitution of most religious orders and congregations, and a devout practice for some of the laity, to devote a regular period of time daily (often half an hour) to personal prayer, apart from the divine office, the rosary, the Stations of the Cross, or other prescribed forms. And it had further become common to take advantage of this period of personal (or "mental") prayer for the practice of meditation. Indeed, it was quite normal to refer to the period of mental prayer as one's "meditation", and so recently as the beginning of this century it was customary in my own monastery to read out in choir, the evening before, suggested "points" for the morning half-hour of "meditation".

Two reasons can be given for this use of meditation in time of prayer. The first is that, by it, the memory, imagination and reason are diverted from the pull of creaturely interests. We come to our daily prayer trailing clouds not of glory but of worldliness, or at any rate of business. But if we can occupy our attention for a time with the mysteries of the faith or with sayings or incidents from the Gospels, there is a chance that this clamour of creatures will be temporarily suspended, and the claim of God on our faculties may be heard more clearly and persuasively. Hence Chapman would argue that, while for an enclosed religious half an hour of prayer might be enough, for people living in the "world" a much longer period would probably be needful; he did not, so far as I am aware, suggest how so long a time might be made available for the busy housewife or the rising barrister. In general, his doctrine about prayer was that the longer one spends on it the better it goes:

> The only way to pray is to pray; and the way to pray well is to pray much. If one has no time for this, then one must at least pray regularly. But the less one prays, the worse it goes. And if circumstances do not permit even regularity, then one must put up with the fact that when one does try to pray, one can't pray—and our prayer will probably consist of telling this to God (p. 53).[2]

The other reason for meditation in time of prayer is, that it provokes pious emotions, feelings, "realisations", which the will can then utilise in "acts" or "aspirations". Recall to the memory

---

[2] From a letter to a layman. The problem here raised obviously deserves further investigation. (1) Has one only prayed well when one *thinks* one has prayed well? (2) Is one's "prayer" to be identified with what happens when one is engaged on a set period of "mental prayer"?

and the imagination the Child in the manger at Bethlehem; picture him shivering slightly in the cold of the winter night, under the vague flickering of a Roman lamp; hear him (in your imagination) whimpering for food. Then reflect that this "helpless" suffering Child is he who, even now while he shivers and hungers, is giving food and warmth to all living things—*per quem nec ales esurit*; and that these sufferings, a prelude to Calvary, are an effect and an expression of a love for yourself that is literally infinite. And now, reverting to the actual present, and knowing that he is here now, by his sacramental presence, by sanctifying grace, or because he is always omnipresent, present and "waiting" for your recognition of him, will you not automatically turn to him with acts of adoration, repentance, gratitude, trust and love? Thus your meditation has passed over naturally into "prayer", the "lifting up of the mind and heart to God". And, as repentance is not real unless it includes a firm purpose of amendment, it seems equally natural that you should pass on to an appropriate "resolution", which should be definite and relevant to your own circumstances. If, finally, you choose, out of the devout thoughts of your meditation, some one that may serve as a motto or "spiritual bouquet", to be recalled to your mind from time to time in the ensuing twenty-four hours, and so to bring your heart back to the pious sentiments aroused in the period of prayer, you will have completed the outline of a type of meditation which must be familiar to many of my readers.

"Meditation", thus understood and practised during set times of "mental prayer", "is an excellent devotional practice for those who can do it". At least at a certain stage of the spiritual way it is "useful, fruitful and possible" (BC, p. 6).

The method of St Ignatius in particular seems an admirable instrument for converting from a worldy life to a devout life. The saint intended his exercises for young men of good education and good abilities, who had not yet given much attention to spiritual things, but could be persuaded to try this month's retreat as an attractive novelty. . . . The same exercises . . . will have a great effect upon those to whom meditation is an untried effort: for the first time the truths which they had learnt in the cathechism and the creed are made real instead of notional. . . . It can be the means of leading to a new life and to any degree of sanctity (*Ibid.,* pp. 6f).

But, argued Chapman, there are limits to the usefulness of this device, and I suppose that in a general way everyone would agree. To begin with, there are the "mystics"; their experiences are often held to be extraordinary and could therefore be left on one side by framers of systems of normal spirituality.[3] Secondly, one comes across people who, from the first, appear to have no "facility" for meditation, at least for formal systematic meditation. Thirdly, there is, in the practice of meditation (or so Chapman argued) a law of "diminishing returns":

The meditations lose their vivacity and their effect by custom. The imagination works less freely on matter which is too familiar, and emotions refuse to arise (BC, p. 8).

The vital point here is the last: *emotions refuse to arise.* It seems sometimes to be assumed that, as progress is made in mental prayer, the strictly "meditative" element will occupy a smaller portion of the "half-hour", but that the extra time thus available will naturally be used for a greater quantity of "affective" prayer, those warm holy sentiments and fervent "colloquies" which are held to be the really prayerful element in the whole exercise.[4] "That would be nice. But it is the opposite of what happens" (BC p. 10). The reader should note this appeal to experience. Chapman was not trying to wean from meditation and emotional prayer those who are intended for that kind of prayer and can find profit in it. He is dealing, like St John of the Cross, with those who are faced with a breakdown in the kind of prayer which they have been taught or have taught themselves—a breakdown which, it is presupposed, is not due to tepidity or ill-health. And his first comment, is, as we have seen, that such a breakdown was to be expected for psychological

---

[3] Chapman had his own explanation of mysticism, and those who are interested may be referred especially to the article "What is Mysticism", printed as an appendix to the *Spiritual Letters.* This is scientia rather than ars; so far as I can see it can be rejected without affecting the practical teaching with which I am here primarily concerned.

[4] The word "affective" is equivocal. As used above, it means "emotional" but in the classical tradition of spirituality it means rather prayer of the *will,* as distinct from both discursive and emotional prayer. It may be suspected that confusion of the two meanings has worked havoc in modern theory.

reasons. We cannot expect that our five-hundredth meditation on the Child in the manger will let loose the same flood of emotion as overcame us when we first seriously applied our imagination and reason to this subject. The novelty has worn off; and it was as a novelty that the subject first enraptured us.

But Chapman offered a deeper, theological, reason for this breakdown, when it occurs in the prayer of those who are really seeking God and trying to lead a good life. He regards it as a symptom of what, with St John of the Cross, he calls the Night of the Senses. Meditation and "affective" (i.e. emotional) prayer, co-operating with the good will of one who is making serious efforts to reform his life, have "consolidated" the *pure will's* love for God, which has now become a "power in the soul". This pure-will love of the soul for God is one in act with "imperceptible contemplation"[5]; it is, in fact, an "infused" love (for we are incapable by ourselves of loving God-revealed as we ought); and its operation, which the activities of the reasoning reason, the imagination, and the emotions, can only (in their direct effect) lessen or interrupt, tends by its very nature to inhibit the (prayerful) activities of these lower faculties. This inhibiting is called by Chapman "the ligature", and he has a favourite example of it:

> Reasoning about spiritual things produces conviction once for all: it can and must be recalled, but cannot be drawn out again for the same time it took to think out on the first occasion. And it is often dry, difficult and tiresome. Even if it were otherwise, the ligature stops it in prayer time, when the simplest words seem to have no meaning, and it proves impossible to understand the Our Father (BC, p. 12).[6]

Chapman ardently denied that what he was talking about was "high mysticism":

[5] The word "contemplation" derives from the Platonic vocabulary of the early Greek Christian Fathers. It emphasises an aspect of prayer to which, in his practical theory, Chapman did not find it necessary to pay much attention, being more concerned with the volitional ("affective" in the classical sense) aspect. But every act of prayer is simultaneously cognitional (or contemplative) and volitional (or affective). The cognitional element can be almost "imperceptible", because the object of prayerful attention is God, and he is beyond our imagining and conceiving; we may be more conscious of the act of will by which we seek to attend.

[6] It should hardly be necessary to point out that Chapman does not allege that it is impossible to *recite* the Our Father, but to *understand* it.

I shall be told that this is mysticism, unproved and improbable. By no means. It is just ordinary religion. . . . What is a Christian to do when he wants to keep a good resolution? Is he to meditate, by using his imagination to rouse his emotions, which in their turn will move his will? No, for emotion is treacherous and short-lived. Is he then to think over all the reasons, and to work out syllogisms to convince him of his duty? Evidently not, for he is already convinced. . . . Every Christian knows the solution of this apparent difficulty: he is to PRAY. We all know that Divine Faith has to rule our human intellect, and that only the prayer of faith will save us, and not our own considerations. Not our reasoning power, not "delectatio" is to draw our will and rule it, but *what we receive from God, infused faith and strength* (BC, pp. 12f; my italics).

And again:

It is dry land, where no water is; and *consequently "sicut desiderat cervus, etc."* Only the desire is a *will,* not an emotion.

All depends on whether you have the courage for so dry a prayer. And yet it has a supra-sensible consolation. It is one long act of love—not of my love to God, but of his to me. It is always going on—but in prayer you put yourself into it by an act of faith.

What I am writing about is a prayer of "beginners", I know nothing about any other. There is nothing high about it. It is for those who have got beyond the stage where they want to *think about* our Lord as absent (pp. 46f).

In fact, these people do not want to "think about" God at all—in time of prayer; they "want God, and not thoughts about God" (cf. p. 118). Their prayer is not spent in "thinking":

The time of prayer is passed by beginners in the act of *wanting God.* It is an idiotic state, and feels like complete waste of time, until, gradually, it becomes more vivid. The strangest part is when we begin to wonder whether we mean anything at all, and if we are addressing anybody, or merely using a formula without sense. The word "God" seems to mean nothing. If we feel this, we are on the right road, and we must beware of trying to think what God is, and what he has done for us, etc., because this takes us out of prayer at once and "spoils God's work"; as St John of the Cross says (pp. 119f).

A word may be required about the phrase "using a formula". The *Spiritual Letters* includes, as an appendix, "A Few Short Rules" for contemplative prayer. These date from 1913, shortly after Chapman had arrived at his "theory", and they tell us the following:

All those who find it impossible to meditate, not from laziness or lukewarmness, and find they cannot fix their thoughts on a subject unless they cease to feel that they are praying, are meant to cease *all thinking,* and only make acts of the will . . . . *Let the acts come.* Do not force them. They ought *not* to be *fervent,* excited, anxious, but calm, simple, unmeaning, unfelt . . . .

The acts will tend to be *always the same.* . . . The *principal* stage consists in this: "O God, I want Thee, and I do not want anything else." This is *the essence of pure contemplative prayer,* until the presence of God becomes vivid. (Then it *may* change, and praise or exultation may be the chief or sole act. But I imagine there is no rule) (p. 289).

I think it is fairly clear that the "formula" of the letter is the verbal content (so to say) of the "act" or "act of the will" of the *Few Rules.* But I also think that in these (not to speak of other) passages Chapman has expressed himself in ways that may be misleading. The unwary reader might infer that his doctrine is that "pure contemplative prayer" *consists in* such formulated "acts of the will"; and, although Chapman says clearly that these acts are "not to be forced" but "allowed to come", the inexperienced practitioner may well find that either he forces an act, or else he is left without any such "act" at all. In fact, I suggest, there are "acts" which "suggest themselves" (what some writers seem to mean by "aspirations"), and there are acts which are deliberately induced ("forced acts"); and whether an individual uses the former or the latter or a combination of the two sorts may be a matter of temperament, circumstance, or grace. But the important thing to realise is that these "acts", whether forced or quasi-automatic, are *not* the essence of pure contemplative prayer; and that Chapman himself, at least in his mature view, did not think that they were.

We get nearer to his real opinion in a letter to an Ursuline nun, dated 1925:

> . . . Hence the *distaste for meditation* which we are conscious of in the time of prayer. We want to use our will to "want God", and not to keep our thought in order. We want to be "wanting God", and detached from everything else. . . . While our will is making its intense (but almost imperceptible) act of love, our imagination is running about. . . . The distractions, which are so vivid to us, are not *voluntary* actions, and have no importance; whereas the *voluntary* action we are performing is the *wanting* God, or giving ourselves to God. . . . The best and usual way to keep it (the imagination) quiet is to repeat certain words, texts, ejaculations. . . . But the *real prayer* is the *act of the will* (wanting, loving, etc.) behind all this. You cannot *feel* this act of the will; but you can know it. . . . We have to learn to live by this higher part of our soul, and to pay no attention to anything else (pp. 18f).

This repetition of "certain words, texts, ejaculations" is, I think, the same as the "acts" of the passage from the Few Rules. If so, it is significant that these acts are here distinguished from the "real prayer". The latter is indeed (rightly) described as an "act"; it is even called an action. But it is an "unfelt" act; it is a "wanting to want" God. We seem "to be idle, mooning, wasting time" (*Ibid.*, p. 179). The "real prayer", then, is neither a "forced act" nor an "aspiration", but something that is more continuous than these, something that goes on during their intermittent recurrence and after they have ceased and during involuntary distractions; something that actuates a "higher part of the soul".

We want a word to denote this "act" of the apex of the soul, this act which is "unfelt" and "almost imperceptible", so that while it is actually going on "we seem to be idle, mooning, wasting our time". St John of the Cross speaks of a "loving attention" to God; but, true though this description of the "act" of prayer in its contemplative aspect no doubt is, it may not at first be of great help to the person who seems to himself to be "full

of distractions, and not praying at all" (*Ibid.*, p. 180). How, such
a person will ask, can I be "attending" to God and at the same time
"full of distractions"? Let us turn to another passage of the
*Spiritual Letters:*

> What *does* matter is the upper part of the soul; but that is
> something which we can't *feel,* but only *know.* But we have
> to make sure that the highest part of our soul . . . is united
> to God, and *nothing else matters* at all in this world. The
> right intention is the only way I can describe it. *The essential
> interior act of religion* is the giving ourselves to God, turning
> to Him, and remaining turned, uniting ourselves to His Will
> and renewing this union as often as we think of it, or simply
> remaining united (p. 175).

It is not clear that in this passage Chapman is speaking specifically about set times of mental prayer. But we shall see later
that he came in the end to attach little importance to the distinction between "times of prayer" and the rest of the waking life of
a devout person (our letter is addressed to a canoness regular
of the Lateran).

The word that we seem to need, and we find it in this passage,
is *intention*. Our intention is precisely the basic determination or
orientation of the pure will in act, and it is what settles the moral
worth of our life. The saying that hell is paved with good intentions is precisely not true. What hell is paved with is velleities
which stopped short of becoming intentions—poor little potential
intentions that aborted and never came to birth. Every priest
knows that, granted the right form and matter, the sufficient
conditions for a valid Eucharistic consecration is ministerial intention. And every priest knows that this is compatible with extreme
"distraction". Intention is the one thing that is completely under
our control. No pious thoughts, imaginations or emotions would
amount to "prayer" if the intention to pray were absent; and on
the other hand, granted the intention of praying, no amount or
quality of distraction (*ex hypothesi* involuntary) can destroy the
reality of the prayer. And an intention persists until it is retracted
or *de facto* terminated by an act of the will, substituting some
other intention.

We are not realistic enough in our discussion of prayer.
Viewed from the human side, prayer is like any other deliberate

self-determination. Intention is what unifies every moral entity.
What makes the difference between a number of venial sins of
theft and an accumulation of small thievings which amount to a
grave sin is that, in the latter case, the materially distinct small
acts are unified by a single intention. The writing of this article
has been done at various times, and has been subject to many
major or minor interruptions. But it has been a single moral act,
because it has been controlled throughout by a single intention;
and the intention has been informed by a single intellectual grasp
of an end to be attained. Of course, when our intention is directed
to a finite external object, circumstances may occur to frustrate its
realisation, and this means that such an intention may fail to
be completely "born". When our intention is directed to spiritual
union with God, no created circumstance can frustrate it; and
God will not frustrate it, because he is *Deus auxiliator,* the
Redeemer of Israel.

It remains to mention the other big distinction between prayer
and some other intentions. It is a truth of philosophy and faith
that only by grace can the creature refer himself, or be referred,
to God as self-revealed. Hence the intention of anyone who prays
in a state of grace is an effect at once of habitual and of an
actual grace. All such prayer is "infused"; and if "contemplative"
means the same as "infused", all real prayer (in a state of
grace) is contemplative.

Those who have studied and understood St John of the Cross
will recognise that Chapman's doctrine of prayer is identical with
that of the great Spanish "mystical doctor", and the *Spiritual
Letters* show that Chapman was conscious of this fact, and of his
debt to his great predecessor.[7] But such teaching was not common,
at least in England, in the first quarter of this century. Some
idea of what we owe to Chapman may be gained by reading the
chapter on Benedictine mysticism in Cuthbert Butler's invaluable

---

[7] There is, however, a difference of emphasis, as suggested above. Chapman
underlines the volitional, affective, aspect of prayer, while St John of
the Cross uses the traditional language of "contemplation", thus emphasising the cognitional side—but it is a "general", "obscure", non-
conceptual, sort of knowledge. As such knowledge tends to elude our
processes of reflexion, the person praying is often hardly if at all aware
that he is "attending" to God. He should be told that he has nothing to
worry about, provided he *intends to attend.*

*Benedictine Monachism* (1919), if we remember that Butler was the representative of a very sound practical tradition of contemplative prayer. Chapman's achievement was to discover for himself, at the cost of how much spiritual struggle, scientific observation, and hard ratiocination, that St John of the Cross had been right after all:

> For fifteen years or so, I hated St John of the Cross, and called him a Buddhist. I loved St Teresa, and read her over and over again. She is first a Christian; and only secondarily a mystic!
>
> Then I found I had wasted fifteen years, so far as prayer was concerned! Naturally I had a gradual revulsion against St Teresa (p. 246, written in 1920).[8]

A further incidental, but by no means unimportant, service was to extract the essence of the doctrine of prayer from the Carmelite, Spanish, sixteenth-century, personal trappings that clothe it in the writings of St John of the Cross himself, and to present it afresh in twentieth-century English dress. Thirdly, I suggest that by giving more emphasis to intention than to attention, Chapman has made the doctrine as a whole less Hellenic and more Christian.

## III

The year 1912, when he formulated to himself his theory of prayer, was an important date in Chapman's life. Another was about 1920:

> I have been reading (for the first time) some of Père de Caussade's *l'Abandon à la Providence divine*. It is extraordinarily good. But, like St John of the Cross, it makes one realise that a simple *remise à Dieu* is not so simple. It is as easy as jumping into a fire, which you had not seen, and has the same effect. It burns your clothes first, then your

---

[8] Anyone who suspects that there is a fundamental contradiction between the spiritual doctrines of the two great Spanish Carmelites is recommended to read "Contemplative Prayer in St Teresa", by Dom David Knowles, *Downside Review*, April 1933 and following numbers.

flesh, and then your bones. It is a fearful thing to fall into the hands of the Living God. But he is Infinite Wisdom and Infinite Love all the same. It is quite a question whether the broad way is any more comfortable than the narrow one (p. 62, 1920).

This discovery of de Caussade meant a lot to Chapman, and as he was a principal influence in England in spreading the knowledge of the eighteenth-century Jesuit, it has meant a lot to many others.[9]

What did Chapman get from de Caussade? In one sense, very little that he had not already worked out for himself, or found elsewhere, as the following quotations, all from dates earlier than 1920, will show:

Be sure that if you give yourself up blindly to God's Will, all will come right, though it may seem all wrong. Do not worry, but be confident (p. 35).

A contemplative is always doing the same thing all day and all night. He is praying, or having breakfast, or talking, or working, or amusing himself; but he is principally conscious that he is *doing God's Will*: the different external activities seem to him a sort of varied outcome of one continuous internal intention (p. 38).

How is it possible to be anxious, worried, self-conscious, bewildered, "with simplicity"? The answer is *abandon*—which is a French word (*une âme abandonnée* always sounds to me like "an abandoned character").

---

[9] Friedrich von Hügel was reading de Caussade away back in the nineteenth century. Chapman's discovery was made in 1920, and he owed it to a *Lady Living in the World* (p. 98). But already in 1914 the Anglican Bishop Chandler, in a remarkable book with the significant title *The Cult of the Passing Moment*, was quoting *L'Abandon,* and taking as his theme the view that the spiritual life is "a communion with God, or a waiting upon God, from one moment to another; with the corollary that fresh and progressive indications of his will may be thus received" (Preface). A copy of Chandler's book came into my possession in 1925, when I knew little of Chapman except as a scholar and a controversialist. When, some years later, I met the influence of de Caussade again in Chapman's own monastery, it was like the joy of meeting an old friend.

The point is that all anxiety, worry, etc., has its seat in the lower (not the lowest) part of the soul—in the imagination and emotions, or even in the intellect; but above this (or below it if you like) is the "apex" or "ground" of the soul, wherein prayer takes place, and union with God (p. 42).

God's will towards us is:
(1) *Voluntas beneplaciti*—(permission).
(2) *Voluntas signi*—(precepts and counsels).
Hence two general virtues—including all others:

(1) Conformity (Rodriguez's name) or Indifference (St F. de Sales' and St Ignatius' name) or *Abandon* (Mgr Gay's name).[10]

(2) Obedience  (a)  to commandments of God and the Church,
              (b)  to counsels, according to our state,
              (c)  to inspirations, according to supernatural prudence.

Also . . . our duty is summed up in giving ourselves to God, as he gives himself to us (p. 233, written in 1911).

Thus, well before 1920, Chapman knew what one may call the bare bones of de Caussade's doctrine. He knew that, more important than the method of your prayer, your one all-governing task in the spiritual life was "to give yourself up blindly" to God's will; not to worry but to be confident; that times of "mental prayer" derived their total value from the same source as times of legitimate amusement—from the acceptance of God's will; that all virtues are included in "conformity" and "obedience"; and he even knew the name for the doctrine: *l'abandon.*

Yet he tells us, in his Introduction to Thorold's translation of de Caussade's *On Prayer,* that there was something in de

[10] Charles Gay, Vicar General of Poitiers, was the author of *De la Vie et des Vertus Chrétiennes considérées dans l'Etat Religieux* (three volumes, 1877). The fourteenth chapter (vol. 3) is entitled "De l'Abandon à Dieu", being preceded by chapters on Charity and Christian sorrow, and followed by a chapter on Fraternal Charity. Gay's treatment of *abandon* is very beautiful, and depends (like de Caussade's) on Bossuet. But, whereas Gay devotes one chapter, and that neither the first nor the last, of his book to *abandon,* de Caussade makes it the whole substance of the spiritual teaching contained in his treatise.

Caussade which he thought was a "novel contribution to ascetical literature":

> We can be perfect here and now by being exactly as God wishes us to be here and now; perfection is not an aim to be realised in a dim and doubtful future, but it is for this minute, this very minute, and not the next minute or two: *hodie si vocem eius audieritis*: this moment is the most precious of all moments, for it is the moment in which we have the power of abandoning ourselves wholly to God's Will. No other moment is in our power. We need not worry about what is to come; by hope we abandon to God the care of the morrow, of our perseverance, of our death, of our eternity; but by charity we abandon ourselves to his Will now. . . . We all knew that it is only in the present moment that we merit, only in the present that we act, only in the present that we love. But (de Caussade) connects this necessary fact with our duty of confidence as to the past and the future: he insists on it as the safeguard against worry and despondency, the great dangers of all dangers, and he expresses it in a startling phrase: "the Sacrament of the Present Moment".

> God is everywhere, and in past and future: he is above all space and time; but to me, it is not the distant but the near, not the past and future but the present moment, which is the veil of God, or rather the unveiling of God. I cannot always tell his Will for the future, but I can never doubt it now; and I can always be sure of being united to his Will now. If we seek him, we have found him.

In de Caussade, Chapman found, then, a synthesis of spiritual truths which he had been discovering piecemeal for himself over a period of thirty years. It was a synthesis developed and presented by an eloquent writer who was also a religious genius of a high order. And it was worked out and applied by de Caussade with astonishing vigour and completeness in the four interdependent spheres of creation, history, redemption and psychology. It was utterly mystical and at the same time utterly Christian and evangelical. And it finally enabled Chapman to overcome the dichotomy which had bothered him for so many years: the painful contrast between the transcendence, infinity, necessity of God and the complexus of this unnecessary, contingent, arbitrary universe of finite realities, within which Christianity is situated, and to which it makes its own contribution of "unnecessary, contingent, arbitrary facts and doctrines" (pp. 205f). Of course he had known all along that there was only one rational "solution" of the contrast:

*God made the Cosmos.*

Why? It was a *very* odd thing to do!

And what an extraordinary universe to invent! Just fancy inventing *matter!* and thinking of such a thing as time—or space! Very clever of him, no doubt—most ingenious, to imagine such curious facts as co-existence and succession. But very arbitrary and absurd—one might say, insane. . . .

Of course there are many odd and (*a priori*) most improbable things besides space and time and matter—such as colour and light, music, right and wrong (conscience), pain, wonder and so forth—not to speak of the moon; and there are many questions one might ask, which philosophy would find it hard to answer, such as why England is not an island, why things don't fall upwards, why I cannot describe heat and cold, why things don't look larger in the distance (pp. 205-8).

A rational solution is one thing. A realised, practical, lived solution is another. And all along there was that discomfort with the arbitrary, driving him to wild humorous outbursts of jeering at its absurdity—the other side of the mastering desire for God:

You remember that I sent you a huge series of papers of theology—a theodicy—a theory of the world on the Christian hypothesis. Now, oddly, I can't say that *any* of that is my real spiritual life. I did not know this till lately.[11] It is my Faith—it leads me to God—it is most useful out of prayer. But in prayer always—and out of prayer also—the mainspring of everything is wholly *irrational,* **meaningless, inexpressible.** "I want God"—and the word "God" has absolutely no meaning. I find so many in this positively absurd and obviously mystical condition; I suppose one "contemplates" without knowing it. Of course it simplifies people's spiritual life into nothing but the desire of God's will. The whole object of life becomes to want nothing but God. *Only there is no reason for it.* The word "God" means *nothing*—which is, of course, theologically correct, since God is nothing that we can think or conceive. St John of the Cross describes the state at length in three places.

[11] He is writing a few months after the invention of the "theory".

Hardly anyone seems to understand it. I could have been in it—
with immense profit—twenty-two years ago, or more. But no
one told me it was possible (p. 248).

What de Caussade brought to this tormented, hungering, spirit
was the lived and life-giving unification of the two contrasted
orders of reality, summed up in the triumphant phrase: the sacrament of the present moment. No longer only *over against* but
utterly *within,* the complexus of created, historical, contingent
finites, as this complexus becomes actual for us in the passing
moment in which alone we are so arbitrarily actually alive, de
Caussade points us to the eternal and the necessary, "made flesh"
for our salvation which is identical with his glory.

The significance of this discovery for Chapman in his personal
life may be dimly conjectured by those who know something of
the disappointments, frustrations, and sorrows of his last years,
in an office which was distasteful to him from the first, and which
prevented so much that he would have wished to do,[12] and of
the last months of a weary illness that brought premature death.
But this is not a biography of Chapman, and it is more to the
point to indicate the effect that it had on his direction of others,
of which a sample may be given from a letter to a Benedictine
nun, written in 1925:

We have to learn in practice what we always knew in theory:
everything that happens is God's Will. God's Will always
intends our good. God's Will is carving us into the likeness of
his Son.

Every moment is the message of God's Will; every external
event, everything outside us, and *even every involuntary
thought and feeling within us* is God's own touch. We are in
living touch with God. Everything we come in contact with, the
whole of our daily circumstances, and all our interior responses,
whether pleasures or pains, are God's working. We are living
in God—in God's action, as a fish in the water. There is no
question of trying to *feel* that God is here, or to complain of
God being far, once he has taught us that we are bathed in
him, in his action, in his Will.

---

[12] "It is really a great blow to become Abbot. There are so many things I
wanted to do. I shall value your prayers . . . that I may not do much
harm" (p. 187).

# The Object of Faith According to St Paul's Epistles

1961

Of all the authors of the New Testament books St Paul impresses himself most vividly on our imagination as a human being of strong, passionate individuality, a man of such force of conviction, of such intellectual and practical power, that it has even been suggested that he was the real inventor of what has become traditional Christianity. It is therefore important to remember that the whole of his Christian life sprang from a certitude which he shared with his fellow-apostles. They were all convinced that there had taken place, in their own lifetime and in Palestine, a set of happenings which were finally decisive for all human history and had repercussions in the sphere of ultimate reality which transcends history. "The ends of the ages have come upon us" (I *Cor* X 11); "the old things have passed away, behold, new things have come to pass" (II *Cor* V 17).

The record of "old things" was found in the books of the Old Testament, accepted as authoritative by the Christians from the first. These "old things" comprised three "moments". In the beginning God had created the world, and man as its denizen and lord, and had seen that they were "good" (*Gen* I). But history had gone awry; and for St Paul, with his Jewish antecedents, there was no doubt that the source of the aberration was a moral deviation, a disobedience to the will of God: Adam had fallen. This moral deviation, with its background of sinister angelic activity, had brought other evils in its train and as its punishment: ignorance in the sphere of religion (Cf. *Rom* II 22: "they, who claimed to be wise, turned fools"), and death (*Rom* V 12). Human history had been distorted and corrupted by this complex of moral, intellectual, and physical evil. Thirdly, however, God had been at work through the ages, preparing the way for a divine remedy. This preparation had taken shape as the Old Covenant, the Jewish dispensation.

And now, in the fullness of time (*Gal* IV 4), God has acted with final decisiveness, crowning the long preparation and renewing the Covenant. He has "sent forth his Son" (*Gal* IV 4), who has died for our sins and risen again to glory. Thus final judgment has been executed on sin; and salvation has become a fact of history, to pursue its victorious course from man's "heart", or inner self, to his body and so to the whole physical environment in which he lives. Because the initial deviation was in the heart of Adam, it is right that the effectuation of salvation should begin in the human heart. Still, it is necessary to remember that the soil from which Christianity sprang was not Greece but Palestine. For those who saw man and creation with Jewish eyes, redemption could not be complete unless it encompassed what we call the material order; Christianity is more than a "cure of souls".

How, or under what conditions, does salvation take its beginning in the human heart? St Paul's clear teaching is that the turning-point, for the adult individual who is to be saved, is his act of faith. This is a completely interior act ("with the heart one believes unto justification", *Rom* IX 10); and it is logically prior to the convert's public profession of faith and to his baptism. St Paul will even say that it is "by" faith that we are justified (*Rom* III 28); but it must be borne in mind that he can use "faith" as a shorthand designation for Christianity as contrasted with Judaism, and rarely considers the problems raised by what modern theologians call "dead faith". His real teaching is undoubtedly that we are justified by the "Cross" of Christ, and that this justification is applied to the individual in baptism; as the Epistle to the Ephesians says, Christ "purified his Church by *bathing* it *in the water to which his word gave life*" (V 26). But it was required of an adult candidate for baptism that he should make public profession of his *faith*. Faith is thus the interior condition *sine qua non* of the individual adult's justification.

Later theology has brought an acute analysis to bear on the concept of faith. It has realised, with the Epistle of St. James (II 26), that faith can be "dead faith"—can belong to one who is not in an actual state of justification. And it has excogitated a definition of faith which is true even in this "limiting case" of a faith which is residual. But St Paul does not normally analyse to this degree; he is not a scholastic theologian. He thinks, and ordinarily writes of faith as a "living faith".[1]

---

[1] There is some advantage in this procedure. "Dead faith" is faith in a most abnormal predicament, like a human being in whom animation is suspended, and the minimal definition which it demands is hardly likely to do justice to what the New Testament has to say about faith. Similarly, it is possible to define the Church in such a way as to abstract from its moral holiness altogether; but the resulting definition, however true, so far as it goes, is dangerously misleading.

Living faith is a faith which "is active through charity" (*Gal* V 6). It is the faith of one who goes forward to accept the basic practical implications of the truth believed, including its first implication: baptism into the Christian fellowship.

What is the truth believed, in an act of Christian faith? Faith, for St Paul, is not purely a question of emotional excitement; nor purely a question of good will, even of good will towards God. It is also, and essentially, an intellectual adhesion to a truth as true. As Bultmann points out, faith and "confession" or profession belong together. And confession is of a truth; it is answering "yes" to a question about objective fact exterior to the person making the confession.

Faith is, indeed, a special kind of intellectual adhesion. In Plato's *Meno* we are given a laboratory demonstration of the fact, or of what Plato takes to be a fact, that *philosophical* (or mathematical) truth is not something that is "handed on" from teacher to pupil by a process of instruction, but something already latent in the pupil's "soul". This kind of truth is brought into reflexive consciousness by the pupil himself, in an intellectually autonomous act. The function of the teacher is to help the pupil to become conscious of his own knowledge; it is not, strictly speaking to "teach" him anything.

In strong contrast to this view of philosophic truth, faith, according to St Paul, is intrinsically dependent on "hearing". It is the acquisition from without of a truth which man, left to himself, would have been for ever incapable of thus attaining. It is, in fact, the assent to a truth revealed by God, a truth which can only be believed as thus *revealed*. It is essentially a religious act, since it not only assents to the truth, but acknowledges the veracity of God who reveals the truth. If, then, philosophy is capable by its own efforts, and without special help from God, of attaining to an affirmation of God within natural philosophic limits, this philosophic affirmation is not, in itself, an act of faith—it would not have come by "hearing".

Since then faith is a *sine qua non* of salvation, and involves an intellectual adhesion to revealed truth as true and as revealed, we may well ask St Paul what is the content of the act of faith. What is this revealed truth, or complex of truths, to which the believer gives his adhesion?

Before seeking an answer to this question, we must remind ourselves that St Paul belongs to the apostolic age, and is himself an apostle. The apostolic age was the age of commissioned eyewitnesses. It differs from every subsequent age, including our own, because since then there have been no commissioned eye-witnesses. And it differs from the period of the original pro-clamation of the gospel by our Lord, since it no longer had the immediate visible presence of Jesus, the hearing of his voice, or the direct vision of his saving acts and sufferings. It relied —as we have to rely—on tradition. But it was privileged, as we are not, to receive this tradition from the lips of eye-witnesses.

Thus, whatever the truth which is the object of Christian faith, the immediate source of this truth, for the converts of the apostles, was the word of the apostles themselves. It was what they preached that the Christians believed.

This is brought out very clearly in a remarkable passage of *Romans* (X 8f):

> The message is close to thy hand, it is on thy lips, it is in thy heart (*Dt* XXX 14); meaning by that the message of faith, which we preach. Thou canst find salvation, if thou wilt use thy lips to confess that Jesus is the Lord, and thy heart to believe that God has raised him up from the dead. The heart has only to believe, if we are to be justified; the lips have only to make confession, if we are to be saved. That is what the scripture says. Anyone who believes in him will not be disappointed (*Is* XXVIII 16). . . . Everyone who calls upon the name of the Lord will be saved (*Joel* II 32). Only, how are they to call upon him until they have learned to believe in him? And how are they to believe in him until they listen to him (better, hear him)?' And how can they listen (hear), without a preacher to listen to? And how can there be preachers unless preachers are sent on their errand (*aposta-lōsin*). So we read in scripture, "How welcome is the coming of those who tell of peace, who tell of good news (i.e. proclaim the gospel) (*Is* LII 7)."

Here St Paul is utilising a selection of Old Testament texts to illustrate his own Christian theology. Deuteronomy speaks of a divine message (*rhema* literally "word"). St Paul explains that this message is "that message of faith which we preach"; it is a message of faith, because it addresses itself to the faith of its hearers. If, he says, you "use your lips to confess" that Jesus is the Lord, while believing "with your heart" that God has raised him from the dead, you will be justified and saved. The prophet Joel says: "Everyone who calls upon the name of the Lord will be saved". St Paul takes this as meaning that he who, in prayer, invokes Jesus as Lord, will be saved.

The argument now proceeds as follows. Such prayerful invocation of Jesus as Lord presupposes that one believes his own claim for himself. You cannot so believe unless you have heard him make the claim (or, alternatively, have heard the claim made on his behalf). But you cannot so hear the claim unless there is some one to proclaim (preach) it.[2] And those who are to proclaim the claim must be (officially) sent on that errand (i.e. must be apostles).

Thus the source of the revealed truth which must be believed if we are to be saved is the official preaching of commissioned eye-witnesses. The function of preaching is apparently identical with that of *evangelizing,* for St Paul quotes, in confirmation of his argument: "How welcome is the coming of those who . . . evangelize good things (*Is* LII 7). Similarly, in *Gal* II 2, he speaks of the "gospel which I preach", and in I *Thess* II 9 he says: "We preached among you the gospel of God." The gospel, then, and the preaching or proclamation have the same content. Just as St. Paul can align preaching and believing (Cf. I *Cor* XV 11: "So we preach, and so you have believed"), so too he can speak of "the faith of the gospel" (*Phil* I 27); and just as the apostles were "sent to preach", so too the apostle Paul was "set apart for the gospel of God" (*Rom* I); in both cases the response required is that of faith (*Rom* I 5; I *Cor* XV 11). A Christian is one who believes in the gospel.

In the passage of Romans X which we have been examining, the gospel or preaching is called the *message (rhema) of faith.* (It is called *rhema* because that is the term for "word" or "message" which St Paul found in the Septuagint version of *Dt* XXX 14). Elsewhere, he uses the more ordinary term *logos* with the same meaning. Thus, in I *Cor* I 18; 23, the *word (logos)* of the Cross is the same as the *preaching* (Cf. "we preach Christ crucified"). It is a word which is "folly" to those who are perishing,

---

[2] Obviously, you might "hear" of Christ from unaccredited sources. But this, in St Paul's view, would not be the normal prelude to *faith,* which requires hearing from some one commissioned to speak. If the translation of the passage in the text above is correct, there is an ellipse in the argument. "Obviously, it is no longer possible to listen to Jesus immediately; hence, his claim must be presented mediately on his behalf." It is possible that we should in fact translate: "And how are they to believe in him, unless they hear of him?"

whereas God has willed to save believers by the "folly of the kerygma" (XV 21). This word is the common possession of all Christians, and its historical origin was in Palestine before the Ascension; so St Paul can ironically ask the Corinthians, supposing that they might resent a ruling of his, whether the word of God originated with them (I *Cor* XIV 36). In *Ephesians* I, 13 the word of truth is identified with the gospel of salvation.

A still more interesting identification occurs in I *Thessalonians*. When the Thessalonians received from St. Paul and his companions "the word-of-hearing of God", they received it not as if it were a (merely) human word, but as a "word of God, which is what it really is" (II 13). The apostolic preaching is thus, in one obvious sense, a word of God. It was therefore entirely fitting that, when St Paul first "evangelized" the Galatians, they accepted him "as an angel (messenger) of God, as Christ Jesus" (*Gal* IV 13-14); compare *Mt* X 40: "He who receives you receives me, and he who receives me receives him who sent (*aposteilanta*) me". There can be no doubt that, for St. Paul, faith plays its part in our salvation precisely inasmuch as it is an acceptance of a "word of God" in its character as a word *of God*. That revealed word of God was, as we shall see more clearly later on, identical with Jesus in his saving historical mission. But in the apostolic age, after the Ascension, this word of God had to be accepted not immediately from Christ but from his commissioned apostles; and it was in fact identical with their preaching.

There had been an earlier time when a man could hear the actual "words" of Jesus; and he who accepted those words as the basis of his life would be building his unshakeable abode upon a rock (*Mt* VII 24-25); those words of Jesus, in fact would "stand" even though heaven and earth should pass away (*Mt* XXIV 35), because they constituted the "preaching" of him who was immediately "sent" by the heavenly Father; they were the word of God. The relation of the converts of the apostles to their preaching is analogous to the relation of an eyewitness to the words of Jesus. In both cases what is heard is the same message from God; in the one case as proceeding immediately from the lips of the Messiah, in the other as coming from the Messiah's commissioned representatives. The mission and preaching of the apostles is an extension to all the world of the mission and preaching of Jesus of Nazareth; like the latter, it is—to use non-Pauline terminology—the sacrament of the presence of God's own voice among men.

We may interpose a reflection here upon our own, and all other post-apostolic times. If the dispensation of salvation was to survive the last of the apostles, from what commissioned source would future believers hear the preaching? This is a point of difference, perhaps, between Catholics and Protestants. The latter would maintain that in the "age of the (post-apostolic) Church" the preaching is to be heard by the individual believer immediately in the inspired scriptures. But there is nothing in the writings of St Paul, or in any other book of the Bible, which suggests this answer. We should rather suppose that, if the preaching of Jesus was handed on to the apostles as his commissioned representatives, then the preaching of the apostles would be handed on to commissioned representatives *of the apostles*. Already in *Ephesians* IV, 11 we read of "gospellers" other than the apostles. Such Epaphras would appear to have been among the Colossians (*Col* 1 7). And Timothy is bidden to "preach the word" (2 *Tim* IV 2), to "do the work of a gospeller" and to "fulfil his ministry" (V 5). Thus the New Testament already traces the outline of a Church which should be apostolic, not in the sense of having living apostles as its immediate teachers, but as depending on the preaching of men whose authority goes back ultimately, through that of the apostles, to the authority of Jesus, whom the Epistle to the Hebrews (III 1) calls "the apostle and high-priest of our confession (i.e. of faith)".

If, then we wish to discover the contents of the faith of the Christians, it follows from St Paul's teaching that we should turn in the first instance to the contents of the preaching of the apostles. In determining what these contents are, according to the epistles of St Paul, we are greatly helped by Dr C. H. Dodd's little book, *The Apostolic Preaching,* a work whose small compass belies its importance for Christian scholarship.

As Dodd points out, St Paul is aware of a distinction between the preaching and the various theological developments of it that might be made by himself or by other Christian teachers. One of the key passages for the preaching is I *Cor* XV 1f:

Here brethren is an account of the gospel I brought to you. It was this that you received from me; on it you take your stand: through it you are saved—if you remember the tenor of that gospel—or was your act of faith all in vain? Among the first things I conveyed to you, and you received from me, was that Christ had died for our sins according to the scriptures, and that he had been buried, and that he has risen again on the third day according to the scriptures, and that he had been seen by Cephas, and then by the Twelve. After that, he was seen by more than five hundred brethren at once, of whom most are alive at this day, though some have gone to their rest. Then he was seen by James, and then by all the apostles. And last of all he was seen by me too, like the last child, that comes to birth unexpectedly. . . . Well then, whether the preaching is my act or theirs, this is the tenor of our preaching and this the tenor of your faith.

The central portion of this passage, from "that Christ had died" down to, and including, "and then by the Twelve" is of crucial importance. It reads like a verbatim extract from an agreed official communiqué. (Note the designation "the Twelve", although obviously they were not at the time more than eleven). It shows that part, at least, of the preaching, and therefore of the object of faith, was Christ's redeeming death according to the scriptures, his burial, his resurrection and some of the resurrection appearances. A Western Christian is reminded of the contents of the second paragraph of the so-called Apostles' Creed. This Creed is a descendant of the Old Roman Creed, and there is good reason to think that the latter took shape, perhaps in the second half of the second Christian century, through the insertion, into an earlier Trinitarian baptismal confession, of "that semi-stereotyped proclamation of the good news which second-century Christians had inherited practically unaltered from the Apostles".[3] If it was this insertion that led to a statement, which the New Testament describes as *preaching,* becoming part of what we call a Creed or a Faith, the fact at least underlines the truth of our argument, that the object of Christian faith, according to St Paul, is in part at least the preaching of the apostles.

To obtain a fuller picture of St Paul's evidence for the contents of the preaching, we must take into consideration some other passages.

In *Romans* X 8f we are told that " the word of faith which we preach" is that Jesus is Lord and God has raised him from the dead. In *Romans* II 16 we learn that, "according to St Paul's Gospel", there will be a day when God will judge men's secrets through Christ Jesus; and when in I *Thessalonians* I 9 we are

[3] J. N. D. Kelly, *Early Christian Creeds,* (Longmans 1950) p130.

told that the Thessalonian response to "the word" or to "our gospel" was to await Jesus "who saves us from the wrath to come", it may be that we can infer that this saving aspect of the Parousia was also part of the preaching. In *Romans* I 2 the gospel is described as being about "the Son of God who was born of David's seed according to the flesh". From such various indications in St Paul's epistles Dodd puts together the following outine of the preaching:

> The prophecies are fulfilled, and the new Age is inaugurated by the coming of Christ.
> He was born of the seed of David.
> He died according to the scriptures, to deliver us out of the present evil age.
> He was buried.
> He rose on the third day according to the scriptures.
> He is exalted at the right hand of God, as Son of God and Lord of living and dead.
> He will come again as judge and saviour of men.[4]

Thus the object of faith includes a core of historical affirmation, with at least the embryo of a theological interpretation of this history (it was "according to the scriptures", and Christ died "for our sins"); it also included a transcendental affirmation (Christ is "at the right hand of God", and is "Lord"), and an eschatological prospect (judgment to come) which implies a framework of ethical monotheism rooted in the Old Testament.

The question may be asked, whether the preaching of St Paul was identical with that of the other apostles. Was there a special Pauline "gospel"? There are, it is true, passages in which St Paul speaks of "my gospel" (*Rom* II 16; XVI 25; II *Tim*, II 8) just as there are others in which he speaks of "our gospel" (II *Cor* IV 3; I *Thess* I 5; II *Thess* II 14). But, at least in some of these, the contrast is not between St Paul and the other apostles, but between the apostle and his hearers. Moreover, there would be room for different emphases in the presentation of the good news; and if St Paul gave special emphasis to the universality of the salvation offered to men in Christ, this would be in harmony with the fact that he, among the apostles, felt that he had a particular mission to the Gentiles (*Gal* II 8f). But the implication of St Paul's whole position is that there cannot possibly be any discrepancy, because the pro-

[4] C. H. Dodd, *The Apostolic Preaching* (Harper 1950) p17.

clamation—whoever makes it among those commissioned to that end—is true, true with the truth of a word of God. As he says about Christ's resurrection (and the same will apply to each item of the preaching): "If Christ has not risen, our preaching is void, your faith is void, we are false witnesses of God"; in other words, the whole Christian religion collapses. He tells us in *Galatians* II 2 that he had referred "the gospel which I preach among the gentiles" to "those of repute" at Jerusalem (apparently James, Cephas, and John), and these had nothing to add. So that in I *Cor* XV 11, after giving an extract from the "gospel which he had offered" to the Corinthians, he can say "Whether I or they (his fellow-apostles), thus we preach". And *Galatians* I 6-9 vehemently repudiates any teaching that is at variance with the one gospel of Christ "If anyone evangelizes you differently from that gospel which you have received, let him be anathema". Thus, in *Ephesians* IV 4, among the various factors which all Christians share in common (one body, one spirit, one hope, etc.) the author can include "one faith".

What historical guarantee have we that there was this identity of preaching among the apostles? Dodd points out that if St Paul received the elements of his preaching, listed in I *Corinthians*, by tradition from those who were already preaching it, he may well have learnt it during his visit to Jerusalem and to St Peter three years or less after his conversion; and in Dodd's opinion the conversion was not more than about four years after the crucifixion. It looks as though the preaching was determined in its main outlines at a period before the dispersion of the Twelve.

It is of great importance to realise that, as Dodd says, "no complete statement" of the contents of the apostolic preaching can be given on the basis of the New Testament alone. St Paul nowhere in his epistles sets out to give such a complete statement. His letters are not, as such, "kerygmatic". When he does give the extensive extract from the preaching that we have examined in I *Corinthians XV*, he does so in order to deal with a specific error held by some of the Corinthian Christians, an error about the resurrection of the faithful; just as when, in the same epistle, he gives his account of the Last Supper, it is to deal with specific undesirable practices in the Corinthian assemblies. In the days of the apostles, if you wanted to learn the preaching in its totality, you turned not to documents but to the living bearers of the preaching, the apostles themselves. But doubtless normally, and when no apostle was at hand, you sought your knowledge of the preaching from your local church and the local teachers. In the nature of the case, each of these communities was composed of people who had been drawn together by their acceptance of the preaching as the answer to life's problem; and the Pastoral Epistles already show us individuals who are not apostles but are entrusted with leadership and doctrinal oversight in the local communities.

It should further be borne in mind that we have not proved that the preaching can be reduced to nothing more than a set of particular statements, largely historical in character. Nor is it yet clear whether the range of faith could, or could not, extend to truths deducible from the preaching by a process of theological thought. We must take our investigations a little further.

St Paul can, on occasion, state the contents of the preaching, or of the gospel, with extreme brevity. "We preach", he says, (I *Cor* 1 23) "Christ crucified"; and this "message of the Cross", which is folly to those who are perishing, is in fact the foolishness of preaching whereby believers are saved. We must assume that such phrases describe the preaching by reference only to a part of its contents, though of course a very important part. I *Corinthians* XV shows clearly that the preaching in fact contained not only the crucifixion of Christ but his burial and resurrection. And in *Romans* X 9 salvation is promised to those who believe that God has raised Jesus from the dead. To limit the object of faith to Christ crucified is to be misled by St Paul's fondness for epigram and hyperbole; he was not really prepared to "know nothing except Christ *crucified*" (I *Cor* II 2).

There is, however, another kind of concise expression in St Paul, in which the contents of the preaching of the gospel, the object of faith, is stated not in an *extract* from the preaching, but sympathetically and inclusively. Thus in II *Corinthians* IV 5 we read: "We preach not ourselves but Christ Jesus as Lord". Compare, in the same epistle (I 19): "The Son of God Christ Jesus, who was preached amongst you through our agency" (II 4); "If your visitor preaches another Jesus whom we did not preach . . ." (*Philippians* I XV); "Some . . . preach Christ out of good will"; and Christ is presumably the unexpressed subject of "was preached among the gentiles" in I *Tim* III 16. Similarly "God's Son" seems to be the object of the verb "to evangelize" in

*Galatians* 1 16; and in *Ephesians* III 8 we read: "This grace was given to me, to evangelize to the gentiles the inscrutable wealth of Christ." There are also several passages in which we read of "the gospel of Christ" or "of the Lord" (*Rom* XV 19; I *Cor* IX 12; II *Cor* II 12; IX 13; X 14; *Gal* I 27; I *Thess* III 2; II *Thess* I 8). In some of these instances, the genitive may be not objective but subjective, the meaning then being "the gospel which Christ proclaimed."

In one passage, however (II *Cor* IV, 1f) we seem to have a clear example in which Christ is the content of the gospel. The Christian missioner (or the Church herself) is there described as "manifesting the truth". There are those who fail to perceive this truth, because "the god of this age" has blinded their thoughts "so that they may not behold the illumination of the gospel of the glory of Christ, who is the image of God. It is not ourselves that we preach, but Christ Jesus as Lord—and ourselves as your servants for Jesus' sake. It is God, who said 'light shall shine forth from darkness,' who has shone forth in our hearts with a view to the illumination of the knowledge of the glory of God in the features of Christ".

We have to remember that, according to I *Thessalonians,* faith is the acceptance of the word of the apostles as being a word of God. In our passage, it is Christ who is preached, and what the unbelievers fail to see is the glory of Christ thus preached. But Christ is the "image" of God, and what they (the unbelievers) therefore fail to perceive is the very glory of God in the visible Christ. It is hard to resist the conclusion that we have here, in all but the very words, the same doctrine as that of the Johannine Prologue: Christ is the Word of God incarnate, and Christian faith is faith in this Word.

But if the object of faith is Christ, the image of God, in whom (according to *Col* II 3) "are all the treasures of wisdom and knowledge", in whom "dwells all the fullness of the deity" (*Col* II 9), it seems reasonable to hold that no verbal formulation of the preaching could possibly exhaust the contents of this object. That Christ died, was buried, was raised from the dead, that he sits as Lord at the right hand of the Father, and will come again to judge all men—all these are essential ingredients of the object of faith; and we remark, in passing, that this shows that the nature of faith does not exclude an at least partial casting of its object into propositional form. As Bultmann rightly observes, "Faith in Christ affirms not merely the presence of a hitherto unknown divine Person. . . . The figure of Jesus Christ is inseparable from . . . his history as manifested in life, death and resurrection. And this history is the historical occurrence of salvation (*Heilsgeschichte*) . . . ; the believer recognises it as having taken place on *his* behalf".[5]

Christian faith is indeed faith *in God as truly revealing*. But this faith in God is indissolubly one with faith in the word revealed, and this revealed word is a historical phenomenon, known—since the Ascension—only through the commissioned word of commissioned apostles and their successors. The individual believer is thus tied, by the nature of Christian faith itself, to those who have believed before him, and it is their faith that he makes his own. But all the historical propositions about Christ in history, when taken together, do not begin to exhaust the inscrutable riches of the "image of God"—the fullness of the object of faith. We seem driven to the position that the object of faith is *Christ as divine truth, entrusted in the totality of his historical work and passion, and in all the implications of this work and passion, to accredited preachers.*

If this is a fair account of the implications of St Paul's teaching about faith, there would be room in the object of faith not only for what Christian tradition has to tell us of Christ's passion and resurrection, and the doctrinal interpretation of the significance of these occurrences, but also for Christ's ministry of teaching and well-doing—all that what we call "the Gospels" have to tell us about him. About these further elements of the object of faith St Paul has little to say. His eye-witnessing was only of the risen Christ, and his tradition was derived from the Jerusalem church when it was still under the overwhelming impression of the death and resurrection of Jesus. Yet I *Corinthians* VII shows us that the "precepts" or "words" of the historical Jesus were a final authority for St Paul, and *Galatians* IV 4 shows that he held that the history of the image of God began with a birth from a woman.

There are other items which St Paul nowhere seems to include explicitly in the preaching or describe as objects of faith, which yet there is reason to think that he would have admitted as such

[5] TWZNT, Vol 6, p 212.

objects. As we have seen, he nowhere sets out to give a complete enumeration of the items of the common preaching; his references to such items are incidental to whatever argument he happens at any moment to be developing. Thus, for instance, the sending of the Holy Ghost as the outcome of our Lord's death, resurrection, and glorification, is never mentioned by him as part of the preaching. It is however basic to his presentation of Christianity: "a man cannot belong to Christ unless he has the Spirit of Christ" (*Rom* VIII 9). The gift of the Spirit is thus the very purpose of redemption, and the realisation of salvation. Now the Acts of the Apostles plainly includes in the preaching the presence of the Holy Ghost in the Church, "as the sign that the new age of fulfilment has begun".[6] We can be confident that this was in fact an item of St Paul's preaching too, though he never explicitly says so.

What, then of baptism? This also has a central place in St Paul's teaching, to which it is indispensable; it is in the waters of baptism that the individual actually receives the justification which is salvation: "You have been *washed,* you have been hallowed, you have been justified in the name of the Lord Jesus Christ and in the Spirit of our God" (I *Cor* VI 11; cf. *Eph* V 25f: "Christ loved the Church and gave himself up for it, to hallow it by cleansing it with the bath of water accompanied by the word."). Baptism is never mentioned as an object of faith or as part of the preaching. But in *Romans* VI 8, after reminding his readers that we have died and been buried with Christ through baptism into his death, St Paul says: "If we have died with Christ, we believe that we shall also live with him". If the life that follows from baptism is an object of faith, it is reasonable to suppose that baptism, as death of our own past, is also such an object.

Like baptism, the Eucharist is never mentioned by St Paul as either part of the preaching or part of the object of faith. But it may be significant that he introduces his account of its institution with almost the same formula as that which prefaces the preaching of Christ's death and resurrection "I received from the Lord, what I in turn have conveyed to you . . ." (Cf. I *Cor* XV 3: "I delivered to you . . . what I also received . . .").

It may be, indeed, that the doctrine of the sacraments was thought of by St Paul and his contemporaries as not part of the

[6] Dodd, *op. cit.,* p 26.

preaching (*kerygma*), but rather of the teaching (*didachè*), the former containing truths which the apostles would present to audiences not yet converted, while the latter was confined to those who had already given their adhesion to the new religion, and were thus ready for more detailed instruction. Modern scholarship has tended to harden the distinction between preaching and teaching. But in fact the distinction may have been one of practical convenience rather than of theological significance. It is probable that the elements of the preaching reappeared in the teaching. And it is equally probable that the teaching was a process of enlarging the content of the object of the converts' faith. St. Paul himself writes, in *Colossians* II 6f: "As you have received Christ Jesus, so walk in him, rooted and founded in him and confirmed in the faith *even as you have been taught*". There is no doubt that, for St. Paul, the sacraments were part of the common treasure of the Church (and not a "Pauline" peculiarity), and they were the objective means by which the salvation and sanctification won by Christ were brought home in act to individuals. That they possess such efficacy was something that could be known only by faith.

The fact is that the Christian lives in a world of new truth which springs from the saving ministry of Christ, but which blossoms out into the gift of the Holy Ghost to the Church and the transmission of Christ's grace through the sacraments. This new world of truth constitutes the one single mystery of Christ (*Col* IV 3), a mystery shrouded in silence during the long ages of time, but now made manifest and known to all peoples so that they may respond to it by faith (*Rom* XVI 25f). A mystery is something that is beyond the inventiveness of human reason; if it is to be known, this can only be by means of faith.

Since faith involves an intellectual apprehension of its object, it follows that both faith and the object of faith are subject to development. Even a single proposition is apprehended only in the measure in which its terms are understood; and each of these terms gains part of its meaning from a context that transcends the proposition itself, a context which is not limited. Still more, if the object of faith is not simply a few propositions about Christ and his history, but is the historical Christ himself in his totality, the process of apprehension is bound to be also a process of growth. It may be that something of this sort was in St Paul's mind when in I *Corinthians,* having stated that his preaching among the Corinthians had not been "in the persuasive words of wisdom", he went on to say that "we do speak wisdom —among the perfect" (II 6). This wisdom of the perfect, of which the Corinthians had shown themselves too immature to be capable, yet seems to be identical, as regards its object or content, with the wisdom of God incorporated in Christ, the object of faith, a wisdom not recognised by "the rulers of this age" when they crucified the Lord of glory (*Ibid* II 4f). If the content of Christian wisdom is the same as the content of faith, it would seem that this wisdom itself is faith developed, faith grown to maturity. In the Epistle to the Colossians St Paul speaks of the poignancy of his desire that his readers should attain to all the wealth of the sureness of understanding, unto a knowledge (*epignosis*) of the mystery of God, which is Christ (II 1f).

Obviously, while every adult Christian can and must make the initial act of faith and thereafter must "stand in the faith" (*Rom* XIV 4; I *Cor* XVI 13), the extent of growth of understanding, the intellectual penetration of the object of faith, will vary enormously from believer to believer.

Using Newman's terminology, we may say that Christ as the revealed word or truth of God and as the object of faith, is an "idea" in process of development. It is an idea which is given not simply and immediately to the individual believer, but to the Church through the mediation of authorised teachers. The measure of the development of this idea at any age in Christian history is not the fullness to which it has attained in any individual mind, but that to which it has attained in "the mind of the Church" as a whole. This developed idea is the real object of faith. The primary believing subject is not the individual believer but the believing community. The individual faith is a participation in the faith of the holy community. It is "through the Church" that the many-sided wisdom of God is made known not merely to human beings but to "the authorities and powers in heavenly places" (*Eph* III 10). The object of faith, then, cannot be limited to the propositions of the original preaching, considered as static entities. These propositions themselves were objects of *faith* only inasmuch as their acceptance was necessarily involved in adhesion to the word of God which was Christ. And as Christ himself lived with a fullness of divine life as the Son of God incarnate, so Christ as the revealed word lives dynamically and expansively in the mind of the Church indwelt by his own living Spirit. So living, the revealed truth tends to express itself in ever new situations, ever new contexts; and it is no more completely separable from its context than the life of the historical Jesus was completely separable from his milieu. In all the developments resulting from this life in changing contexts, the word of God remains the object of faith; to reject its developments is, logically, to reject the word itself which lives only in its developments. The distinction between Christian faith and Christian *gnosis* is not an ontological one; it is the distinction between defined and undefined doctrines.

Faith, then, according to St Paul, is the act and habit by which one accepts the revealed word of God (a) as such a revealed word; and (b) as the basis of the whole of one's freely-willed life. Its object, the revealed word of God, is Christ in the fullness of his redemptive action, suffering, resurrection and glory, and in all that gives to these occurrences their saving efficacy. But this object, at the same time, is Christ *as proclaimed and preached* by his commissioned representatives; the Christ of the official *kerygma* and the official *didachè*. *Kerygma* and *didachè* are partially expressible, and partially expressed, in propositions; and when they are thus officially expressed, these propositions are to be believed—they are "of faith". Faith, however, does not restrict itself to the acceptance of these propositions. It adheres, not only to the propositions, but to the fullness of the *kerygma,* which is the fullness of the living Christ. The Church and her members, in seeking to penetrate the meaning of this object of faith, find themselves going on from the faith of the "little ones" to the wisdom or gnosis of the "perfect"; there is a tendency to development which is inherent in faith's object, considered as an "idea". Such developments are "theology" unless or until they are taken up by the preaching and teaching authority and made part of the explicit *kerygma* or *didachè*—whereupon they enjoy the same standing as the propositions of the original *kerygma.* Faith is the faith of the Church in logical priority to the faith of any individual member. The individual is a believer insofar as he adheres, even beyond his full understanding, to the faith of the Church, whose own understanding is itself progressive and never, therefore, perfect in this age in the measure that it will be perfect in heaven. Finally faith, which is normally "living faith", is an act of religion, because the revealed word is believed as and because it is the revealed word of God. In modern parlance, God *qua* revealer is the formal object of faith. And if it is "by faith" that we are "justified", that is because faith disposes and enables us to accept baptism, whereby justification is actually effected.

# Spirit and Institution in the New Testament

1961

The words Christian and Christianity are sometimes used in our Western culture to denote a moral attitude or form of behaviour of which the speaker approves. Thus you may find someone describing as "Christian" an act of material charity, or a habit of what is called "honest doubt". To use the words thus is to depart from their original meaning. The word Christian is first found in the New Testament (*Acts* XI 26; XXVI 28; I *Peter* IV 16), and there it indicates members of a new human grouping. It is probable that the word was not invented by the group itself, but was a nickname pinned upon its adherents by observers from outside. If so, it may be that by the time St Peter's first epistle was written it was already becoming a title of pride in the eyes of the group: "If a man is punished for being a Christian, he has no need to be ashamed of it; let him bear that name, and give glory to God."

In what follows I shall use these two words in their original sense. By Christianity, then, I mean the religion (or set of religions) which derives from that historical group with which the New Testament brings us in contact—the group's own name for itself was "the Church" or "the Church of God".

In this sense, Christianity is a fact of history; a fact, indeed, of the present moment, but with a long story going back to the days at Jerusalem shortly after the crucifixion of Jesus of Nazareth. Christianity "has long since become public property":

Its "sound has gone out into all lands", and its "words unto the ends of the earth". It has from the first had an objective existence, and has thrown itself upon the great concourse of men. Its home is in the world; and to know what it is, we must seek it in the world, and hear the world's witness of it.[1]

The world's witness of Christianity has been very varied, and often very hostile. But it has had its critics also from within. The most radical of the domestic criticisms runs more or less as

---

[1] Newman, *Essay on the Development of Doctrine*, pp. 3f.

follows: The one and only thing that matters in Christianity is the challenge of God to the human spirit, and the grace-enabled response, which must always be an individual's response, to that challenge. The essence of Christianity is—or should be—the resulting habit of loyalty to God, based on a recognition of one's total dependence on him:

> From our side this committal (of self to God) is all. Everything else is God's work through Jesus. In him God gives himself to each one. God rules within, by guidance and power, setting the task for each and giving the ability to carry it out. Thus life *is* communion with God. The distinction between secular and sacred goes. What is wrong must be cut out. All that is good is his service. . . . Viewed as God's gift to us, as his revelation in Jesus, it is inexhaustible. . . . It is both natural and supernatural. Natural, because it is what man was made for; and supernatural, because it is only possible as power for it comes from God.[2]

This, then, is what matters in Christianity. But, it is said, historical Christianity by contrast has been impenitently institutional, an *externalized* religion. It has maintained, and given importance to, hierarchy, sacraments, and liturgy. It has proclaimed the authority of a visible Church "outside of which there is no salvation". It has imposed dogmas, it has lent its protection and sanction to a human philosophy. It has a long, unending record of political interference. All this constitutes what may be called the outer shell or integument of historical Christianity. It is alien to its essence, which it has concealed and thwarted, "stifling the Spirit" (I *Thess* V 19).

The greatest upheaval that Christianity has ever sustained from influences within its own ranks, the sixteenth-century Reformation, was in large measure inspired by the spirit of such a criticism of institutionalised Christianity. But the heirs of the Reformation did not escape from institutionalism; they only substituted one set of institutions for another. The Christian West used to know, and suffer under, one Church. The Reformation has left us with a number of churches; institutionalism has not been transcended but propagated.

It cannot be denied that Christian institutions—like civil institutions—have been the occasions of great evils in human

2 W. E. Wilson, *Essential Christianity*, pp. 130 f.

history and in the realm of the spirit. But, since *abusus non tollit usum,* the question of the status of Christian institutionalism is not settled by that admission. I believe that the criticism is based on presuppositions which are not ultimately valid. But, for that very reason, an adequate answer to it would involve an examination of the nature of man and of that willed human response to God which is religion; and such a philosophico-religious investigation is outside the scope of this particular enquiry. I propose to myself a more limited object. I wish to ask whether Christianity, even at the most primitive stage of its development discoverable through our documents, even as it sprang from the ministry of Jesus, was ever "a religion of the spirit" in the sense demanded by the criticism.[3]

## I

Of course, if by "a religion of the Spirit" we do not mean to *exclude* institutionalism, but only to remind ourselves that Christianity is not *merely* institutional, it would be absurd to pretend that New Testament Christianity is not a religion of the Spirit. The response which the New Testament demands to the challenge of the Good News from God is nothing less than a total self-committal to God thus addressing us; a self-committal which is essentially interior. This response is what St Paul calls "faith" (*pistis*). Faith is a word which has had a long history in Christianity since St Paul. We are here concerned not with what it may have meant to Augustine or Thomas Aquinas or Luther, but with its meaning in the Pauline epistles.

For St Paul, faith is a reality of the inner world of the spirit, and is distinguishable from all outward consequences, effects, or manifestations: "With the heart we believe unto justice; but with the mouth confession is made unto salvation" (*Rom* X 10).[4] The *confessio fidei,* the external and public profession that we accept the Good News as from God, is one thing; belief itself, faith, the actual personal acceptance, of which the profession of faith is a manifestation to others, is another thing. It is a thing of the heart. And it is implied that where this interior reality of faith is withheld, there is no "justification", no possibility—it

---

[3] On the wider issue, cf. F. von Hügel, *Eternal Life,* the chapter on "Institutional Religion and the Conclusions"; also, E. Cuthbert Butler, *Religions of Authority and the Religion of the Spirit.*

[4] St Paul is expounding *Deuteronomy* XXX 14.

might seem—of a right, grace-transformed, relationship of man with God.[5] We are "justified as a consequence of faith" (*Rom* V 1).

This Pauline faith is something more than an act or habit of the intellect. It is not located by St Paul in the reason (*dianoia*), but rather in the heart (*kardia*). We must, however, remember that for him, with his Jewish and Old Testament background, the heart is not man's emotional or affective equipment as contrasted with his cognitive and ratiocinative faculties. It is not on the same level as, or on a more superficial level than, reason. It is deeper, more radical, than discursive reason. It is the human person focused in the most interior self; what later mystical writers will call "the apex of the soul". It is probably identified (in *Ephesians* III 16 f) with "the inward man". Faith is born and lives in this most interior sanctuary of the human person. It commits the individual to God, who speaks the Good News to him, there where the individual is most inwardly, and incommunicably, himself.

Faith is, indeed, a human act, though doubtless an act permeated by, and originating in grace.[6] But it is vigorously con-

---

[5] St Paul is not here considering the question of the salvation of infants, or of those who reject the Gospel "in good faith".

[6] It is curious that hardly any text of St Paul states precisely and undeniably that faith is God's work in us (*Eph* II 8 is differently expounded by modern exegetes). In II *Corinthians* IV 13 it is not clear whether faith is a presupposition or a consequence of the Spirit. The faith which is mentioned as a particular charism in 1 *Corinthians* VII 9 can hardly be simply identified with the faith which belongs to *all* Christians. The faith which is mentioned as "fruit of the Spirit" in *Galatians* V 22 is treated as parallel with "goodness", "meekness", and so on, and so seems more specific than that faith which is the basic presupposition of all human worth in the supernatural order. Similarly, it is doubtful whether the faith which is "measured out" to individuals, according to *Romans* XII 3, is that faith by which we are all "justified". Nevertheless, the logic of Paulinism, for which man's salvation is wholly God's act, would seem to require that the faith by which we accept the Gospel is something given by God. Faith is, in fact, at once the indispensable condition for the reception of grace, and itself also an effect of grace. St Paul was led by the history of his own conversion and by the needs of his anti-Jewish polemic to emphasize almost exclusively the former half of this complex truth. But cf. 1 *Timothy* I 14: "Now the grace of God hath abounded exceedingly with faith and love which is in Christ Jesus", on which C. Spicq (*les Epîtres Pastorales, ad loc.*) comments: "Along with grace, and as its direct emanations, have been manifested faith . . . and love.'"

trasted by St Paul with "the works" of the Law. It is not an act of strenuous, external, merit-seeking, obedience, but an act of surrender, or receptivity, of allowing God to act upon "the inner man". St Paul was a convert from Pharisaic Judaism, and to him the difference between his new and his former religion was that Judaism sought merit by works, while Christianity by faith accepted justification.[7] Thus, for him—and even in an epistle like *Colossians,* where the controversy with Pharisaic Judaism is no longer the central issue—the whole of Christianity finds its stable foundation in faith (I 23). Charity, it is true, is even greater than faith (I *Cor* XIII 13). But it is faith that finds vent for action through charity (*Gal* VI). And charity, like faith, is essentially an interior reality; it is poured out in our *hearts* (*Rom* V 5; cf. II *Thess* III 5) and appears to be something radical and fundamental to the inner life of the faithful (*Eph* III 18).

The noun "faith" (*pistis*) is not found at all in St. John's Gospel. It occurs once in the Johannine epistles and four times in the Apocalypse. These statistics, however interesting to the literary critic, mean nothing theologically; the verb "to believe" (*pisteuein*) is used more often in the Fourth Gospel than in all the Pauline epistles taken together.

In fact, the Gospel and epistles of St John agree completely with St Paul that faith is basic to Christianity and to salvation. The first epistle of St John sums up what God requires of us as being "that we should make our act of faith in the name of his son Jesus Christ, and that we should love one another" (III 23). "Everyone who believes that Jesus is the Christ is born of God" (V 1). Over against Christianity there is the unregenerate world: "the whole world about us lies in the power of evil" (V 19). The victory which has overcome the world is, precisely, our faith (V 4): "Who is it who overcomes the world but he who believes that Jesus is the son of God?" (V 5). It is as believing

[7] To point the contrast between the two religions, St Paul allows himself to say that, whereas the Jew sought to justify himself by his works, the Christian is justified "by his faith" (*Rom* III 28). But his real teaching is that the Christian is justified by *God.* The Christian's faith is not the agent, but the condition, of his justification. This distinction between agent and condition is important when it is a question of relating the function of the sacraments, and indeed of the redeeming death of Christ, to that of faith.

in the name of the son of God that Christians "possess eternal life" (V 13).[8]

As for St John's Gospel, it moves from the affirmation in the prologue that the Word made flesh gave power to become children of God to "those who believe in his name" (I 12) to the concluding statement of its own purpose (in chapter 31): "These things have been written down, that you may believe that Jesus is the Christ, the son of God, and that (so) believing you may have life in his name." And between these opening and concluding statements it is mainly composed, till we reach chapter XIII, of dramatic representations of the birth and preservation, or the rejection or loss, of faith. It goes without saying that this Johannine faith is an interior reality, the condition of our reconstitution as no longer mere products of human generation, but re-born "sons" or "children" of God. Faith's intellectual quality may be more emphasized in St John that in St. Paul; on the other hand, its moral conditions are strongly stressed—it is moral defects which explain why some fail to believe.

The Pauline and Johannine writings are the literature of a young and missionary religion, and it is natural that they tend to concentrate on the initial act of faith whereby a man "turns from idols to serve a God who is living and genuine" (cf. I *Thess* I 9). But this act is only the starting-point of a *state* or habit of faith. Christians can be succinctly described as "believers" (e.g. I *Thess* II, 10, 13). And this habit of faith, once engendered, can grow (II *Cor* X 15).

It has been usual in the past to look to St Paul and St John for theological articulations of New Testament Christianity, though today we are more aware than of old that the Synoptic

---

[8] It does not seem relevant to our inquiry that the *object* of faith in the Johannine writings is often the Messianic or filial status of Jesus; whereas Pauline faith tends to have as its object the death and resurrection of Jesus. Personal and circumstantial factors condition the way in which a thinker will state basic Christian truth. St Paul inherits the outlook of the primitive Church at Jerusalem, its attention riveted on the overwhelming fact that the crucified Jesus had been raised from the dead. An evangelist, concerned with the ministry of Jesus, starts from the drama of contemporary acceptance or rejection of the claims made in and through that ministry, already before the crucifixion. I do not think that either St Paul or St John would have thought that the other was teaching as true anything that was inconsistent with his own convictions.

Gospels and Acts are themselves steeped in theology. The idea of faith, and the word itself, are not absent from these Gospels. The word sometimes occurs in sayings which it is reasonable to regard as editorial. Thus, "Give us more faith " (*Luke* XVII 5) is probably an editorial introduction to the sayings which it leads up to. Similarly, it is just possible that *Matt* VIII 10 and *Luke* VII 9 ("Not even in Israel have I found so great faith") may be an editorial introduction to the saying which follows it in *Matthew* ("Many shall come from the East and the West . . ."), which may be intrusive in this context. Often, the faith of a person who is about to be healed by Jesus (and in one case, *Matt* IX 2, the faith of his companions) is mentioned or commented on; it may be that in several of these instances also the mention of faith is editorial or accretive.[9] There is, however, good evidence of the association of faith with miracles in *Matt* XIII 58 (cf. *Mark* VI 6): "And He did not perform many miracles there (*sc.* in Nazareth) *because of their unbelief.*"

But the demand for faith is, in fact, the very nerve of the Synoptic argument. St Mark sums up the proclamation of the Good News by Jesus in the words : "The time is fully come and the Reign of God is at hand; *repent and believe in the good news*" (I 15). The wording of this summary is, in my opinion, an editorial revision of the briefer version preserved in St Matthew: "Repent, for the Reign of the Heavens is at hand."[10] But there can be no doubt that the Marcan version expresses the nature of the challenge of the Good News from God. Jesus came before the public in his ministry as having a commission from God, as one who had been "sent", cf. *Matt* X 40 (= *Mark* IX 37; *Luke* IX 43), XV 24. He brought from God a message of

[9] The primitive Christian community, to which we owe the Synoptic tradition, was not interested in what today is called "faith-healing" as such. It will have seen our Lord's cures as Messianic signs, prefigurements of the spiritual blessings of "the last days", in which it knew itself to be already living. Since the preliminary condition for the reception of these blessings was faith, it was natural to emphasise the faith of the sick people who were cured by Jesus. It is not easy to fix on any particular Synoptic miracle of healing in which the reference to this faith is clearly original. Possibly the vivid Marcan account of the healing of the epileptic boy is a reproduction of an oral account by Peter: "Come, have pity on us, and help us if thou canst. But Jesus said to him, 'If thou canst! To him who believes, everything is possible.' Whereupon the father of the boy cried aloud, 'I do believe: succour my unbelief' " (IX 22-4).

[10] For a critical comparison of *Mark* I 14 f and Matt IV 17, see my *The Originality of St Matthew,* p 123 f.

Good News, the good news of the eschatological Reign of God. It is because what he preaches ("these words of mine", *Matt* VII 24, 26) is a message from God that it can become the unshakeable basis, the rock for human living. The Good News is, in fact, the proclamation of the Messianic Reign ("Blessed are your ears, because they hear; many prophets and just men have desired . . . to hear what you hear, and have not heard", *Matt* XIII 16 f). Clearly, the only way in which this message could become effective, the indispensable condition for the success of Jesus' mission, was that its truth as a message from God should be accepted by the public to which it was addressed. Such acceptance of a message as divine is faith. Jesus was not urging his public to have faith in God, *tout court*. He was inviting it to believe in a particular Act of God, embodied in his preaching, his work and his person.[11]

And here it may be noted that just as, for St Paul and St John, faith was the condition of a "resurrection from the dead" or a "new birth" of the human personality in its most interior reality, so acceptance of Jesus' gospel would entail a reconstruction of life in harmony with his prophetic reinterpretation of Old Testament religious morality. The Great Sermon (*Matt* V-VII; *Luke* VI 20f) doubtless has editorial "interpolations" in one of our documents, as it has suffered from the editorial pruning knife in the other. But there can be little doubt that, taken together, these two records allow us to form a substantially true conception of the inwardness and the infinite horizons of our Lord's moral and religious teaching. The simile of the house built on a rock with which the Sermon concludes is curiously like the notion of a life "rooted in, and *founded on,* love" (*Eph* III 17), and it recalls to our minds the Johannine notion that "our faith" is "the victory that overcomes the world" (I *John* V 4 f). There can be no dispute that Jesus proclaimed a "religion of the spirit".

## II

It might seem natural, at this stage of our investigation, to try to determine in greater detail what was the content of the Good News in which Jesus invited his public to believe, and to com-

---

11 There are striking similarities between the religious movement disclosed in the Dead Sea Scrolls and the Christian movement. But they are insignificant compared with one enormous difference; the Dead Sea sectarians never claimed that the Messianic Act of God was taking place in their midst.

pare it with the content of the gospel as preached by the apostles afterwards. But it will be more to our present purpose to ask: To whom was the message addressed? From whom was the act of faith demanded? To neglect this question, or to give it a hasty answer, might lead us to overlook a factor which is vital to our understanding of the position of Jesus of Nazareth in the world's history, and of the religion which he founded.

Jesus belonged to the Jewish people. That great people is still with us today; and still today, as in the days of the early Roman Empire, it is in common estimation, and as viewed from the outside, a singular people. Various reasons may be, and doubtless have been, offered—again from outside—to explain this singularity. But, as is so often the case, the real explanation is a religious one, and we can turn to Jewish witness for a statement of it. Leon Roth, in his fascinating study, *Judaism, a Portrait,* has insisted that what is really essential to Judaism is its conviction that the Jewish people is the "holy community". As the holy community, its constitutive bond is not precisely racial homogeneity but the practical acceptance of the Torah as divine:

> The "household of God" is the community of Judaism. Its root loyalty is not to a person or an aggregate of persons but . . . to a Teaching. This Teaching is the "Law . . . of Moses" . . . . Judaism knows Moses not as lawgiver but as prophet . . . indeed, as the greatest of the prophets; and "his" law is not his at all: it is God's. . . . The Teaching dropped the teacher's name. It is no longer for Judaism, as in the Bible, the Torah *of Moses* . . . but, barely and anonymously, Torah. (p 17-19.)

Roth is able to illustrate this notion of Judaism not only from Maimonides but from Josephus, and there can be no doubt that such was the Judaism of the first century A.D.

Many human groups have, in history, claimed to be this holy community of the Covenant through Moses. The Samaritans still survive—reduced now to tiny numerical proportions—and it would appear that they claim, as against the Jews, to be the authentic People of God. The same claim is made, not only by them and by the Jews, but by at least two great Christian bodies, each for itself. The notion of the holy community may, in fact, be said to have proved itself one of the most stubborn and persistently influential of all human ideas and convictions. And it should be noted that each of these claimants—as is essential to the very notion—maintains that it itself is the one authentic or legitimate continuation, in contemporary history, of the community of the Exodus from Egypt and the Convenant of Sinai.

The Dead Sea Scrolls have been described above as though they were the literature of a sect. But it should be observed that, for the member of the Dead Sea group, this group was itself, in contradistinction from the Jews who still worshipped in the Temple at Jerusalem, the true People of God's covenant. Like the Samaritans, the Dead Sea community did not deny the basic notion of Judaism, the idea of the holy community. But, like the Samaritans, they *identified* the holy community with their own group.

Modern Judaism, however, is descended from the much larger body which, in New Testament times, still acknowledged the legitimacy of the Jerusalem priesthood. Within this body, which we may for convenience describe as the Great Tradition of Judaism, there were divergent tendencies, wings, parties. Our own Gospels tell us of the "Pharisees" and the "Sadducees". But although a famous English version of the Bible speaks of the "sect" of the Pharisees, it is most important to remember that these parties were all within the one community, and each acknowledged the members of the others as being thus within. You could say, if you like, that there were High Church Jews, Low Church Jews, and Broad Church Jews. But all these acknowledged and belonged to what you would then have to describe as the one Jewish "Church". The community of the Dead Sea Scrolls, on the other hand, were *outside* the community of the Great Tradition, whose right to the title of the People of God they would hotly dispute.

There can be no shadow of doubt, unless our documents are utterly misleading, that Jesus was not only of the Jewish race, but lived and worked in the Great Tradition. The originality of his insights found expression through the traditional terms and concepts of the Jewish faith and theology, the divine authority of which, in its Old Testament crystallization, he assumed throughout. He proclaimed the Good News of the Reign of the Heavens; both the terms of this phrase are rooted in the Old Testament. When he sent his discreet but quite definitely affirmative reply to John the Baptist's question: "Art thou he that should come?" he implied that he was fulfilling the Jewish Messianic expectation. His own favourite self-description was, it appears, "the Son of Man", and it cannot be doubted that this is a description derived from the Book of Daniel (Ch VII). Even when, as on the question of divorce, he taught a doctrine that was at variance with that of the dominant schools of casuistry, he is represented as grounding his teaching on a thoroughly rabbinical solution of an objection derived from the Old Testament (*Matt* XIX 4-8; cf. *Mark* X 2-9), and—more profoundly—on his own exegesis of a text from the Book of Genesis. And in the very sermon in which he sets forth the spirit of the religious ethics of the New Covenant, he emphasized, St Matthew tells us (V 17), that he had not "come" to undo "the Law and the Prophets".

All this shows Jesus as standing within the general "universe of discourse" that goes with the notion of the holy community. But there is evidence, too, that he accepted the identification of that community with the community of the Great Tradition. He taught in the ordinary Jewish synagogues of Galilee. He sent a cured leper to register his recovered health before the priests (which no member of the Dead Sea community would have done). He illustrated his attitude to the precept "Thou shalt not kill" by the picture of a man about to offer his "gift" at the "altar". Though he found himself in controversy with both Sadducees and Pharisees, he is said to have bidden his hearers obey the Scribes and Pharisees, because they occupy "the chair of Moses". He describes the altar as consecrating the gift, and the Temple as God's dwelling-place. And in Jerusalem he showed his holy zeal for the Temple by casting out the money-changers. It is entirely consonant with this general impression, derived from the Synoptic Gospels and the traditions they incorporate, that St John's Gospel represents him as saying to a Samaritan woman: "You worship you cannot tell what, we worship knowing what it is we worship; *salvation, after all, is to come from the Jews*" (IV 22).

On the basis of that loyalty to the holy community and its Torah, which was essential to the Great Tradition, there was room, as we have seen, for a variety of emphases. It appears that Jesus would have seemed to his contemporaries to belong to the Apocalyptic stream of orthodox Judaism, to the "school of thought" that laid stress upon the Messianic hope, and interpreted that hope within the context of the Pharisaic belief in the angels and the resurrection of the body. The precise originality of his own message, seen in this general framework of thought, lay in its implication that the Act of God, to which Apocalyptic thinking looked forward as to the very *raison d'être* of the holy community, was already taking place in his ministry, and that he himself was "He that should come".

It cannot be questioned that this was originality in its most tremendous sense. It explains the popular impression that here was one who "taught with authority and not as the scribes"; and it justified the concern aroused by his ministry in authoritative circles. And, after all allowance has been made for the effect on the primitive Christian tradition of the Church's own controversies with Judaism, it can hardly be doubted that Jesus himself, at least as the ministry drew towards its denouement, published the most searing criticisms of those who controlled the thought and practice of the Great Tradition. This, however, makes it all the more significant that he is never represented as having criticized Jewish institutionalism precisely *as* institutionalism. Indeed (and the point is vital), in so far as an actual historical holy community is itself an "institution", involving an institutional machinery and officialdom, *he could not criticize institutionalism as such* without undermining the very basis of his own message. In claiming to be "He that should come" to re-establish the Reign of God in God's own people, he was committed to the validity of the notion of a People of God, and committed to its identification with the actual community within which he worked: "My errand is only to the lost sheep of the house of Israel" (*Matt* XV 24).

We have thus reached a very important preliminary conclusion: The message of Jesus was necessarily addressed, not to individuals as merely human beings, but to the Jewish community of the Great Tradition *as a community*. If you will forgive the comparison, the very nature of his claim places him, in the eyes of a historian, not on the level of a revivalist preacher addressing himself to individuals without reference to their "denominational" allegiance, but on that of a Luther in the period before his formal breach with the Roman Catholic Church. It made him essentially a figure of the world's public history.

### III

It is only when this conclusion has been reached and assimilated that we can fully appreciate the "dialectical moment" in the development of the story of the gospel, when it became clear that the appeal of Jesus to the faith of the holy community, whose leading representatives were among the Scribes and Priests, was destined to "fail". This "failure" is the theme of *Matt* XI—XII, though it is there taken in conjunction with a critique of the reality of the response even of the common people.[12] Doubts about the possibility of reconstructing a "biography" of Jesus should not blind us to the fact that a phase of affirmative expansion in his ministry was followed by a phase of relative withdrawal and concentration upon a more limited task.

What, it may be asked, would such a "failure" signify, if our Lord's claim was true, if he really was "He that should come"?

In the first place, it would mean that the Great Tradition, in its role as the holy community, had lost its *raison d'etre*. The holy community was indeed the "chosen people" of God. But, as Leon Roth points out (*op. cit.*, p 16), "it is so easy to claim to be of the chosen people, and to forget that the choice means duty, not privilege. . . . Yet the Biblical appellation of the Jews is not the 'chosen' but the 'holy' people, that is, a people set apart for a special vocation. Thus Judaism is . . . not what some or all Jews happen as a fact to do. It is what Jews should be doing (but often are not doing) as members of a holy people. It is not a product but a programme, and the Jews are the instrument of its fulfilment."

The "programme" of Judaism is, according to the Messianic hope, a programme for the future. To the extent that Judaism's meaning is found in the Messianic hope—and the Apocalyptic hope of the Reign of God, when taken in its full depth, places the *whole* meaning of Judaism in that hope—to that extent a community which had rejected its Messiah would have lost its vocation and its role in the providential ordering of history. If it survived, it would survive as an empty husk—an "Israel according to the flesh", to use Pauline terminology, but no longer the holy community.

---

[12] The fact that St Matthew is here utilizing a common theme of primitive Christianity ("his own received him not") is not sufficient to justify scepticism about the reality of the cleavage between Jesus and official Judaism. This cleavage could be eliminated from critical history only by a *tour de force* upon the documentary evidence.

But would it survive? Had not Israel's continuing existence been a result of the special providence of God?

Thou art thyself my king and my God, who commandest the saving of Jacob. Through thee we will push down our enemies with the horn: and through thy name we will despise them that rise up against us. For I will not trust in my bow: neither shall my sword save me. But thou hast saved us from them that afflict us: and hast put to shame them that hate us (*Ps.* xliii 5-8).

This conviction that the Lord God is the lord of history, and that he is, as it were, committed by his own covenant to the protection and preservation of his holy community, because it is his instrument of predilection and the focus of his government of mankind, is a dominant theme of Isaias, and the basis of the message of deutero-Isaias.

A Judaism, however, which had rejected its Messiah could no longer claim this special divine protection. This is what gives its profound significance and appropriateness to our Lord's apocalyptic prophecy of the fall of Jerusalem and the destruction of the Temple. There is no need to suppose that this, as recorded by the evangelists, is nothing more than a *vaticinium post eventum*. If Jesus was really in earnest about his Messianic claim, such a prophecy was a logical inference from official Judaism's rejection of that claim. The "glory would depart" from Jerusalem and from the House that had been God's dwelling-place; and the forces of destruction, that way-lay every human achievement, would find that at last they were attacking a city with no divine defender. Israel had rejected the very Act of God. So much the worse for Israel.

Yes, but if the holy community rejected the Good News, would that not also be "so much the worse" for the bearer of the news, the one who claimed to be "He that should come"? What is a Messiah without a Messianic community? He would be a "relative" without a "correlative". If the holy community existed only for the sake of the Messiah and his age, can we not also say that there would be no function for the Messiah except in and through the holy community which had accepted him as such?

It seems to have been foreseen by Jesus that, his claim being what it was, its rejection would spell his own destruction. The critical historian may certainly ask himself whether those predictions of his passion and death which the evangelists put on to the lips of Jesus have, as they stand, been given a precision and colouring which they did not originally have. But there is no need to suppose that the tradition of such sayings does not rest on any basis of forebodings actually uttered by Jesus himself. The charism of prophecy was hardly necessary for him to see that, if he persisted in his public work and claim, the authorities would be goaded into action; and in that rough age the result—since he did not propose to defend himself—was predictable. Look at the matter from the point of view of those who had failed to "believe in him". What surer way was there of demonstrating that this was not the Act of God than to contrive that the holy community should officially disown him? There is truth, if not strict historical truth as that term is understood by modern scientific historians, in the picture of the leaders at Calvary, saying: "He saved others, but He cannot save Himself! Is He the king of Israel? Let Him come down from the cross, and then let us believe in Him" (*Matt* XXVII 42 = *Mark* XV 31 f; *Luke* XXIII 35).[13] He did not come down. Had not the gospel disproved itself by the acid test of its own appeal to the holy community?

## IV

Thus the rejection of the Act of God spelt death for the divine Messenger, no less than it entailed the "death" of the holy community which had rejected him. But, if the claim of Jesus was true, *death could not be the end*: "My word . . . which shall go forth from my mouth . . . shall not return to me void, but it

[13] For a discussion of the reliability of the Christian tradition that the Sanhedrin encompassed the condemnation of Jesus by Pilate, cf. P. Benoit, *"Le Procès de Jésus,"* and *"Jésus devant le Sanhedrin,"* in *Exégèse et Thèologie,* vol. 1, p 265-311. On the other side, cf. P. Winter, *"On the Trial of Jesus"* (*Studia Judaica,* Band 1). It should be observed that, for the Jewish leaders, if they decided that the claim of Jesus was untrue, he was something worse than a "heretic". History has only too many examples of the handing over of heretics to the secular arm. The Sanhedrin would have been in a specially difficult position, since the Roman government did not pose as the arbiter of Jewish religious disputes. The Jews must produce some charge which would pass muster in a Roman court; and, if the charge was palpably incapable of being substantiated, must bring pressure to bear on the governor.

shall do whatever I please, and shall prosper in the things for which I sent it" (*Isaias* LV 2). In the very measure in which he was certain of the truth of his own message and its divine authority, our Lord must have known that its "failure" was only an appearance. And he will not only have known it, but have made it known. Scholars still ask themselves whether the predictions of his resurrection in the Gospels are, or are not, predictions "after the event". They may, in their present form, have been coloured by memories of the event; but (like the predictions of the passion) they are in substance guaranteed by the fact that Jesus, who doubtless could so easily have saved himself by renouncing his claim, refused to do so. He could refuse only because, for him, his death was not the end.

But the resurrection of the Messiah would be a pointless theatrical device, unless there were to be a "resurrection" of the holy community also. The victorious Messianic message must find its lodgement in the faith of the Messianic community.

Hence we see the vital importance of the "dialectical moment" in our Lord's ministry which took shape in the selection, choice, training, commission, and empowering of "the Twelve", and the promise that they should be "judges of the twelve tribes of Israel" (*Matt* XIX 28).

For although "they that were His own" had not "received" the word of God, there were some—a group which St Paul, using a term borrowed from the Old Testament prophets, would call a "remnant"—who had received him. They had done so by individual acts of faith and adherence. But they shared a common faith in a single object, and were fashioned by Jesus into a "little flock" (*Luke* XII 32), thus becoming a collective group to whom, as to the true and believing Israel, the Israel which had acknowledged the Act of its God, the continuing holy community, God would "give the Reign". And, since a community requires at least a minimum of organization and "government", the Twelve were to be the new leaders of this community.[14]

---

[14] It could be argued that the "sending out" of the "apostles" which is at the base of the Synoptic record of the ministry (*Matt* X 5f; cf. *Mark* VI 7f; *Luke* IX 2f) was of merely transitory significance, a passing phase of the ministry of Jesus himself. But the fact that the apostles were from the beginning twelve in number is probably connected with the traditional designation of the holy community as the "twelve" tribes of Israel. The apostles were thus the spearhead of the transformation of the expectant into the Messianic holy community.

There seems to be no ground in history for supposing that, after our Lord's crucifixion, there was any proclamation of the Good News previous to the conviction that he had in fact risen from the dead;[15] indeed, both St Paul and *Acts* seem to suppose that an essential qualification of an "apostle" was that he should be able to render eyewitness testimony to the risen Christ.

But if, in the loneliness of Calvary, the holy community had been reduced to bare identity with the one Suffering Servant of the Lord, the resurrection of the Messiah was pregnant with, was in a sense identical with, the resurrection of the holy community. And from the first discoverable moment we find the new and triumphant version of the Good News on the lips of the leaders of what our documents now call "the Church of God", the *ecclesia* of the new redemption from an apocalyptic "Egypt". It was "the Church of God" which, according to the Epistle to the Galatians, St Paul had persecuted during the short interval between the Lord's resurrection and his own conversion. But the thing is more important than the name. It must constantly be borne in mind that the resurrection of the Messiah would have been "in vain" without a "resurrection" of the holy community also. And obviously there was no resurrection for that community in its material identification with unbelieving Jewry. No, the "little flock" had entered upon its prerogatives and its mission, and a new age had opened in world history.

True, the Temple still stood, the Jewish priests still performed the ancient sacrificial rites, new born babes and proselytes were still being initiated by circumcision into the community that found its common religious life in this liturgical system; and Moses was still being preached in the synagogues. For a time, too, the followers

---

[15] Dr. Dodd's reconstruction of the earliest attainable form of the *kerygma* includes the resurrection of Jesus among its constant items. More recently, in "The Appearances of the Risen Christ: an Essay in Form-Criticism", (in *Studies in the Gospels,* ed. D. E. Nineham, 1955), he has argued that *formally* "there is nothing to distinguish the Gospel narratives of the resurrection appearances from the 'Paradigms' and other concise narratives on the one hand, and the 'Novellen' or 'Tales' on the other, which occur in other parts of the Gospels, and they merit the same degree of critical consideration, not only in their aspect as witnesses to the faith of the early Church, but also as ostensible records of things that happened" (p 35). It may be added that the specific mention of the burial of Christ, in the "kerygmatic" passage in *1 Corinthians* XV, seems to me to lend force to the view that the belief that Jesus had risen was related not only to the appearances but to the discovery of the empty tomb.

of the new "Way" still frequented the Temple and synagogue and were allowed to do so. The logical consequences of a new insight are not always immediately translated into action, not always even immediately drawn by the reason.

Logically, however, if the Good News is true, there was already a fundamental breach between the Church and the continuing Great Tradition of Judaism. To the eyes of a Jewish or an unbelieving historian it will appear that the Church was already logically "in schism" from what St. Paul calls "Israel according to the flesh"—just as the sect of the Dead Sea Scrolls was in schism. But if Jesus was the Messiah, as the Church now proclaimed, then the Great Tradition, in rejecting the Messiah, was in schism from the Church of God, and its public worship had lost its authority.[16]

The holy community, an actual historical group that is a group precisely *qua* religious, must have both public religious rites and liturgy, and an authorized ministry for its liturgical worship. But already, in the early days of the Jerusalem church, Peter and John, according to *Acts* IV 19, had appealed from the voice of the Sanhedrin to "the voice of God". The "old things" had passed away, and "He that sat on the throne" had "made all things new".

From the earliest period to which historical research and criticism can take us back, the Church of God had its ministry (the Twelve), its initiation rite (baptism), and its liturgy (the Eucharist). Psychologically, it might matter a great deal, but theologically it would not matter at all, if those who followed the Way were "cast out of the synagogues" as, according to their tradition, the Lord had foretold; for, under the leadership of the Twelve, they were all "of one heart and soul" in a new fraternity (*Acts* IV 32) which they identified with the true Israel of God. And when that other prediction was fulfilled, and the Temple lay in ruins, they could dispense with the sacrifices of the old Torah, since they had "a cup which they blessed" and "a bread which they broke" (I *Cor* X 16). And already, in a crisis which almost shattered the brotherhood, they had decided in

---

[16] Already, then, the true holy community was divorced (in principle) from those observances which had made Judaism a national religion. The Church was already "catholic", though it may not have realized this at once.

principle that, though one must be baptized, one need not be circumcised.

## V

Liturgy, sacred rites, and a hierarchy, in a Church which claims to be the unique beneficiary and vehicle of salvation, obviously add up to institutionalism. Thus it seems to me that primitive Christianity, at its earliest discoverable stage, was already not only a religion of the spirit, but also an institutional religion. Is it possible to link this institutionalism with the ministry of Jesus, or is it the first stage of a corruption of the original gospel? The question takes us to the very heart of the problem of Christian origins.

In recent years the "quest of the historical Jesus" has seemed to have found itself, at least temporarily, in an impasse. It has brought us, in fact, or so it may appear, into contact not with the historical son of Mary of Nazareth, but rather with the primitive Church, its institutions and its beliefs. A whole generation of scholars has been largely concerned with determining what conditions in the mind and circumstances of the primitive Church are implied by, and will explain, the contents and pattern of the Gospels and the pre-evangelic tradition.[17] It is as though we had been reading Mommsen, not to learn about the history of Rome, but to discover the *Weltanschauung* of the Germany of Mommsen's age. Shall we ever be able to take the jump which will bring us past the early Church to Jesus himself? The problem is in essence a historical one, but it has pastoral overtones.

Everyone must admit to himself that the early Church is an effect requiring an adequate cause or causes.[18] Nearly everyone admits that the historical Jesus is, at least, the major cause of which we are in search. But is he, in himself, an adequate cause of whatever the early Church regarded as essential to its own religion; or was that religion an amalgam of the message of Jesus and other factors in the immediate environment or the subjective conditioning of the early believers? Basically, this has been the

---

[17] This is the problem of the *Sitz im Leben,* not of Jesus himself, but of what, if the word can be used in a purely neutral sense (not implying untruth), may be called the primitive Christian myth.

[18] In modern Oxford this assertion perhaps calls for an apology to the spiritual heirs of Hume.

great problem of New Testament scholarship for over a hundred years. But the terms of the problem have been altered, greatly to the advantage of traditional convictions, by the progress of scholarship, and not least by the fact that it is no longer possible to suppose the great time-gap between Jesus and the writing of the major New Testament books, which Strauss held to be necessary for his own hypothesis. The main features of traditional Christianity—those, at least, with which we are here concerned, as determining it to be a religion not only of the spirit but of institution—go back to the pre-Pauline Church of Jerusalem.

For the traditional believer, however, this advance is not yet sufficient; he cannot be indifferent to the question of whether or not the gap between the primitive *ecclesia* and the son of Mary can be closed. And, on the other hand, as a historian he cannot deny *a priori* the possibility of a primitive corruption. After all, we have, in the story of the Gentile-Jewish controversy at the time of St Paul, clear evidence that *either* the universalists were encompassing a revolution, *or* the Judaisers were yielding to the fascination of influences which were essentially pre-Christian and sub-Christian. But our question concerns the moment before that controversy had broken out. Had sub-Christian influences *already* entered into the substance of Christianity, before it turned to the world beyond Palestine?

I want to suggest that possibly the time is ripe for scholarship to attempt the final leap.

I have already put forward the view (not a very novel one!) that the "little flock" of the disciples of Jesus is the embryo of the Church. And I have suggested that the Twelve, the embryo of ecclesiastical hierarchy, is a group of dominical institution. It has, of course, been pointed out already by others that the designation of Judas the traitor as "one of the Twelve" can hardly be supposed to be an invention of the apostolic Church.

There is one Gospel passage which I must approach with the warning, or the reassurance, that I am not trying to make a "denominational" point: the promise to Simon Bar-Jonas in *Matt* XVI. I need not waste time in arguing that this passage is an authentic part of the genuine text of St Matthew, or that its language seems to be a direct translation from Aramaic. Nor do I mean to use the passage here to vindicate any special standing among the Twelve for Peter. I wish, however, to make two points about this group of sayings.

(a) *"On this rock I will build My Church, and the gates of Hell will not prevail against it."* This saying reminds me of two other statements attributed to Jesus, both of which we have already considered in other contexts.

The question has been raised about this saying, whether it supposes that the Church is to conduct a victorious war of aggression against the gates of Hell, or whether the forces of Hell are envisaged as the aggressors, and the Church as the victorious defender of its established position. It seems to me that this question may be answered by reference to the other Synoptic passage where Jesus is said to have used the figure of a building founded upon a rock: "and the rain fell and the floods came and the winds blew and beat upon that house, but it did not fall; it was founded upon rock" (*Matt* VII 25  *Luke* VI 48). Here, clearly, the house is the victor over the aggression of nature. Now, if the saying in *Matt* XVI was not fashioned by the same mind which composed the finale of the Great Sermon, it was fashioned by someone else upon the model of that finale. In either case, the composer of the second saying (about the Church) was thinking of the gates of Hell as performing the same role with reference to the Church as the forces of nature played against the house of the Sermon's finale.

The Sermon teaches that the good disciple of Jesus has built his personal, ethico-religious life on the "words" of Jesus, words which will not "pass away" (*Matt* XXIV 35=*Mark* VIII 31; *Luke* XXI 33), because they are a divine message, a word of God. Such a disciple has thus found, in a word of God the lord of history, creator of nature, giver of the Covenant, a source of stability which no created powers can undermine.

Similarly, then, the saying in *Matt* XVI teaches that the Church will have a stability which will triumph even over Hell's aggression, because it has been founded by the Lord's Messiah on the rock of his own choosing. But this is to attribute to the Church that supernaturally guaranteed abidingness which the prophecy of the destruction of the Temple would deny to the Great Tradition of Judaism. Thus our saying answers the tremendous problem raised by the predicted downfall of the Great Tradition. For, though man cannot bind God to fidelity, it is the basic conviction of Judaism that God has bound himself to the holy community; this is the meaning of the Covenant. The greatest of secular empires has a birth-certificate which is also a death-warrant. But the holy community does not die—or, if it dies, it dies to rise again in greater glory—because it is the peculiar choice of the Lord of history. If then Jesus, from a standing-point within the Judaism of the Great Tradition, prophesied the downfall of the holy community *as identified with that Tradition,* he was bound to transfer the abidingness of the holy community to some other body, different from the community of the Great Tradition, yet able, like it, to claim continuity with the *ecclesia* of the Exodus and the Israel of the prophets. The fact that the saying in *Matt* XVI does precisely this—or rather promises to do this—is, for me, an *a priori* argument for its genuineness as a saying of Jesus; and this argument is strengthened by the literary similarity with the finale of the Great Sermon.

(b) But if Jesus was realistically determined to perpetuate the holy community in his "little flock", the question of government was bound to arise. And if he was "He that should come", bringing with and in himself "something greater" than the Temple (*Matt* XII 6), then all government in the reconstituted holy community must be exercised directly by himself or by derivation from him. From this point of view, it is only what we should expect, that our passage appoints Simon Bar-Jonas to a position of authority, giving him "the keys of the Reign of God". Simon's authority will not be something intrinsic to his person as Simon, but derived from "the great shepherd of the flock" (I *Peter* V 4). Precisely as thus derived, this authority, though wielded by a man, will be heavenly authority, drawn from the same sphere from which alone the rock-function and the permanence of the holy community derive: "whatever thou shalt bind on earth shall be bound in heaven". It cannot be a coincidence that the second occurrence of this binding-and-loosing metaphor in St Matthew is in the second passage which explicitly mentions the Church by that name.[19]

The holy community, we have argued, needs not only government but rite and liturgy. There may be room for argument whether the pattern of the Eucharist as given in St Paul and—somewhat differently—in St Mark or St Matthew is directly of dominical origin. There can hardly be any question that a Eucharist rite was "instituted" by him at the Last Supper. As regards the rite of baptism, it is true that the only New Testament books which directly refer this to Christ's institution are St Mark (in the appendix to Ch. XVI) and St Matthew. But it is probable that the emphasis and shape given by the Synoptic tradition to the narrative of our Lord's own baptism by John the Baptist means that the early Church saw this as a sort of prototype of the Christian sacrament. St John's Gospel, also, besides the conversation with Nicodemus, has a curious statement that the disciples of Jesus were baptizing during his own ministry.[20] In any case, the use of baptism as an initiation rite was so universal and, so far as we can judge, so primitive in the Church that there seems good reason to think that it rested on the authority of Jesus.

## VI

In the preceding paragraphs we have been led into an area of controversial details. I want now to go back to the more basic

[19] Dr Dodd has shown that there is good reason to think that St Paul knew, and made use of, the teaching contained in *Matt* XVIII 15-18. In that case, the pericope is at least not a product of the closing years of the apostolic age, when, it might be urged, the "spirit" was losing ground far and wide to "institutionalism".

The whole passage in *Matt* XVI 13-20 is profoundly *theological* and "Christological". A question about the public reaction to the person of Jesus leads up to Simon's confession of faith which, though made by a man, is attributed to divine revelation. The Church, built by Christ on the rock, is to have a stability which, as we have seen, is given by God and guaranteed by Christ. The authority which Peter is to wield will derive from Christ, and his authoritative decisions will embody the decisions of "the heavens", i.e. God. Thus Peter will be the mouthpiece of divine authority. This authority will be mediated to him by Christ and it will be remembered that, according to *Matt* XI 27, all revealed knowledge of God is mediated by "the Son," the object of Simon's confession of faith in St Matt XVI 16.

I may add here that I do not attach great importance to the *word* "Church" in these two passages of St Matthew. Whatever word was used in the Aramaic original (the Aramaic equivalent of "synagogue" has been suggested), it would inevitably be rendered by a Christian translator as *ecclesia*. The question is, if it be granted that Jesus spoke of building (on Peter) something against which the gates of Hell would not prevail, what can he conceivably have proposed to build except the holy community? On the possibility, in a Jewish context, of the metaphor of "building" a community, cf. O. Cullmann *Saint Pierre*, ed. 1, 173 f.

[20] On St John's own principles, this could not, of course, have been fully sacramental baptism, since "the Spirit was not yet given". But it could have been the historical embryo of Christian baptism, as the "little flock" was, in my opinion, the historical embryo of the Church.

issue, and to try to make clear why I think that the question whether Jesus was the founder—or refounder—of what, in one aspect, may be correctly called an institutional religion does not depend simply on the answer which, as historians, we may be inclined to give to these problems of detail.

Dare I say that I think that some people talk or write as if Jesus were not really a complete human being[21]—so complete as to belong, as human beings must belong, to a real concrete environment which acted on him and in which he acted? He was as genuinely human as the Emperor Augustus; and I venture to suggest that he had his feet as firmly planted on *terra firma.* Issuing from his ministry—*post hoc* if not *propter hoc*—there came a great spiritual and institutional religion, as deeply rooted in the Jewish past as it really transcended it. We know a good deal about the Palestinian environment in which Jesus lived and died. We know that its religious culture was uniquely mono-theistic. But we also know that the real *geistiges Band* of Judaism was the conviction that the Jews were the People of God's choice, the one holy community. We know that the main body of the Jews identified this holy community with the Great Tradition centred in the Jerusalem priesthood and cultus. There is every reason to believe that Jesus, in the early stages of his public life, accepted this identification.

Did he, or did he not, claim in some real and matter-of-fact sense that the Messianic Reign of God was being inaugurated in his work?

I should myself admit that there is an element of ambiguity in this question. If most Jews expected the Messianic age to be intro-duced in a single flash of divine lightning, it is clear that Jesus saw his own work as a process in time. Hence, there could be a sense in which, while he was really introducing the Reign of God, that Reign was not a *fait accompli* till his ministry—and, as it turned out, his passion and resurrection—were accomplished. Granted this qualification, are we not now in a position, not merely as believers but as historians, to affirm that he *was* making this astounding claim? I know that this is a most momen-tous question—the most momentous question, perhaps, of all with which we are faced by history. Can we refuse to it the

---

[21] Of course I believe that he is God the Son. But that is a matter of faith rather than of historical science.

answer Yes, without importing into our historical judgement a factor of hesitation or scepticism that arises from some other sphere of thought?

But suppose that the answer is Yes. And suppose that Jesus was intelligent enough to realize that his claim, his new insight, involved a wealth of logical and practical consequences. Then see him in his actual environment and, remembering that his ministry was to end on Calvary, consider whether he must not have foreseen that "failure" as vividly as Julius Caesar foresaw the implications of his proposed passage of the Rubicon. His claim was of a nature that presupposed the truth of the belief in the holy community. Unless the holy community conceded the truth of the claim, unless it "believed in the Good News", the claim was itself void, and the word which had gone forth from the Most High must return to him void. With his rejection by the Great Tradition in prospect, was it not inevitable that he should use the short time left to him to fashion, in the very womb of that Tradition, a realization of the idea of the holy community which would preserve continuity with the community's past but would be newly conditioned by the community's corporate faith in his claim and in the message he had brought, the message which he *was*? But if there was to be a community, there would have to be social structure and provision for community acts. If we do not always clearly realize the inescapable implications of the Messianic claim, it is because we are heirs not only of Jerusalem but of Athens, for whom it is not immediately absurd to suppose that a Jewish Messiah could conceive of the holy community as a bodiless ideal.

Of course, everything that I am here saying presupposes that, while Jesus accepted defeat in the factual sense of accepting martyrdom, he did not accept martyrdom as the end, either for himself or for the holy community. There was, in other words, if I am right, a vision[22] in the heart of Jesus to which Christian faith corresponds. But just as our faith should make us more, not less, realistic about the environment, so, I suggest, this vision will have made Jesus entirely realistic about his own situation and

---

[22] The Messianism of Jesus was, in one aspect, a prophetic Messianism. The prophet Isaias had "seen the Lord" in a vision which inaugurated his prophetic mission. Jesus is reported as having said: "None knoweth the Father save the son." Such a knowledge of God, in a Jewish context, entails knowledge of the divine redemptive purpose.

his own work. If, despite the Jewish leaders, that work was the work of God and therefore bound to triumph, it followed that provision must be made for the time after the passion. Looking at the thing as a historian, I do not think that Jesus despaired, "lost faith", before the end. As a Christian, I do not believe he despaired *at* the end.

## VII

The question with which we set out was, whether we could find a stage at which Christianity, or its prelude in the ministry of Jesus, was a religion of the spirit, but not yet a religion of institution. If I am right, no such stage can be discovered. Institutionalism was embedded in the presuppositions of our Lord's ministry and was incorporated in its intended result.

But it is important to remember that, if Christianity has institutionalism in its essence, it is *also* a religion of the spirit. It was here that St Paul found the great contrast between his new religion and the Pharisaic Judaism to which he had previously adhered. Doubtless, Judaism too was a religion of the spirit, requiring of its practisers an interior allegiance to the presuppositions of the Torah; and, if such allegiance was forthcoming, a proselyte could be admitted to the holy community whatever his racial origin or cultural background. In fact, however, not only were circumcision, and the aspect of Judaism as a national culture, a barrier to many Gentiles, but there was a strong racial current in the Judaism of the Great Tradition. In theory, God could raise up children unto Abraham from the stones of the desert, but in practice things did not easily work out like that. Christianity, by the very circumstances of its origin in a rejected Messiah, and of its early breach with the Great Tradition, was both logically universalistic and soon became "catholic" in practice. This universalism is the consequence of its faith, of its being a religion of the spirit.

And this is perhaps the place to remind ourselves that we have here given little consideration to the question of the *content* of the Good News. To describe Jesus as the founder of an institutional religion is, in my opinion, true; but it is so far from being the whole truth that, expressed thus without qualification, it sounds like a grotesque misrepresentation. For nearly two thousand years the Church has been engaged in a deepening penetration of the significance, the bearings, and the potentialities of the Gospel; and the growth of understanding will presumably go on till the Second Coming of the bearer of the message. Still today, as in the time of St Paul, the Church can pray that her children may be filled with that knowledge of God's will that brings all wisdom and spiritual insight with it (*Col* I 9).

It is no light matter, nor is it altogether a comforting thing, to decide that Christianity cannot escape from its destiny to be an institutional religion. The record of institutional religion is writ large in history, for all to see, and if we can point to the basic claim of Jesus as evidence that he accepted institutionalism in principle, the critics of religious institutions can remind us that he himself is recorded as having developed a tremendous invective against those who in his own day were of repute in the institution of the Great Tradition.

But if Christianity is institutional, it is also, as a great English layman has taught us, both "intellectual" and "mystical". Each of these three "elements" of religion poses its own problems; each needs to be balanced and checked by the other two. As regards the institutional element, Christianity has long since recognized that even excommunication is a sentence which, though it be passed by legitimate authority, may yet be unjust. *Abusus non tollit usum.* And if that seems to some a rather lame conclusion to the whole matter, then let us remind ourselves that our Lord himself was the Great Excommunicate, handed over to the secular arm for the imposition of the supreme penalty. At that moment, before Jesus could utter his *consummatum est,* it could be argued that the High Priest in Sanhedrin was still the legitimate highest authority in the holy community. Has institutional religion ever more nearly succeeded in "quenching the spirit" than when—so the Gospels tell us—the priests extorted from Pilate that unjust sentence of death? But we, who can look beyond Calvary to Easter morning, we who see in that death and resurrection the redemption of Christ's Mystical Body—what can we do, as we "survey the wondrous Cross", but join in the Church's paradoxical song: "O happy fault"?

# Collective Bias and the Gospels

1962

In Lent, 1961, Professor D. E. Nineham gave four broadcast talks on the Gospels, and these have been published in book form.[1] They are an attempt to show those who are not specialists how the Gospels (mainly the Synoptic Gospels) can be understood in the light of the findings of modern critical scholars. It is important for scholarship, as well as for the general public, that such attempts should be made, and Prof. Nineham is to be very warmly congratulated on his performance. The book, in fact, fulfils its purpose so admirably that I propose, after a brief outline of its contents, to forgo further compliments and to concentrate on complaints, of which the target will be rather the modern scholars than Prof. Nineham himself. But first, what has modern scholarship, according to this author, to tell us about the origin of Christianity? The four following paragraphs correspond with the four chapters of the book.

(1) Jesus of Nazareth is represented by modern scholarship as a teacher, or rather as the herald of good news from God, the good news of the advent of God's Kingdom or Reign, seen in the general context of the Jewish Messianic hope. This message presented itself to the listeners in Palestine as a challenge to prepare themselves to stand face to face with God. It implied a tremendous crisis, as is indicated by a number of parables and sayings. What folly it would be, these parables and sayings imply, not to "repent" or rather to adapt one's life radically to the imminent encounter with God! Obviously, the Kingdom of God must be given absolute priority in the arrangement of our lives and interests.

(2) Most of Jesus' contemporaries refused to take the challenge seriously. How could this very ordinary man be the messenger of the greatest crisis of all? Some of our evidence suggests that Jesus replied to this question by pointing to the Messianic character of his wonderful works. But elsewhere we get the impression that he simply appealed to the self-

---

[1] D. E. Nineham, *A New Way of Looking at the Gospels. Four Broadcast Talks* (S.P.C.K., 1962).

authenticating nature of his own message; and, "if they will ask God, he will help them to a right decision". As for the expected marvels that should accompany the advent of the Kingdom of God, our Gospels suggest that Jesus did not reject the belief in them, but taught that they would be associated with the *final* Coming. But many modern scholars would hold that the pictorial details of Jesus' alleged predictions are due to the imagination of the early believers and are not in the fullest sense part of the teaching which Jesus himself gave.

(3) *Who* was Jesus? Did he, actually or virtually claim to be "the Messiah", or "the Son of Man", or "the Son of God"? The third of these titles would not necessarily mean more than the first, and some scholars go so far as to doubt whether Jesus even claimed the simple title of Messiah. As regards the second title, some scholars say that Jesus could at most have claimed to be "the Son of Man elect, so to speak". Anyhow, we can see that the general Gospel picture is of Jesus as God's special "agent for the work of salvation". (Prof. Nineham even says that "all scholars can fully agree" about Christ's unique relationship to God; but do they agree about this? And if they do, are there not some who would mean no more than a Hindu might concede concerning this celebrated Jewish *guru*?) Whatever Jesus thought of himself, he felt that "he had the power and the duty to begin God's great and final battle against the powers of evil . . . . And he was moved to choose and train a body of disciples to help him in his work, and perhaps to carry it on after his death". Prof. Nineham seems inclined to think that Jesus foresaw his death "as a ransom for his fellows".

(4) What has our Lord's message of the Kingdom to say to us in the twentieth century? Well, we believe that God is the Lord of history, "with whom in the end all men must settle their account". And we are certain that we shall die. (So far, be it observed, we are in the position of the Jews before the gospel.) We, too, need to be awakened to the critical situation in which these truths place us. We need to realise that "it is a terrible thing to fall into the hands of the living God", but that, if we choose the childlike attitude of complete voluntary dependence on God, we shall find that he is indeed not only a King but a Father. Jesus teaches us that God does not merely welcome the repentant, but takes the initiative in seeking out the sinner; and so does our Lord, God's agent. In absolute reliance on God we shall find

release from our fears; for God is not only limitless in love, but limitless in power. Jesus demonstrated in his life, and supremely in his death, what it means to put all one's trust in God's love and power. "If Jesus on the Cross was to have any future—if all that he had said and done was to have any lasting meaning and validity, they must be given entirely by God. And there, too, you have some inkling of the meaning of the Resurrection."

It is important to bear steadily in mind that, in these talks, Prof. Nineham did not set out to give his own interpretation of the Gospels. Rather, he was reporting on the present state of Gospel scholarship; a difficult task, if only because, of course, scholars differ profoundly from one another, and it is not easy to strike an average. They differ in their presuppositions. There are probably still scholars who, deep down, *presuppose* that Jesus was not God incarnate, and that miracles have never happened. There are scholars who presuppose that the correct intellectual framework within which to view Christian origins is German Existentialism. There are also scholars who, deep down, presuppose that the true findings of scholarship must be in harmony with the essentials of the traditional Christian faith. Differing in their presuppositions, scholars differ in their results. And I believe that there is one profound cleavage between scholars which prevents us from adding up their results and striking an average.

So far, however, as it is possible, I think we can admit that Prof. Nineham has given a very fair statement of the overall picture of Gospel scholarship at the present time though I am not sure that he has paid sufficient attention to continental Catholic scholarship. But I wonder whether he would agree with me that this picture should have been given with an explicit warning to the ordinary hearer or reader? I should say that the overall picture reflects a *bias*. Scholars who, fundamentally and by presupposition (whether conscious or not), disbelieve the traditional faith are bound to seek to present an intelligible reconstruction of Christian origins on a purely natural basis. And scholars who fundamentally are orthodox in belief are sometimes almost neurotically anxious not to claim more in favour of their faith than the bare minimum which the evidence actually *dictates*. Now the overall picture of the findings of modern scholarship results from the combined influence of the radicalism of the disbelievers and the anxious minimalising of the believers.

These two influences combine to produce a *collective bias*. The actual results of scholarship at a given time are therefore less favourable to orthodoxy than they ought to be.

An illustration of the operation of the bias may be given from this book itself. On p. 20 Prof. Nineham writes: "Whatever we think of the Nature miracles—walking on the water and the like —there can be little doubt that Jesus did by some means work cures of various sorts; even his opponents could not deny the evidence." (Observe the coy attitude to "Nature miracles", the evidence for them may be good or bad, but the very idea of them is repugnant to some scholars.) But on p. 26 he tells us: "To us, the value of miracles as evidence is bound to be limited. In the first place, at this distance of time, it is not always possible to be sure that a particular miracle happened, or happened exactly as described; and even if we are convinced that Jesus healed and cured people" (notice the "even if", and compare it with the "little doubt" of the previous quotation) "to us, with our know-ledge of natural science, psychology and modern medicine, the significance of the fact will probably appear rather different from what it did to the first century Jews"—here the Nature miracles have dropped out of view altogether. Taken together, these two quotations present modern scholarship in an interesting light. To deny that Jesus effected remarkable cures (remarkable, it may be added, for their rapidity and independence of methods of treat-ment) would, in the light of the historical data, be to make oneself look foolish. But, granted the fact of the cures, scholars—some of them—are still uneasy. The shadows of Hume, and of the nine-teenth-century conception of natural laws which cannot be subject to interference, cross on their subconscious; miracles are "non-U". So first it is pointed out that we cannot always be sure that a *particular* miracle has occurred—at least "exactly as described". Secondly, we are given a rather airy reference to modern science, medicine, and psychology. The general reader is left with the impression that miracles are "out".

Yet very little reflection is needed to realise that, in the first place, the evidential value of the miracles does not depend on our ability to be sure that one particular miracle-story is quite "true" to the facts, or indeed true at all. It depends on whether there is good evidence that that *sort* of occurrence—astonishing cures— accompanied our Lord's ministry; and this is something which Prof. Nineham (as the spokesman of modern scholarship?) feels constrained to admit. Secondly, the vague reference to modern science, medicine and psychology, is more specious than convincing. That Jesus used, in his cures, a twentieth-century equipment of scientific, medical, and psychological knowledge would of course be "miraculous" in itself, and it is not seriously suggested. Is it then suggested that modern scientific and medical knowledge (as apart, for the moment, from psychological knowledge) can explain the characteristic Gospel stories of healing, for example, the giving of sudden sight to the blind (without a surgical operation), hearing to the deaf, speech to the dumb, normal functioning to the paralysed? I doubt if the suggestion could be seriously maintained, and I should like to meet the scientist or doctor who, without instruments, could reproduce the phenomena. So it all boils down to the appeal to modern psychology. All Jesus' healings, it must be contended, were of functional, not organic disorders; they were effects of therapeutic suggestion, performed by a therapist who had made no study of modern psychology. And we look around the world, and ransack the African jungle, to find a modern healer who operates in the same way and with the same multifarious success. (Our search will be complicated by the difficulty, when we get to the jungle, of excluding preternatural agencies in the ministry of the witch-doctors and medicine men.)

I think we can make one further point about this unfashionable subject. The appeal to modern psychology surely carries with it the implication that Jesus—since sensible scholars will not argue that he was a charlatan—was himself deceived by his healing powers. He must have known that, in the cultural context in which he lived, his cures would lead people to believe that he was a miracle-worker, with all that that implied when he was himself proclaiming the Kingdom of God. Yet he continued to work the cures; and was, therefore, himself deceived by them. But if we believe that his basic claim was true, can we really be comfortable about the complicity of divine Providence in this misleading combination of a true claim and spurious (because not really miraculous) miracles? Or, to put the matter another way, what guarantee is left, if Jesus was deceived about his cures, that he was not deceived about his basic claim?[2]

To this last question Prof. Nineham will reply that, whatever we think about the cures, the claim itself is "self-authenticating". But this seems, if we may judge by the fourth chapter of his book to amount to little more for us today, than that we can see for ourselves that Jesus was correct in proclaiming that each of us stands ultimately before the judgment-seat of a God who is both King and Father, infinite love combined with infinite power. And this reduces the whole truth of the good news to something which has no necessary connection with, or dependence on, our Lord and his ministry at all. St Paul would have held that it is something which the conscience of the veriest pagan could have told him at any time, without the help of any gospeller. We find ourselves, in fact led—as it were inadvertently—to a position which I find it difficult to distinguish from advanced radicalism. Jesus was a deluded genius who stumbled on the truth of our chronic human predicament in face of the Infinite. He was just another John the Baptist, who saw a little more clearly than John had done that God is not only terrible but kind.

Thus collective bias has had its inevitable consequences. The good money of docility to the evidence has been driven out by the bad money of an appeasement policy, and the "average" result of scholarship becomes identical with extreme radicalism. It only remains to explain the feeding of the Five Thousand as an optical illusion, and to suppose that the daughter of Jairus and the widow's son were not dead but suffering from syncope. But perhaps the empty tomb on Easter morning will still be somewhat embarrassing.

Another possible source of bias is the starting-point which Prof. Nineham has chosen: Can we find the general theme that runs through the teaching of Jesus? The question almost inevitably

---

2 Could it be argued that Jesus, while aware of the danger that he would be regarded as a thaumaturge, continued to work cures out of charity towards the sick, permitting the misunderstanding as an unintended secondary effect of his behaviour? It would have been a risky course for one who proclaimed the Kingdom of God; and more so if, as will be argued below, he claimed to be the official inaugurator of that Kingdom. Moreover, I am not prepared to dismiss as unauthentic the saying, for instance, in which Jesus is represented as meeting the suggestion that "he cast out devils through Beelzebub", not by repudiating his exorcisms, but by using them as proof of his proclamation of the Kingdom of God. There is also the reply said to have been sent to John the Baptist when his envoys enquired whether Jesus was "he that should come". If either of these sayings is authentic—and they can hardly be rejected except on *a priori* grounds—then it is clear that Jesus *exploited* the miraculous appearance of his cures. I should add that I can appreciate a feeling of reserve about the diagnosis of the so-called states of demonic possession, but this does not affect the sensational character of the "exorcisms".

suggests that Jesus' *teaching* constitutes his significance for history and religion. It could be argued that there is at work here an influence from the Reformation emphasis on "the word" in contrast to "the sacraments". But perhaps the bias goes back even further.

The primitive Christian Church was a missionary body. As it came into contact with the Hellenistic world, it almost inevitably presented itself as a superior philosophy, a philosophy to end all philosophies. Even earlier, in its first period in Palestine, it concentrated its efforts on proclaiming the "word" of the resurrection and Messiahship of Jesus. From this point of view, the Church seemed to exist in order to preach an evangel. And when the Gospels came to be written they were soon conceived of, and perhaps were already conceived of by their authors, as crystallisations of this evangel. How natural, then, to present Jesus primarily as the prototype of the Christian evangelist, as the Man with the Message. And of course he was this. But was this *all* that he was; and was his message directed towards the same recipients as that of the Church? The fact is, I hold, that he was more than a teacher. And I think the early Church became by degrees more reflectively aware of this fact, until at length, in the Prologue of the Fourth Gospel, the word of salvation is identified not merely with the teaching of Jesus but with his historical person. God's "message" to mankind was more than a prophetic utterance; it was the person who first delivered the prophecy. I should wish to argue that this Johannine interpretation of Jesus (already anticipated in the Pauline letters) was not a corruption of the primitive essence of Christianity, but the victory of that essence over a less complete understanding of it. Jesus, I suggest, was not "sent" precisely to preach the Kingdom of God; he was sent to *inaugurate* it by historical action and suffering. But of course the preaching formed an essential part of his historical action.

We have to take the notion of the Kingdom of God seriously and to see it in its *Sitz im Leben*. Prof. Nineham agrees that the meaning of the term, as used by Jesus, includes the notion of "the decisive intervention of God in the world's activities, and the lasting state of affairs which this was expected to bring about" (p. 6).

Now this whole notion of the Kingdom of God belongs to a cultural and religious milieu in which it was axiomatic that the Jews were the People of God, the Holy Community. In that milieu, the expected Kingdom of God was the concern of the Jewish people as the Holy Community.[3] The expected Kingdom of God was so much the concern of this people as a collective whole that it meant the embodiment with a new and unprecedented completeness of the theocracy in and over this People, this community. The "intervention of God in the world's activities" as focused in the People of God, and the resultant "state of affairs" was to be realised in that People. If the Gentiles were to benefit from the Kingdom, they could do so only through some relation to the Holy Community. There is no sign that Jesus ever attempted to detach the notion of the Kingdom of God from its essential connection with that of the People of God.

This implies, I take it, that Jesus saw his lifework as the reformation of the Holy Community, a reformation involved in his proclamation of the imminence or advent of the Kingdom of God. If this point is somewhat obscured from our superficial gaze in the Gospels, this may be the result of the bias in the primitive Church. The Church's mission to the Gentiles was precisely *not* a mission to the Holy Community. The Gentiles belonged to what, in Jewish and Christian eyes, were unholy communities, the kingdoms of this world. And the Church, following in the wake of the Hellenistic Jewish missionaries, saw itself as endeavouring to save individuals, as brands from the burning, from the furnace of God's wrath against this unholy world. It was natural that the men of the Church, including our Evangelists, should unconsciously present Jesus as doing the same sort of thing—as primarily concerned with the conversion of individuals. It was all the more natural since, even before the mission to the Gentiles got under way, the Church, after Pentecost, was engaged in converting individual Jews. By that time, Jesus having been crucified and having risen from the dead, the Jewish People had lost their status as the Holy Community. The new Israel was in existence.

But before the crucifixion, the Jewish people of the central tradition retained their status as the Holy Community. There is

---

[3] It should be observed, as Leon Roth has pointed out in *Judaism: a Portrait*, that "holy" in this context does not mean "morally good", but "dedicated" or "consecrated" by the good God to a divine purpose. This consecration incidentally involved a summons to be good, but it was not itself conditional upon a full response to that summons. The purpose, and the summons, were logically prior to the response and essentially independent of it.

no evidence against the natural assumption that Jesus recognised this status (unlike the Dead Sea Sectarians who denied it, as of course, by implication, the most primitive Church did). Hence, in order to inaugurate the Kingdom of God the attempt must be made to get his teaching, his claim, and his person accepted at his own evaluation of them by the Holy Community *as such,* by the actual Jewish politico-religious collectivity. Jesus' mission, as he himself conceived it, was not, if we are to speak precisely (and precision is absolutely vital here), to individuals considered as individuals (whether Jews or Gentiles or just human beings) but to the Jewish People as the Holy Community. This vital fact goes, I think, completely unnoticed in the reconstruction of Christian origins by modern scholarship, at least as described by Prof. Nineham.

If, however, Jesus' objective was that his mission should be recognised by the Holy Community, this means that his work will have taken the form of a campaign directed towards a climax. Of course, the Holy Community was a society composed of individual members, and every (orthodox Jewish) recruit to Jesus' cause could be regarded as a hopeful strengthening of the forces behind the campaign, as a partial victory. So there were individual conversions. Jesus aimed at them and welcomed them, and the primitive Church saw these incidents as foreshadowing its own missionary successes. But, in the campaign of Jesus' mission, they were incidents *en route.* The decisive engagement must take place in Jerusalem, vis-a-vis the religious authorities of Judaism.

It is a fact of history that the religious authorities rejected—or, at the very least, did not accept—Jesus' claims; the campaign seen at the level of phenomena, was a failure. My point here is that, *if Jesus was not mistaken,* if he really was the inaugurator of the Kingdom of God, the result of his historical work must have been, at the deepest level, not a failure but a success. And this means that it must be looked for primarily, not in individual conversions to a belief in the almighty providence of a good God, but in the continuing existence throughout history of a re-formed Holy Community. And the relevance of Jesus to our own age will depend on the possibility of the incorporation of each of us, and of humanity in its whole breath and depth, into that Community of the Old yet ever New Covenant.

Who then, is Jesus? It appears to me to be a weakness of

modern scholarship, as presented to us by Prof. Nineham, that, while it asks this question, it hardly answers it. And why should the question be worth asking, if what matters in the gospels is nothing more than a reminder that we are at each moment confronted with God, the almighty, the all-holy, the all-merciful? But if what matters is the identity and the nature of the continuing Holy Community, then the question of the personal status of Jesus within and over against it may be as urgent as our Gospels represent it as being: *Who do men say that I am . . . Who do you say that I am?* Is Jesus "just" the chronologically first member of the renewed Community? Or is he, further than that, "just" the Man in whom the implications of that membership, the new relations with God established by the advent of the Kingdom of God, are perfectly realised and, if this were all, how can we know that he was more holy than a Francis of Assisi or a Curé of Ars? Or was there really something "unique" in his "relationship to God"? If so, can we take any steps towards grasping what that uniqueness was?

I must acknowledge that I think modern scholarship's agnosticism at this stage of enquiry is deplorable. Take the issue of Messiahship, which is the real crux. The Gospels themselves make it clear enough—if they are to be trusted on the point—that Jesus rejected the vulgar connotations attached to the title of Messiah: just as he rejected the vulgar interpretation of "the Kingdom of God". But into the latter term he poured a fresh content. Did he not, perhaps, at any rate assume, in regard to the Kingdom of God as rethought by himself, the role which traditionally belonged to the Messiah vis à vis the Kingdom?[4]

I think modern scholarship, by and large, would hold that the Church, *from its very beginning at Pentecost,* proclaimed Jesus' Messiahship. When we thus speak of the primitive Church, it is well to remind ourselves that we mean a group of people with the Twelve and the Brethren of the Lord at its core. To this group we owe virtually all that we know, or can hope to discover about "the historical Jesus". It is not unreasonable to suppose

[4] A distinction may be desirable here. Insofar as Jesus claimed that, in his own ministry, the Kingdom of God was *in fieri* rather than *in facto esse,* to the same extent he may have claimed that he himself was Messiah *in fieri*—one might almost say *in petto*—until his resurrection. It has been thought that traces exist in the New Testament of a primitive stage in the Church's preaching or teaching in which it was held that Jesus had *become* Messiah by his resurrection.

that their memories of Jesus became to some extent coloured by their subsequent Christian experience, and that they quoted his sayings somewhat altered to suit the requirements of the contemporary situation. But have we really sufficient grounds for thinking that what for them was basic in their presentation of him, his own Messianic claim, is something which they read back into the facts on no other grounds than their post-Pentecostal belief? St Paul was an early convert to the Church; he appears to have been living in Jerusalem and near enough to the centre of events, just before his conversion, and he was Jew enough to appreciate the issues involved. He accepted the Messiahship of Jesus as absolutely basic to the new religion, and accorded to the words of Jesus a decisive value which implies that, already in his ministry, he was the arbiter of man's destiny.[5] The Fourth Gospel, in those deepest strata which underlie its special religious terminology and thought-world, has the Messianic claim, for and of Jesus, at its very roots. And then turning back to the Synoptic material is it not unreasonably radical criticism to reject the really overwhelmingly abundant data which state or imply that Jesus assumed, in relation to the Kingdom of God, a role which was Messianic in fact if not in name? I feel about this much as Prof. Nineham feels about the cures: there can be "little doubt" about it. The point needs, of course, to be argued at length. But suppose, in illustration of the *status quaestionis,* we take a saying which Prof. Nineham presumably accepts as authentic, since he quotes it as suggesting a distinction between the Son of Man and Jesus: "Every one who shall confess me before men, him shall the Son of Man also confess before the angels of God" (*Luke* XII 8). How could a prophet or herald of the Kingdom of God thus insist on the importance of "confessing" himself if he were no more than a prophet? Could Isaias or Jeremias conceivably have said such a thing? Could John the Baptist? Or Peter or Paul? It could only have been said by one who held himself to be in a Messianic relation to the Kingdom of God. Of course, once this implication is realised, the critic may revise his view of the authenticity of the saying.[6] But other sayings are waiting round the corner, and he will find himself rapidly embarked on a slope which leads to something like historical scepticism.

[5] The second half of this sentence is called for, since it could be argued that Paul regards the actual Messianic status of Jesus as dating from the resurrection. But then, Paul clearly regarded Jesus as the Son of God (which, if it did not for him connote the Messianic office, connoted something much more tremendous) from the moment of his birth: *When the fullness of time was come, God sent forth his Son born of a woman.*

If the Synoptic Gospels are to be trusted on the point, the title which Jesus did frequently use of himself (and it has a Messianic connotation) was "the Son of Man". There are scholars, as Prof. Nineham points out, who think that Jesus could not have designated himself by this term, since it "could only mean a supernatural figure due to appear right at the end of the world in a blaze of majesty and glory". However, the evidence that Jesus used the term (whether of himself or not) is, in my opinion, remarkably strong. Its almost complete absence from New Testament documents, except in sayings attributed to Jesus, is hard to explain otherwise.[7] But did he use the title of himself? It is objected that "anyone living an ordinary life, as Jesus did" could not possibly designate himself by a term of such apocalyptic glory. I suppose few objections could be more blatantly question-begging. If orthodoxy is true—and this, in the end, is the question —Jesus was one living an ordinary human life, yet destined to come "again" in glory to judge the living and the dead. To argue that he could not have used the title of himself is suspiciously like assuming that the Incarnation is impossible. It is a clear instance of bias.

There is, however, more to be said, and it is relevant to the question whether Jesus *would* (not *could*) have used the title of himself. "The Son of Man", prior to the use of the term by Jesus, is a figure belonging to a world-picture dominated by the notion of the Kingdom of God. It is conceded that Jesus proclaimed the Kingdom of God. Since we must, I think, allow that Jesus used

[6] The saying as given by St Luke seems to be related to versions of it extant elsewhere in the Synoptic Gospels. They do not all use the term "the Son of Man", but they all emphasise the importance of confessing "me" *sc*. Jesus. However, it could be argued (mistakenly, I think) that all the Gospel recordings of the saying derive from *Mark* VIII 38, where it is given in the form: "Whoever shall be ashamed of me *and my words* . . . the Son of Man shall be ashamed of him, when he comes in the glory of his Father with the holy angels." The critical master-stroke will be to argue that the original saying ran: "Whoever shall be ashamed of my words . . ." the reference to "me" (before "my words") being a primitive Christian addition. I personally believe that it is the "me" which is original, the "and my words" being an addition made in the Church of Rome and showing the early influence of Christian missionary *bias* (the Church was a *preaching* organisation). "Me . . . the Son of Man" is a better antithesis than "My words . . . the Son of Man".

[7] St Paul's teaching that Christ is "the second Adam" may be an attempt to express in tolerable Greek (for the expression the "Son of Man" is almost intolerable in Greek) what he took to be the meaning of the title. He may, then, have known that the title was put on the lips of Jesus in the tradition crystallised in our Synoptic material.

the title "the Son of Man" (whether of himself or not is the immediate question at issue), it is clear that he ratified the expectation which was not universal among the Jews, that this person would inaugurate the Kingdom of God in its final coming. We are now forced back upon the question: did Jesus preach only that the Kingdom of God was imminent; or did he teach, or imply, that it was already in process of inauguration in his own ministry and person? This would seem to be the real *crux* of New Testament scholarship. Prof. Nineham leaves the question unanswered when he writes: "Jesus . . . came into Galilee proclaiming that the actual moment of God's action has arrived, *or at any rate has come very close. In any event he makes it clear that in the lifetime of the people he is talking to, the rule of God will be here*" (p. 7; my italics). The real dividing line among critics is indicated somewhere among these alternatives.

Was there a basic difference between John the Baptist's preaching of the Kingdom of God and the preaching of the same Kingdom by Jesus? For John, the Kingdom was still fully in the future, however imminent. What of Jesus? I do not wish to deny, rather I affirm, that Jesus did point to a future coming of the Kingdom to coincide with the end of this world's history. But I believe that he further proclaimed or implied—and here he differed from John—that that post-historical coming had, in the purposes of God, an *historical,* real but mysterious, anticipation; and that his own ministry and person were essentially involved in that anticipation. Indeed, I believe that his teaching was pregnant with the implication that the inauguration of this historical Kingdom, really identical with the Kingdom which it mysteriously anticipated, was actually taking place in and by his ministry. There was, indeed, a sense in which, before his death and resurrection, even this historical Kingdom was "not yet"; it was, that is to say, not *in facto esse* but *in fieri.* But in another sense, in that sense in which the adult man is already present in the child, it was already there. In holding this view I am not, as Prof. Nineham is aware, alone. It is the view of Dodd and Cullmann, to mention no other contemporary scholar. Between accepting and rejecting this view there is no middle course for scholarship. And the issue cannot be dismissed as of secondary importance, a detail about which we can differ and yet preserve a common front of scholarship.

But if Dodd and Cullmann are right, we find ourselves realising that what the Son of Man (according to the teaching of Jesus) is to the post-historic Kingdom, that Jesus is in reference to the historical anticipation of the Kingdom; he is the inaugurator. And if, as is certainly the case, the historical Kingdom is, in the teaching of Jesus, identical with the post-historic Kingdom which it mysteriously—sacramentally—anticipates, it is probable that the inaugurator of the historical Kingdom is identical with the inaugurator of the post-historic, i.e. with the Son of Man. If this is not in fact the case, Jesus was committing himself to a piece of ephemeral mythologising when he taught that there would be a "Son of Man". It is only by severe (and, I venture to suggest, critically unjustifiable, surgery upon the Gospel data that we can escape the view that Jesus did so identify himself with the Son of Man. The attempt to escape is, I think, due either to bias or to a rejection of Cullmann's view of the twofold coming of the Kingdom. As to this, it will be enough for the moment to point out that, whether or not our Lord taught this twofold coming, the teaching is there in the Gospels and pervades, in different expressions of it, the New Testament.

Obviously, if Jesus claimed to be identical with the Son of Man, so that the Son of Man "had not where to lay his head", had come "not to be served but to serve", was destined to suffer and to die, he was introducing a very profound modification into the traditional view of this figure; just as, if he taught the mysterious anticipation of the Kingdom of God, he was profoundly modifying the current view of that Kingdom. I think that those older scholars were right who suggested that, in fact, Jesus synthesised "the Son of Man" with the Isaianic "suffering servant of the Lord". It is certain that the Church in New Testament times used the Isaianic figure in its interpretation of the significance of Jesus. But at the present day it is fashionable to cast doubt on Jesus' own use of this figure to describe himself.

The doctrine of the twofold coming of the Kingdom and the twofold coming of the Son of Man is the product of a religious insight of genius. It lies at the very heart of the Christian religion considered as a historical phenomenon. It is the same doctrine as the classical Christian doctrine of the state of grace as a real, but mysterious, anticipation, under the veils of faith and within the stage of our human probation, of the life of the blessed in heaven in the enjoyment of the Beatific Vision. It is the doctrine which differentiates Christianity from Judaism, and it is, therefore, if true, the justification for the existence of the Church as an entity separate from the Jewish people as such. If we admit that this doctrine originated with Jesus himself in his historical life, we have a sufficient clue to the whole of his ministry and his martyr-witness. Unless we make this admission we are without a clue to the original meaning of his life, and the logical link between him and the religion which looks back to him as its Lord and founder is broken.

It may be objected that these are theological considerations irrelevant to an historical enquiry. But there is an issue involved which is intrinsic to the historian's problems. If Jesus was not the creator of the Christian religion, and if the picture of him which the Synoptic material enables us to reconstruct is unhistorical, what has happened to the authentic picture of the Galilaean agitator? He is undiscoverable beneath the mask that the Christian tradition has imposed upon his real features. Whenever the traditional picture has been rejected by scholars, the attempt to find "the historical Jesus" has ended in an *impasse,* or its results have been deservedly discarded by subsequent scholarship. This is true of the liberal Protestant Jesus, and is now true of Schweitzer's Jesus of "thorough-going" apocalyptism. And who invented the traditional picture of him, a picture that does not dissolve as we gaze upon it but seems to acquire three-dimensional consistency? Who invented the Christian religion with its basic dynamic insight? Both the picture and the insight are pre-Pauline. Who was the theologian-poet, the great Anonymous, in the Church of Jerusalem in the first five years after Pentecost, who has changed the course of history by annihilating the memory of the real Jesus of Nazareth and substituting for him a tremendous genius who never existed? How was this achieved, how was the new picture and the new idea "sold" to the primitive Jerusalem Church (including the Twelve); and how did the Anonymous effect his own disappearing trick? To these questions, the somewhat lame answer of the liberal wing of contemporary scholarship is: there was no Anonymous; everything was done by the creative collective imagination and thinking of the primitive Church. But it should be noticed that, at this ultimate stage of the argument, we are no longer in the realm where scholarship can claim the right to dictate to us. It is a matter of fact, that, in our experience, great creative insights are not the product of collective imagination; they are the acts of individual intelligences. I am reminded of Quiller Couch's observation that the English ballads cannot be the product merely of a cultural complex but must have had authors who were individual human beings. A "creative collectivity" may take responsibility for a myth which is not a source of new life but the precipitate of wishful thinking. But it has never created, within the limits of five years or so, a figure which has at once obliterated a real historical person for whom it has been substituted, and has become the dynamic force of a great world-religion. To suppose that Christianity is a tree that has sprung from such a root is at least as improbable—if I may borrow a comparison from Harold Riesenfeld[8]—as to explain modern psychology without appeal to the creative insights of a Freud, a Jung, an Adler.

The third Synoptic title of Jesus considered by Prof. Nineham is "the Son of God". I should agree with Prof. Nineham that *a priori* this term could mean no more than Messiah. He will, however, perhaps agree that there is practically no evidence, and little likelihood, that it was being currently used in that meaning in the days of Jesus. If that is so, then, if Jesus used the title himself, he was presumably provoking a theological question in his hearers' minds; and there seems to be no evidence in the Synoptic Gospels that he took any measures to prevent their reading into the title a more than Messianic significance.[9] And if

[8] *"Bemerkungen zur Frange des Selbshewussteins Jesus"*, in *Der historische Jesus und der kerygmatische Christus* (Berlin, 1960). I venture a translation of two passages from this striking article: "Who is the creator of this Picture (of Jesus)? We might find a distant analogy in the founders of the great psychoanalytical schools of our age. Here certainly it is not a question of anonymous enthusiasts, whose contributions have gradually produced a system, but of highly self-conscious, creative, personalities who have expressed the consistency and shape of their conceptions. New Testament Christianity is too powerful in its unity of intellectual content and outer form (a unity which is manifested in the durability of the Picture in the history of the Church) to be convincingly explained without the intervention of an equally powerful creative personality. And compared with this Picture, the recent portrayals of Jesus' person are altogether too shallow and limited (?*befangen*) to be psychologically credible." "We may take Alexander the Great as an analogy. The role played by the king of Macedonia and lord of a world-empire in history and romance is the consequence of what the historical Alexander not only was, but (above all) willed. We owe the literature about him not only to the interest and imagination of his admirers, but above all and primarily to the impression and force derived from his person and self-consciousness. Despite the embellishments and distortions (in the literature) we cannot get away from the effect of the historical person and the will of his personality. And this is also shown by the way in which the Alexander-literature differs in form and content from, for instance, the representations of the world of saga, of prehistoric heroes."

[9] But cf. *John* XI 34-36.

he was claiming to be the inaugurator of the Kingdom of God, was there not a real danger that this particular title *would* suggest something a good deal more tremendous than a merely Messianic role? The subsequent development of the Christian understanding of the term, even in New Testament times (cf. for instance, the Epistle to the Hebrews) shows that the danger may have been a real one. If the famous saying in Matthew XI 25-30 is authentic, then as we meditate upon the implications of "none knows the son truly except the father, and none knows the father truly except the son, and those to whom it is the son's good pleasure to reveal him,"[10] we surely find it hard to resist the conclusion that Jesus positively invited his disciples to give this title a meaning which is frightening even to us in the twentieth century.

But suppose we concede that the title has no such overtones. In that case, it is a Messianic title. And in that case, if Jesus claimed to be "the son of God", he did claim to be Messiah, despite all the scholarly hesitations, relayed to us by Prof. Nineham, about the actual term Messiah and even the title "the son of Man". And the Messianic claim is the really vital one.[11] Are we then to reject the evidence which suggests that he claimed or accepted the designation "the Son of God"?[12] Perhaps the greatest obstacle to such a rejection is that it would probably involve denying that Jesus spoke of "*my* father" in that special way which appears to be his in the Synoptic material. We should have to suppose that, if Jesus used this mode of speech at all, he meant no more by it than that God is the universal "Father" and *therefore* his own, just as he was *also* Peter's "own" Father. It was the liberal Protestant contention that the essence of the gospel was the universal fatherhood of God and the universal brotherhood of man. But Prof. Nineham, at least, does not need

---

[10] The avoidance of capitals may serve to indicate to my readers the possibility that Jesus is speaking in general terms: "Only a father truly knows his son, and only a son truly knows his father; others may have the son's knowledge communicated to them, but only if the son chooses to communicate it." If, however, Jesus was thus speaking in general terms, he seems to invite his hearers to apply the general principles to God and himself.

[11] What really matters is that Jesus claimed to be exercising the "Messianic" role of God's commissioned agent for the inauguration of the Kingdom of God (as our manuals of Apologetics put it, he claimed to be "the envoy of God", *legatus Dei*). Once we *accept* that claim, and its implication that the Church is now the covenantal Holy Community, we can turn from scholarship to the teaching of the Church to discover how much more than merely an envoy he was.

to be reminded that it has recently been strongly urged that "there is no ground whatever for asserting that Jesus taught" this doctrine; rather, the evidence is that he taught that those who accepted the new dispensation *became* adopted sons of God through the relation given to them in this dispensation, to himself, the (unique) Messianic Son of God.[13]

Having used Prof. Nineham as my stalking horse, I want once again to emphasise that he does not commit himself to the positions which he presents as current in critical circles today. He has given a very fair picture of the present state of Gospel scholarship. I have indeed suggested that he might have warned his hearers and readers about the bias which affects this scholarship. And I will now add that I fear he was attempting what, in one important respect, is an impossible task. There can be no *average* result attainable by adding together the findings of those scholars who maintain and those who deny that Jesus claimed to be actually inaugurating the Kingdom of God; just as you cannot strike an average between good and evil, between truth and error. But my main purpose has been precisely to accuse modern scholarship of the collective bias of which I have written above, and to maintain that, could we but get rid of the bias, we should see that the verdict of critical history must be that Jesus claimed to be "he that should come" and to be establishing on

---

[12] Some of the implications of this rejection may be noted here. The Matthew-Mark version of the Voice at the baptism of Jesus must go. In the Lukan account we must accept the less well-attested reading: "Thou art my God; this day have I begotten thee", and indeed we must reject this too, since it implies the *Messianic* sonship. We must also reject the Voice at the Transfiguration. We must dismantle the Matthew-Luke accounts of two of the Temptations of Jesus, which hinge on the idea that Jesus accepts the designation "the Son of God". We must get rid of, or explain away, the saying referred to above: "No man knoweth the son, etc." We shall be in some difficulty over the parable of the Wicked Husbandmen. And we shall have to do some severe surgery on the Synoptic account of the "trial" of Jesus before the Jewish leaders. (Incidentally, how do those who would deny that Jesus claimed to be at least the Messiah explain his behaviour before the Jewish leaders and before Pilate? Why did the leaders allow this innocuous Galilaean holy man to go before Pilate's tribunal? And by use of what legal fiction did Pilate order his execution? We are told that the superscription on the Cross was "the King of the Jews": how was this accusation arrived at, if Jesus made no claim to be Messiah? And was Jesus morally justified in failing to exculpate himself, as he could so easily have done?)

[13] The words quoted above are from H. F. D. Sparks, "The Doctrine of the Divine Fatherhood in the Gospels", in *Studies in the Gospels*, edited by D. E. Nineham, p. 260.

earth, in mysterious anticipation, the final Kingdom of his
heavenly Father.[14]

[14] Those who doubt the propriety of hinting at scholarly bias may be
referred to a recent paper on "the priority of Mark" (William R.
Farmer, "A Skeleton in the Closet of Gospel Research", in *Biblical
Research* VI, 1961). Dr Farmer writes of the earlier history of the study
of the Synoptic Problem (especially in Germany): "The whole question
of the fate of various hypotheses concerning the gospels was intimately
bound up with the fate of the theological schools and ecclesiastical parties
which found one or another of these hypotheses useful. As for the
orthodox, they weren't really interested in any critical hypothesis. They
preferred to stick to the Bible. But that does not mean that they did not
exercise an influence upon the history of the Synoptic problem. Indirect
though it was, this influence was great." And if the general reader is
scandalised by such suggestions of bias, he may be reminded that bias
is hard to exclude from historical and literary criticism, precisely when
beliefs of tremendous moment are at stake. There would be much
"biased" criticism of Thucydides, if it mattered enormously to us today
whether his presentation of Greek history is true.

# Belief and Reason in Science and Religion

1964

The relations between science and religion have been hotly debated in the past, and are still capable of arousing interest and indeed of stirring passion. Religion is praised as humble faith or decried as craven credulity. Science is denounced as proud rationalism or extolled as the triumph of reason. I wish to ask here whether science in fact excludes from itself every element that could be described as belief; and whether religion excludes from its domain the operations of the critical intellect.

But first it may be prudent to clear up an ambiguity in the terms themselves. By religion here I do not mean an alleged pure essence of religion, never perhaps found in human history; and by science I do not mean a Platonic idea of science. I am referring to science as a historical phenomenon in the contemporary world, one of the most powerful factors in the environment which we men have actually created for ourselves. And by religion I shall also be referring to actually existing religion. Indeed, since there are many religions on the contemporary stage, it may be convenient to aim at full concreteness by confining our attention primarily to the religion with which I am best acquainted, and in which in fact I happen to believe: the Roman Catholic religion —though much of what I shall say about religion would, I hope, be acceptable to many Christians who are not Catholics.

I

It is characteristic of science that it takes its stand on data that are either immediately sensible or are themselves known as inferences from sense data; the movement of a sub-atomic particle, if it cannot be known by immediate observation, can be known indirectly by some of its observable effects or concomitants. Starting from such data, science tries to find a hypothesis, a possible way of understanding the observed data. Thus, the phenomena of the apparent motions of the stars and other heavenly bodies are a set of data which invite the quest of an explanation. Here, of course, a short cut may be taken, and appeal made to the activity of alleged, but unobservable entities such as demons or gods. Such an explanation is not scientific, in our modern use of the word, because it is an explanation extrinsic to the sphere of observable data; what science seeks is immanent intelligibility. In this connection it could be asked whether Newton's gravity was a strictly scientific hypothesis. But the Ptolemaic hypothesis to explain the heavenly motions was strictly scientific. It was a possible way of understanding the then available data. Its elaboration involved the beautiful theory of epicycles, and for many centuries it seemed, as to Thomas Aquinas, the best way of doing justice to the appearances, of "saving" them, as the jargon put it, but Thomas did not forget that there might yet be found a better way of explaining the phenomena.

When a hypothesis has thus been reached—and it always involves going beyond the data from which it started to an act of understanding them in a "law" which is not itself a possible object of sensation—the scientist looks for verification. This means that he looks about for further data in a region where, if the hypothesis is correct for the original data, it ought to hold good. He will try his hypothesis out on this new set of data; and, to the extent to which it fits them, it is confirmed or verified. When I was a youth, Einstein had published his theory of relativity, and had pointed out that, if it were true, there should be some consequences hitherto unobserved or at least unrecorded. One of these was a displacement of light from stars appearing close to the orb of the sun in a solar total eclipse. It was possible to work out the amount of displacement required for the truth of the hypothesis, and men of my age can remember the excitement with which we waited for the next total eclipse of the sun. They will also remember that, when allowance had been made for the statistical likelihood of inaccurate observation or atmospheric refraction, the results were sufficiently favourable to the hypothesis. So far, then, it was verified.

Thus science moves from observation, through insight, understanding and hypothesis, to verification. This is a rational process. It responds to data in an insight or act of understanding, to which it gives conceptual expression in the formulation of a hypothesis; and it concludes by verification. Another "test" is coherence with the structure of already acquired knowledge or theory.

There are unproved presuppositions in science. Its sensible data, to begin with, are of course unproved and incapable of proof. They are mere fact. You do not prove mere fact; you undergo it. Science is not the refusal to accept mere fact, but the refusal to rest in it as brute fact. This refusal is the core of scientific behaviour, but it does not alter the given, pre-rational, quality of the data; it remains true that science starts from unprovable, though undeniable assumptions and that therefore its rationality is a dependent rationality.

It may be added here, as a digression, since materialism often appeals to science, that sense data are inescapably mental facts. They are experiences of experiencing subjects, and they can never be divested of this mental quality. Materialism, is, in short, a gigantic confidence trick. It asks us whether there can be any room in a world which is certainly material for the reality and activity of immaterial spirit. But the truth is that spirit, the activity of mind, is primordial. We may indeed ask whether there is any spiritual activity entirely divorced from a material conditioning; but we know that we neither have nor can have any material data that are not essentially conditioned by mind.

A second presupposition of science is that understanding is relevant, indeed universally relevant, to sense data. This is the presupposition which inspires the refusal of science to rest in mere fact as being brute fact. It is a presupposition, because if it were absent, scientific behaviour would not begin. It is true that, *a posteriori*, science can point with pride to the verification of its hypotheses (or, which is the same thing, to the truth of its predictions) as in the nature of subsequent confirmation of this presupposition: the "laws", so to call them, in which scientific understanding is formulated do appear, when we put them to the test, to hold good in that objective universe with which sense experience seems to put us in touch. There is thus, within limits, a verifiable coincidence between the rational laws and the data of sense. But could not this coincidence be accidental? None of us, of course, believes that it is, but if we ask for proof that it is not, clearly science cannot supply the proof. In other words, science makes a presupposition about the rationality of the universe which has sometimes been expressed as the principle of the uniformity of nature or of natural law.

It may be a particular aspect of this presupposition which is implied by the notion and the quest of verification. Verification presupposes that, as it has been expressed, "similars are to be similarly understood". This principle requires rather careful formulation. All triangles are similar. But a right-angled triangle is understood in one way, and an acute-angled triangle is understood in another. Yes, but all triangles, when each is considered simply as a triangle, are similarly understood; all, for instance, have—on the basis of Euclidean geometry—the sum of their interior angles equal to two right-angles. A careless use of the principle of similarity can lead one into error, as we have been warned by the discovery of heavy water. But tricky as the principle is, it is a necessary presupposition of science. Science is sure, not only that rational explanation is everywhere relevant, but that the same explanation holds for two different sets of data, provided that the two sets differ only insofar as they are not numerically the same set—or only in other ways irrelevant to the purpose in hand. It is a condition of laboratory experiment that differences that might be relevant are either excluded or have "allowance" made for them: if you wish to study the virus of scarlatina you try to secure a pure laboratory culture. Now the principle that similars are to be similarly understood is one which we all accept. Deny it, and all scientific induction would be impossible. But science cannot prove it; it is something which is not proved by science but presupposed. If it is questioned, science can only appeal to some extra-scientific discipline, such as philosophy, or to self-evidence.

These presuppositions of science are, no doubt, in a scientifically inexpugnable position. How would you set about casting doubt on them? You would begin by pointing to some data that science had overlooked, or to which justice had not been done. You would have to apply your understanding to these data; and having elucidated their significance you would have to universalise their message. In so doing, you would yourself be operating with the presuppositions which you sought to overthrow. You would be relying on the validity of the human cognitive process, and that is what the scientist relies upon. In other words, scientific process being reasonable, it cannot reasonably be doubted.

But just as science rests on unproved assumptions, so also there are questions which it necessarily leaves unanswered. One such question arises if we hold that biology is really a science, distinct from physics and chemistry. Living things, it may be held, while they do not contravene the laws of physics and chemistry, yet manifest and express a further set of laws which are not deducible from physical and chemical laws, though they may be conditioned by them. If this is so, then the question arises of the unification of these various scientific viewpoints in a higher synthesis; and this question is one which science itself cannot answer but which the scientist, being an intelligent man, can recognise.

Doubtless some would argue that the so-called laws of biology are mere appearance; in other words, that biological fact will prove capable in the long run, or is in principle capable of being reduced to chemical, and ultimately mere physical, fact. I do not myself think that this is probable; I think it is itself a misunderstanding of the very real truth that biological fact presupposes physical fact as its condition. But at least we cannot reduce the laws of intelligence to physics, because, if reason thus lost its intrinsic autonomy we should have deprived science of one of its basic presuppositions. This is another way of saying that materialism, including scientific materialism, is excluded. We are left, then, with the type of questions which Aristotle relegated to the treatise which comes "after physics" and which are therefore known as metaphysical.

We can now raise another question, still more far-reaching, of which the answer, whether affirmative or negative, would take us right outside the realm of science. What we can and must ask is the explanation of the existence of the entities which science experiences, understands, and judges; or, if objection is raised to the stating of the question in that way, what is the explanation of the fact that sensible data occur? And what, again, is the explanation of the existence of intelligences which experience, understand, and judge? Why are there sense data? Why do they give rise to hypotheses and laws of lesser or greater probability? And why is there anyone to have sense experience, to enquire, to understand, to formulate laws, and to verify them? Why is there anything at all? That something exists we know, in virtue of the fact that we entertain the question: Does anything exist? For the mind cannot entertain itself with nothing; nor can a question be entertained by a non-existent consciousness. It is one of the glories of our age that science has progressed so far in understanding what exists, or in rationalising sense data. But because it necessarily starts from the fact of what exists, science itself cannot face the further question of why anything exists. And this means that the life of science bathes in an ocean of mystery, not only in the sense that there are many scientific questions as yet unanswered or even not yet raised, but because, transcending the range of possible scientific truth, there must always be a sphere which is for science one of unanswerable questioning. Mystery is what we know to be unknown; and the scientist knows that he leaves unanswered the question whether there is a reason for existence, and, if there is, the further question what that reason is.

Science, then, is an intellectual activity which involves presuppositions and leaves unanswered further questions. To speak thus is not, it may be objected, to show that science depends on belief or faith, since the scientist's acceptance of sense data and of the principles of reason is not so much an act of faith as an ineluctable necessity; while his inability to answer the further question about the reason of existence involves him, precisely as a scientist, in a necessary suspension between belief and disbelief. But further, we have now to show that science as a historical phenomenon and a characteristic of our age is intrinsically conditioned by belief.

What then do we mean by belief or faith?[1] True belief is a kind of knowledge, though not that kind of knowledge which the popular mind associates with science and calls scientific knowledge. Thus, let it be granted that the square root of 3,094,081 is plus or minus 1759. A teacher who was given this correct answer by his pupil might wish to know how he had reached it, and the true answer to this question might be one of two; either the pupil had worked out the answer by the correct arithmetical rule which he had himself learnt and understood and tested; or he had been told the answer by someone whose accuracy and reliability he had good reason to trust. In either case he had attained to truth. But in the former case he had attained it by pure immanent intellectual process, while in the latter case he had attained it by reliable information—on authority, as we say. In the latter case he has true belief, in the former he has immanently generated knowledge. There is no difference in the quality of the truth, whichever method is employed. A correct answer to a sum is not less correct because it is not a piece of immanently generated knowledge. The difference lies in the mode of attaining and possessing the truth. Similarly, a man may know

[1] Theology distinguishes between natural belief and supernatural belief, or faith. This distinction does not affect the ensuing argument.

that water is $H_2O$ either because he has done the relevant experiment under the required laboratory conditions, or because he has learnt the truth from a good chemistry textbook. In the former case he has immanently generated knowledge of the truth; in the latter he has true belief.

We are living in a scientific age. What does this mean for the vast majority of our contemporaries? Insofar as modern science directly adds to their store of knowledge, this is almost entirely because they believe the scientists, not because they have immanently generated knowledge of the truths of science. When the ordinary listener hears, in a wireless programme, that thanks to the American space-probe we now know the constitution of the atmosphere of the planet Venus, he has acquired some scientific knowledge, but obviously he knows nothing about the atmosphere of the planet by immanently generated knowledge of his own; he knows it by belief. For the ordinary man, then, and this means for all of us as regards far the greater part of our interests, to live in a scientific age is not to live in a period when reason has superseded faith, but to live in an age of a different sort of faith from that of the Christian centuries—if it is correct to speak of such. Today, we turn for the supply of our beliefs to the empirical scientists rather than to the philosophers or the Church. Obviously this makes a considerable difference to the furniture of the common mind of the age. But it makes no essential difference to the way in which the common mind acquires its knowledge. We have turned, insofar as we have substituted science for religion, simply from one set of beliefs to another.

It will, of course, be urged that, while the ordinary man in a scientific age remains a believer, the scientists themselves, to the extent to which they are such, have left the realm of belief for that of immanently generated knowledge. I may accept on faith that water is $H_2O$; but the scientist knows it with immanently generated knowledge. He knows it, because he has done the relevant experiments and has checked his results. He may not be doing the experiment at this moment, but he has an indubitable memory of it and of its result.

But, when we turn from the individual scientist and the limited horizons of his own immanently generated knowledge to the great historical phenomenon of the science which we all believe and of which some of us are practitioners, the case is more complex. The scientist is not a completely isolated individual, in no way dependent on the help of other past or present scientists. On the contrary, science in history and today is a vast human collaboration, international like the Catholic Church, though of course, like the Church, revealing national differences and even, perhaps, some stresses between East and West. No single scientist has immanently generated knowledge of the whole field, or even of a large part of the whole field, of contemporary science. Each is a specialist in one or two fields, and in a very narrow sector of such a field. And within the narrow sector in which he himself works, even within the particular piece of research that he has made peculiarly his own, the scientist is dependent on the results of others to such an extent that it is extremely difficult, if not impossible, to distinguish what in his knowledge is purely original. The truth of a scientist's findings may depend on such things as whether the specimen he has been testing is of a certain provenance and purity, whether his slide-rule and other instruments are accurate and whether the general background of knowledge of his subject, which forms the context of his own experiment, is worthy of the reliance which he places upon it.

If, on the other hand, it is required of a scientist that he shall restrict himself to immanently generated knowledge, then the progress of science as a major historical phenomenon will be so retarded as practically to become unimportant.

To sum up, we may say that science is a rational process, depending on prescientific data, operating on rational principles which it cannot itself justify, and giving rise inevitably to questions which transcend its own competence; so that all scientific knowledge is bounded by a sphere of mystery in which beauty and moral goodness have as much right to exist as science can claim for itself. And as an historical phenomenon, and a characteristic of our age, science is shot through with belief, and presents the ordinary man with a field for the exercise rather of faith than of reason. Moreover, its own progress and apparently inexhaustible fecundity depend upon a great moral fact: the intellectual integrity of its practitioners, and their mutual trust.

## II

It would be disingenuous to deny or to minimise the contrast between science and religion. Whatever the presuppositions and limitations of science, and however much scientists in fact depend on belief, it remains that what is characteristic of scientific process as such is its intrinsic rationality. The characteristic of religion, on the other hand, is that faith is intrinsic to it. This is expressed in the baptism service, in which the minister begins by asking the candidate for baptism: What do you seek from the Church? And the candidate—or his godparent if he is an infant—replies: Faith. Traditionally, a Christian is a baptised person; baptism is a rite administered by the Church, and the Church requires from the candidate an external profession of faith in the Church's message. It is assumed that this profession is true, and therefore that the candidate has faith.

But faith, for the Christian, is not—as regards his life in this world—a provisional and passing phase of religion, one to be succeeded, as he goes forward, by immanently generated knowledge of the truth of what he had at first only believed. Such a process from belief to immediate knowledge is, in principle, always possible in the world of science. If a man is dissatisfied with his belief that water is $H_2O$, then he may go to the laboratory and perform the experiment which will give him immanently generated knowledge of it. But there is no way, in this life, whereby the believer may transcend the horizons of faith. On his deathbed, whether he be sinner or saint, fool or great theologian, the Church will still invite him, as part of his preparation for the last journey, to profess his faith in her teaching.

Is there then any room for processes of reason within the sphere of religion? The existence of theologians and of theology suggests that there is. And already in the New Testament we find the first fruits of man's rational reaction to the content of the Christian faith. St Paul was, among other things, a hard-thinking man. The contrast between him and, let us say, the author of St Mark's Gospel is not a contrast beween degrees of faith; it is very much a contrast between a faith which accepts and a faith which reasons upon what it has accepted. It is to be observed that a Christian believer does not merely believe in God; he believes in God's self-revelation in mankind's historical experience, and particularly in that strand of history and tradition which culminates in the historical life of Jesus of Nazareth and is then carried to mankind at large by the Church which he founded. It has been well said that the three great realities for a Christian as such are God, Christ, and the Church. What is the believer's relation to them? Basically and normally it is a relationship of complete personal commitment, and is thus something more than a pure intellectual assent to a set of propositions about them. It is a commitment which involves not only his intellect but his will; and the resultant relationship is in some ways analogous to the relationship of a lover to the person he loves rather than to that of the scientist to his hypotheses. But emphasis upon the will-and-feeling elements of faith must not blind us to its intellectual element. It is an axiom of philosophy that nothing can be willed unless it is also known. The believer does not adhere to God revealed in Christ except insofar as he really does *believe* that God has spoken to mankind in Christ and as Christ. And such a belief will normally become the starting-point of an unending intellectual process of growth in understanding of the revelation.

I wish to suggest that in this process of intellectual growth, which we call theology, the revelation has the same place and function as sense data have in science. It is the unquestioned—because for faith unquestionable—*datum* which sets problems for our understanding and gives rise to hypotheses, that is to theological theories and eventually systems. The process is no less rational than are the processes of science; it is the starting-point which is different. Even the starting-point of theology has an element of sensation. The Christian revelation was, as has been said, something that occurred within human historical experience, and all such experience has its foundation in the senses. The author of one of the New Testament books describes the revelation as "what we have heard and seen, and our eyes have gazed upon". But these initial sense-experiences are the starting-point for theology, not inasmuch as they are mere fact, but inasmuch as they are accepted by faith as pregnant with a special divine message or self-disclosure. This acceptance underlies the whole of the subsequent theological process of understanding them, and of building upon them a self-consistent understanding of human experience in its relationship to God the revealer.

We have seen that the scientific process proceeds from the elaboration of hypotheses to their verification. Is there anything corresponding to verification in theology? I think there is; but a preliminary clarification may be desirable here. For faith there is no question of veryifying *faith*. As we have seen, theology presupposes faith, and no science verifies its own postulates. The question of theological verification is therefore a question of verification within the presuppositions or postulates of theology; it presupposes faith all along.

A scientific hypothesis, granted that it is internally self-consistent, has to satisfy two external tests. It has to show that it can be held along with what we already know; and in this connection it is further desirable that it should be consistent with whatever else we hold to be probable. And secondly, as we have seen, it is subject to verification by appeal to fresh sets of data.

A theological theory or system is also, of course, subject to the test of coherence with what we otherwise know or have reason to think probably true. It will be asked to show this coherence not only within the general field of theology itself, by its ability to combine with other accepted or reputable theological theories, but, beyond the borders of theology itself, it should also cohere with the ascertained or probable truths of philosophy, general history, and science. For instance, a polytheistic theory of the Trinity would contradict what philosophy has to tell us; some crude opinions about the Real Presence might be disprovable by natural science; a crude view of the implications of the inspiration of Scripture could be countered by an appeal to the science of history.

Is there, then, a test for theological theories comparable to the test in science of verification by appeal to fresh sets of sense data? I suggest that the comparable test in theology is an appeal to the religious experience of the believers. A theological theory will be confirmed if it proves to be spiritually fruitful, it will be suspect if its spiritual results are unsatisfactory. This is an appeal to what theologians call the *sensus fidelium*. It must be admitted that it lacks the precision of scientific verification, if only because religious experience cannot be treated quantitatively or mathematically. Lacking such precision, it cannot be applied mechanically but requires that those who apply it should themselves be spiritually appreciative, well-informed, and of good practical judgment. It has a somewhat close analogy in the appeal to the consensus of opinion in the evaluation of works of art. As the greatness of Shakespeare is proved by the esteem that he calls forth from all and sundry in every age and culture, even from those remote from his own; and as a man without musical sensibility may yet feel sure that the reputation of Mozart must rest on something more than subjective inclinations; so a theological

237

opinion which proves fruitful in the life of a wide variety of believers in a diversity of circumstances, and whose fruitfulness has stood the test of time, is to that extent verified.

It was observed above that the believer, as such, looks for verification not of his faith but of the theology which seeks to give rational articulation to his faith. It remains to ask whether there is any rational bridge between religion and the rest of man's rational life. Is faith a consequence of a leap from the natural order into an order above nature—a sheer leap that is intellectually unjustifiable? We have seen that scientific knowledge arises upon the basis of sense data which are indeed pre-rational but are yet ineluctable. It would be possible to argue that something similar is true of all our natural knowledge, even though in pure mathematics the starting-point in the senses, necessary though it is to stimulate thought's origin, seems to be rapidly transcended. We have also seen that the object of Christian faith, the revelation of God, was itself an historical occurrence apprehensible, in its materiality, by the sense of the Christian eye-witnesses. What we are now asking is whether there can be any rational justification for faith's unique *interpretation* of religion's historical data.

It would, I think, be hard to show that a direct unmediated enlightenment by God of the human mind, enabling it to grasp and accept faith's interpretation, is impossible. But it is interesting to find that as early as the New Testament age Christianity was not content to rely on such immediate illumination. "Men of Israel", we read in a speech put upon the lips of St Peter by the author of the Acts of the Apostles, "Jesus of Nazareth was a man duly accredited to you from God; such were the miracles and wonders and signs which God did through him in your midst, as you yourselves well know" (*Acts* II 22). This is an appeal to rational grounds for making an act of faith in the revelation thus "accredited" or attested. It may indeed be disputed whether the sort of grounds adduced by the Bible here or elsewhere remain solid enough at the present day to afford a basis for faith; just as we may wonder whether such grounds, however solid in appearance, could justify faith if the content of the alleged revelation did not commend itself to man's moral sense and to antecedent probabilities: the Emperor Vespasian is alleged to have restored a blind man to sight, but we do not today think that this proves much about Vespasian. And since grounds of credibility are relative to the subjective conditions of the person who is being invited to believe, they will vary from age to age and even from man to man. The principle, however, behind the appeal to such grounds is important. A man who has valid grounds for believing has his faith integrated into his total life of responsibility, and his religion can, in its turn, illuminate the rest of his human experience and guide his activity. Nevertheless, it is true that such a man, having recognised his duty to believe, accepts the content of his faith from the source of revelation and does not test it in detail by detailed verification.

We have seen that science pursues its operation in a circumambient area of mystery. It is for philosophy or metaphysics to seek to determine something of that mystery and it is held that philosophy can bring a man to the point from which the only reasonable further step is an acknowledgement that the heart of that mystery is the Absolute Reality and *Summum Bonum* which believers call God. Then revelation enters upon the scene to give a self-disclosure of the supreme mystery beyond the reach of natural philosophy. If the revelation is seen to be duly accredited, and if a man, again following the dictates of reasonable responsibility, makes his act of faith, then there is a roundedness in his total apprehension and response to reality which neither science nor philosophy by itself is capable of giving. But within that totality of response, the autonomy of science remains intact. It is part of the faith of a believer that nothing that is true for science can be false for theology, nothing that is true in theology can be disproved by science.

# The Constitution on the Church and Christian Reunion

1965

From the earliest days of announcement and preparation, two conciliar themes were closely interwoven. The Council sought to promote a renovation of the Church and its accommodation to the contemporary world in which its pastoral and apostolic activities are set. It also sought to pave the way for the union of all Christians in one visible fold. These may be described as respectively the immediate object and the more remote aim of the Council. And it may be added that one purpose of the renovation and accommodation, the *aggiornamento,* is to facilitate Christian union.

Both the immediate aim and the remoter object are of a pastoral character, and the Council never forgot that it was above all a "pastoral" Council. On the other hand, it was never allowed to forget that sound doctrine and theological thinking are themselves pastoral in their purpose. Theology, according to St Thomas, transcends the distinction between the speculative and practical sciences and is "eminently" practical. Those who best understand the problems of Ecumenism are aware that one of the greatest obstacles to Christian union is our failure to agree about the nature of the Church which Christ founded; and those who see *aggiornamento* as requiring no mere surface adjustment in the field of Canon Law and administration, but a radical re-appraisal of the Christian Gospel and its implication, would be among the first to agree that this requirement cannot be met without a clear vision of the Church herself, in her nature, her functions, her God-given mission. When, therefore, in opening the second session of the Council, the Pope proposed to the conciliar Fathers an effort, on the part of the Church, to attain a deeper and truer reflective understanding of what the Church herself is, he was suggesting something that was directly relevant to both the object and the aim of the Council.

A scheme of a Dogmatic Constitution on the Church had been drawn up by the relevant Preparatory Commission of the Council. It was circulated and debated towards the end of the first session and encountered very considerable criticism, especially for what was held to be its too juridical approach to its subject. The scheme was silently withdrawn in the interval between the first and second sessions, and the Constitution which has now been published as an Act of the Council is a revised edition of the *schema* which was prepared, as a replacement of the first, by the Doctrinal Commission in the early months of 1963. What bearing have the contents of this document on the aims and problems of Christian Ecumenism?

It is sometimes objected against the Catholic Church that she sees and presents herself in a too exclusively institutional, juridical, indeed legalistic light. Insistence on her institutional character has in fact been much in evidence in Catholic theology since the Reformation. What was thought to be an exigency of polemics has tended to become the central theme in the Catholic theology concerning the Church, and it has been objected against us that we have conceived of her too much on the analogy of a natural society, of a temporal state, and have obscured the unpredictable operations of the Holy Ghost. If we have not forgotten about him altogether, we have tried to limit him to the *ex opere operato* action of the sacraments. Such criticism is not necessarily derived from a depreciation of the sacraments. Not only the Eastern Orthodox but many Western non-Catholics, and especially an important element in the Anglican Communion, have a profound vision of the Church as a *sacramental* reality. And they have criticised us as having subordinated the sacramental to the jurisdictional and the administrative: "Whereas the episcopate is a sacramental function of the Church . . . the Papacy is a juridical and administrative one which is imparted by the administrative act of election." Dr Mascall, from whom I quote, further argues that juridical and administrative power is so concentrated, by the modern Roman system, in the Pope that "it is the Pope and the Pope alone who exercises in his own right pastoral oversight over every diocese and every individual Christian.[1] Such criticisms from the West could be paralleled from Orthodox writers, and it has even been said that the First Vatican Council "abolished" the episcopate in the Latin Church.

A further criticism has been alleged against the conventional ecclesiology of the period just preceding the Council (and indeed we have something here that goes back at least as far as Bell-

[1] E. L. Mascall, *The Recovery of Unity*, (Longmans, 1958) p. 208.

armine). It is said that we have seen the question of the unity of the Church far too exclusively from the angle of the unity of a universal historical society with a single governmental centre, far too little from that of a mystery which is fully embodied in every local Church and is actualised in the Eucharistic celebration in which the bishop represents his people before God.

It was always possible to point out that there was nothing in our dogmatic bases, not even in the decisions of Vatican I, to necessitate this picture of the modern Catholic Church. But there was certainly much in the concrete facts of our daily life to give plausibility to the picture. And there were tendencies alike in the sphere of Canon Law, or at least canonical practice, and in that of ecclesiological thinking, which supported the picture. Differences between the churches at the level of dogma must of course never be underestimated. But there is truth in Küng's argument that the reason why the Western Reformers rejected the principle of the papacy was that they were scandalised by the concrete operation of that principle in their own day.

The ultimate remedy for what we must consider a misunderstanding of true Catholicism will not be attained till the *practice* of the Church has been renewed. But both the Vatican Councils have shown us the practical influence of theology and doctrine. It was after the conclusion of the First Vatican Council that Roman thinkers began to develop a unilateral theory of power in the Church. G. Alberigo has shown that, for instance, a strong collegial theory of Church government was not only held in Roman quarters before the Council, but was deliberately allowed for by the official advocates of the papal primacy and infallibility at the Council itself. It was after the Council that some writers lost contact with earlier tradition, to such an extent that it was argued that even an Ecumenical Council's authority was solely communicated to it by the Pope. Pushed to an extreme, this tendency would mean that the papacy is the only fount both of all canonical jurisdiction and of Christian power in the Church. Bishops would become receivers of such power from the Pope, and exercise it by delegation from him. Presbyters would similarly receive and exercise power immediately from their bishops but ultimately from the Pope, while the laity would be passive subjects. Alien though such a tendency was from the mind of the sober papalists of Vatican I, it has been, if not created, at least encouraged by the fact that Vatican I proclaimed a doctrine about the Pope which was not complemented by a similarly elaborated doctrine about the episcopate.

On the other hand, the renewal of theology and biblical studies of the last fifty years has been in large measure behind the practical successes of the so-called "progressive" champions in Vatican Council II. We may therefore hope that what the Council has enacted, especially in the *Constitution on the Church,* will in time produce practical results which will help to discredit the caricature of Catholicism which has made our dialogue with the separated brethren and their churches so difficult.

The nettle has in fact been grasped by a magisterial exposition of the Catholic doctrine of the episcopate. This exposition gravitates round two poles: the nature of episcopal consecration, and the real, God-given and not Pope-given, authority of the episcopal "Order" or "College".

We are taught by the Council that episcopal consecration conveys the "fullness" of the ministerial priesthood, itself a participation of the priesthood of Christ. It is a priesthood of sanctifying, teaching and governance, to be exercised within the divinely structured fellowship of the Church, and therefore by members of the episcopal Order. This Order represents to the Church to-day the "college" of the Apostles, and as Peter was the head of the college, so the successor of Peter is the head of the Order. And as the apostolic college, by divine ordinance, had supreme and universal authority over the Church but was itself bound to Peter by the necessity of preserving communion with the Rock on which the Church is built, the Shepherd who feeds all the sheep of Christ, so the episcopal Order or college has a like universal supreme authority, to be exercised only with the consent of the Pope who is not merely a member of the college but its head.

The crux of this whole doctrine is to be found in the statement that episcopal consecration gives to the new bishop a *"munus"* of governing. In other words, a bishop's teaching authority is not derived simply from the "canonical mission" given to him by the Pope; it derives from the very sacrament of Order in its fullness as episcopal consecration and character. The essential function of the Pope, which is implied in the insistence on the necessity of "hierarchical communion" with the episcopal college and its

243

head, is a unifying and co-ordinating one.[2] The episcopal office is for the sake of the Church and is therefore to be exercised within the Church; and in order that its exercise by hundreds or thousands of bishops within the single fellowship may not produce chaos, it is of divine appointment that the Pope shall be, in the last resort, the arbiter of communion and therefore the arbiter of the exercise of this governing function. The Pope is not the source of all power—even of all power of government—in the Church; he is the ultimate arbiter of the exercise of a power which inheres (and is not derived from the Pope) in the college of bishops.

What could be the consequences in practice of this doctrine, which though not a new one has been newly reaffirmed, and reaffirmed in full cognisance of, and allegiance to, the papal doctrine of Vatican I? The doctrine means, of course, that a bishop is not "merely" a diocesan ruler. He is a diocesan ruler only in virtue of the fact that he is, in logical priority, a member of the episcopal college and therefore one who shares a universal authority. His concern can never be limited to his own diocese but must extend to the whole Church and to the missionary needs of the whole world. Naturally, his links will be more immediately with the bishops of his own country or region. He will not think of himself as related to the universal Church only through his relation to the successor of Peter; horizontal relations become important for him. And the Constitution on the Church itself reminds us how this "collegial instinct" led to local conjunctions among the bishops of antiquity and especially to the patriarchal system of Church government. It adds: "Similarly at the present day, episcopal conferences can do varied and fruitful service in giving practical effect to the collegial sense." If extreme practical centralisation has alienated the minds of many of our Christian brethren from the Catholic Church, the perspectives here opened up are surely promising for the future of ecumenical relations.

It will be objected that, nevertheless, the Pope's autocracy remains intact, since without his consent the episcopal college cannot enter into full exercise of its powers, cannot in full actuality rule the universal Church. And, so long as we confine ourselves rigidly to the juridical level, this is true. It is a consequence of the fact, pointed out by the Council of Aquileia in A.D. 381, that "the rights of communion derive from Rome".

[2] *De Ecclesia* cf. n. 27.

But perhaps it is hardly fitting that those who have accused the Vatican of juridicism should wish to be able to rely on juridical safeguards against autocracy. The Pope's ultimate legal liberty of discretion, which is undoubted, after, as it was before, the promulgation of the new Constitution, has to be seen in a wider context of moral obligation and of custom.

Morally speaking, just as the Pope cannot destroy the existence of the episcopal college, so he may not in practice disregard its existence. There is an analogy here with the obligation that rests on him, in matters of dogma, to consult with his fellow-bishops; not a legal obligation, but a moral one, and one which was conspicuously observed before the definitions of the Immaculate Conception and the Assumption. The moral obligation to make the episcopal college an effective reality is brought into fresh evidence by the explicit teaching on the existence and nature of the episcopal college that is set forth in the Constitution. And if it is further objected that, after all, the Pope himself is the only judge of the implications of this obligation in concrete circumstances, it must be replied that it is of the nature of Christianity that its legal and juridical aspects are subordinate to the personal and moral aspect; and that in practice no "polity" will work well without the good will of those who live under and in it, and of those who hold office in it.

In practice, and particularly in a perspective of ecumenical hope, the possibilities now before the Church are immense. It should be possible, by a prudent and daring application of the principle of subsidiarity, to take in hand a massive programme of "decentralisation". Whatever the utility of the centralisation which has been increasing ever since the beginning of the fifth century, it is not something that is *demanded* by the divinely-given structure of the Church; on the contrary, it has tended to obscure one aspect of that structure. It would indeed be foolish to attempt an archaeological restoration of the state of things in the Church of the fourth century or the sixth. But there is no difficulty in principle in following the policy advocated in the debate on the decree on the Catholic Oriental Churches by Abbot J. Hoeck of Scyeyern, which would lead to a modern form of patriarchal government for the Church, in which the function of the papacy would again be seen as something in the nature of an *ultimate* court of practical and doctrinal appeal, while the direct, day-to-day governmental activity of the Vatican would be confined to a geographically and numerically much diminished Latin patriarchate. Such a development would not only facilitate the re-establishment of communion with the Orthodox East; it would offer a solution for corporate reconciliation certainly with the Anglican Communion and perhaps with other greater Western Christian bodies.

It is not only by its great chapter on the Church's hierarchical constitution that the new document will be of service to the ecumenical cause. It contains also the basis of a renewed vision of the Church's unity as centred not only in the papacy but in the Eucharist. Contrasting the Eastern outlook on Church unity with a one-sided exposition of the Western idea of unity as focused in the successor of Peter, Archdeacon Allen observes: "(For the Greek Orthodox) each sacramental centre constitutes the Church in its fullness . . . ; the bishop of each local sacramental centre . . . is not a substitute for the personal priesthood of Christ in the Church; on the contrary, he is the image of Christ . . . and does not take Christ's place, but effectively participates in and makes present the invisible but very present reality of which he is the image." This is a sacramental, as distinct from a juridical or administrative, vision of unity. If it were taken to exclude the other vision, it would fail to do justice to the deep-seated Christian conviction that the universal People of God is, and is morally bound to remain, outwardly united in a visible (and, we should add, structured) communion. But the two viewpoints are not mutually exclusive.

The *Constitution on the Church* lays down the foundations for such a sacramental view of Christian unity. "As often as the sacrifice of the Cross . . . is celebrated at the altar, the work of our redemption is put into operation. And at the same time by the Eucharistic bread the unity of the faithful who compose one body in Christ, is represented and made real" (Chap. I, n. 4) *"Porro corpore Christi in sacra synaxi refecti, unitatem Populi Dei, quae hoc augustissimo sacramento apte significatur et mirabiliter efficitur, modo concreto exhibet"*: "Strengthened anew at the holy table by the Body of Christ, they manifest in a practical way that unity of God's People which is suitably signified and wonderfully brought about by this most awesome sacrament." (Chap. II, n. 11). *"Haec Christi Ecclesia, vere adest in omnibus legitimis fidelium congregationibus localibus, quae, pastoribus suis adhaerentes, et ipsae in Novo Testamento ecclesiae vocantur*

*. . . in quavis altaris communitate, sub Episcopo sacra mysterio, exhibetur symbolum . . . unitatis Corporis Mystici, sine qua non potest esse salus. In his communitatibus . . . praeses est Christus, cuius virtue consociatur una, sancta, catholica et apostolica Ecclesia"*: "This Church of Christ is truly present in all legitimate local congregations of the faithful which, united with their pastors, are themselves called churches in the New Testament . . . in any community existing around an altar, under the sacred ministry of the bishop, there is manifested a symbol of that . . . 'unity of the Mystical Body, without which there can be no salvation'. In them . . . Christ is present. By virtue of Him the one, holy, catholic, and apostolic Church gathers together." (Chap. III, n. 26). And presbyters, representing their bishop in a local congregation, *"universalem Ecclesiam in suo loco visibilem faciunt"*: "make the universal Church visible in their own locality." (Chap. III, n. 28). Thus we are encouraged to see the Church, not simply as an international society with a super-local government, but as a sacramental mystery made fully actual wherever Mass is legitimately celebrated, and above all where the local bishop, surrounded by his clergy and the faithful, is himself the celebrant. The universal *koinonia* (fellowship) is thus made actual at a particular place and time, and the international Church is to be seen not only as a *societas fidelium* (society of the faithful) but as a *communio ecclesiarum* (communion of the Churches). It is immediately apparent how well this vision of the Church harmonises with the teaching on the sacramental origin of the bishop's *munus regendi* (duty of governance) and on the universal authority of the college of bishops.

Modern Catholicism has not only been accused of juridicism, legalism and excessive centralisation. It has been charged with clericalism, and this is a charge which comes perhaps with especial frequency from our Protestant brethren. The *Constitution on the Church* should help to mitigate this charge. After its opening chapter on the Mystery of the Church, it at once proceeds to a chapter on the People of God. It is significant that it is only after this chapter that our attention is directed to the hierarchical structure of the Church. The People of God is a scriptural appellation of the Church, which is composed of baptised believers who form *"genus electum, regale sacerdotium, gens sancta, populus acquisitionis . . . populus Dei"*: "a chosen race, a royal priesthood, a holy nation, a purchased people . . . the people of God" (Chap. II, n. 9). And the organically structured character of this "priestly fellowship" is said (*Ibid.* n. 11) to be "brought into act by the sacraments and virtues". It is within this total vision, focused on baptism, that the "ministries" within the Church find their place and their reason. "*Christus Dominus, ad Populum Dei pascendum semperque augendum, in Ecclesia sua varia ministeria instituti, quae ad bonum totius Corporis tendunt. Ministri enim, qui sacra potestate pollent, fratribus suis inserviunt, ut omnes qui de Populo Dei sunt, ideoque vera dignitate Christiana gaudent, ad eundem finem libere et ordinatim conspirantes, ad salutem perveniant*": "Christ the Lord instituted in his Church, for the constant nurturing and growth of the People of God, a variety of ministries, which work for the good of the whole body. For those ministers who are endowed with sacred power are servants of their brethren, so that all who are of the People of God, and therefore enjoy a true Christian dignity, can work towards a common goal freely and in an orderly way, and arrive at salvation." (Chap. III, n. 18). "*Munus autem illud, quod Dominus pastoribus populi sui commisit, verum est servitium quod in sacris Litteris 'diakonia' seu ministerium significanter nuncupatur*": "Now that duty, which the Lord committed to the shepherds of His people, is a true service, and in holy writ is significantly called 'diakonia' or ministry." (*Ibid.*, n. 24). The bishops in particular are reminded that "he who is greater is to become like him who is less and he who presides is to be as it were minister" (*Ibid.*, n. 27). Since by far the larger number of those who make up the People of God are laymen, the chapter on the hierarchy is followed by one on the laity. No attempt is made to define the laity but they are here described as all the faithful except those in sacred orders and those who belong to the "religious state". Like the other members of the Church, the laity are vivified by God's Spirit. They share in Christ's priesthood. Christ fulfils his prophetic function through them, and makes them his witnesses, instructing them by the *sensus fidei* (sense of faith) and the grace of the word (n. 35). They can, and sometimes duty impels them to, express their view on what concerns the good of the Church; and their pastors are encouraged by the Constitution to "make willing use of their advice" and to give them due freedom of action, paying earnest attention to their wishes.

Mention has been made in the preceding paragraph of the *sensus fidei*. Some Russian Orthodox thinkers, led by Khomiakov, have emphasised, to a degree which to us Westerns seems exaggerated or at least too exclusive, this aspect of the Church's life. But the notion of the *sensus fidei* is also traditional in Western theology, and the Constitution affirms that *"Universitas fidelium qui habent a Sancto, in credendo falli nequit, atque hanc suam peculiarem proprietotem mediante supernaturali sensu fidei totius populi manifestat, cum ab Episcopis usque ad extremos laicos fideles universalem suam consensum de rebus fidei et moribus exhibet"*: "The body of the faithful as a whole, anointed as they are by the Holy One, cannot err in matters of belief. Thanks to a supernatural sense of the faith which characterises the People as a whole, it manifests this unerring quality when, 'from the bishops down to the last member of the laity', it shows a universal agreement in matters of faith and morals." (n. 12). It is added that the People of God, under leadership of the teaching body, by means of this sense of faith *"fidei indefectibiliter adhæret, recto iudicio in eam profundius penetrat eamque in vitam plenius applicat"*: "clings without fail to the faith, penetrates it more deeply by accurate insights, and applies it more thoroughly to life." (*Ibid.*).

It may be observed, in passing that, valuable though this treatment of the *sensus fidei* is, it could be further developed. The Constitution stresses the *infallibility* of the sense of faith when the whole People of God agrees in matters of faith and morals. Such infallibility is parallel to the infallibility of the magisterium in some of its pronouncements. But the magisterium has authority which extends beyond the area of infallible teaching; and it may be suggested that the *sensus fidei* similarly has an authority more extensive than that which is infallibly guaranteed. It is, moreover, well known that the *sensus fidei* is consulted by the magisterium when the need arises of determining some point of doctrine; and Newman, in a celebrated article, showed how, amid widespread failure on the part of the teachers of the Church in the fourth century, the *sensus fidei* preserved and maintained true doctrine. The notion of the teaching, as contrasted with the learning, Church must never be pushed to a point at which the rest of the Church is merely passive to the oracular utterance of the bishops.

It is obvious that the magisterium, as such, is a static, traditionalist, conservative element in the Church. But the Church combines in a wonderful harmony, not without tensions, a static and a dynamic element. The dynamic element proceeds from the "special graces", *"quibus Spiritus Sanctus omnis ordinis fideles aptos et promptos reddit ad suscipienda varia opera vel officia, pro renovatione et ampliore aedificatione Ecclesiae proficua"* "whereby the Holy Spirit makes the faithful of every rank fit and ready to undertake the various tasks or offices advantageous for the renewal and upbuilding of the Church." (n. 12). It is the task of the pastors of the Church *"non Spiritum existinguere, sed omnia probare et quod bonum est tenere"* "not to extinguish the Spirit, but to test all things and hold fast to that which is good." *(Ibid.).* It is obvious that these "special graces", these *charismata,* as the Constitution calls them, are often given, for the good of the Church, to priests, bishops and Popes. One thinks of St Jerome, St Augustine, St Gregory the Great, and in more recent times of Newman, Suhard, John XXIII. But they are not essentially attached to hierarchical status, and are often given to lay people; to a St Therese, a Friedrich von Hügel, a Brother Lawrence. They are the unpredictable, original, creative factor in the Church. They make it impossible, as was pointed out in a striking speech in the Council, to foretell the course of the Church's history, of that "history of salvation" which did not cease with the end of the age of revelation, but is continually carried onwards by the action of the Spirit of Christ. It is for this reason that the Church is not only an ancient mystery, but an ever-renewed mystery of human-divine encounter.

It is in this context of the life of the Spirit, indwelling and welling up from the depths of baptised humanity—which exists only in individual, personal subjects—that the sacraments attain their full meaning. Modern Catholic theology, in reaction once again against the Reformers, has laid great emphasis on the *ex opere operato* efficacy of the sacraments. But it has never, in its central stream, denied that the fruitfulness of the sacraments is conditioned by the dispositions and response of those who approach them, collectively and individually. Here the teaching of the *De Ecclesia* can be usefully supplemented by that of the *De Liturgia.* A vision begins to take shape of a vast interplay of objective sacraments and subjective goodwill, of a process from faith through sacraments-of-faith to faith, from grace to grace, of the great Pauline doctrine that only the Spirit of God can plumb the abyss of God, our Redeemer and our goal.

To the heirs of the Reformation it has often seemed as though true religion, in the practice and to some extent in the theory of

Catholicism, has been overlaid, even corrupted, by the *cultus* of the saints and above all of our Lady. The Constitution deals with these issues in its last two chapters. In Chapter VII the *"cultus"* is seen as an expression and a deepening of the "communion" which binds all the redeemed together, whether on earth or after death, in a growing union in Christ. We look to the saints who have gone before us into glory as to exemplars of that transformation into the likeness of Christ which is our common vocation. But we also have intercourse with them and seek their intercession, in order that they, like our fellow-Christians who still share our pilgrimage, may help us on our course through their prayers. But at the same time we are reminded that the whole purpose of the *"cultus"* is *"pleniorem Christi et Dei laudem"*: the fuller praise of Christ and God.

The same prudent, sober, positive attitude governs the chapter "On the Blessed Virgin Mary, Mother of God, in the Mystery of Christ and the Church". Here then is of course a full and explicit adherence to the Church's defined doctrine. But there is also a fully deliberate refusal to anticipate future developments, or to commit the Church to positions advocated by only some streams of theological thinking. The Constitution gratefully acknowledges the maternal charity shown to us by the Mother of our Redeemer, and mentions that she is invoked in the Church under the titles *Advocata, Auxiliatrix, Adiutrix, Mediatrix.* But it at once sets out to obviate mistaken notions: *"quod tamen ita intelligitur, ut dignitati et efficitati Christi unius Mediatoris nihil deroget, nihil superaddat. Nulla enim creatura cum Verbo incarnato ac Redemptore connumerari unquam potest; sed sicut sacerdotium Christi variis modis tum a ministris tum a fideli populo participatur, et sicut una bonitas Dei in creaturis modis diversis realiter diffunditur, ita etiam unica mediatio Redemptoris non excludit, sed suscitat variam apud creaturas participatam ex unico fonte cooperationem"*: These, however, are to be so understood that they neither take away from nor add anything to the dignity and efficacy of Christ, the one Mediator. For no creature could ever be classed with the incarnate Word and Redeemer. But, just as the priesthood of Christ is shared in various ways both by sacred ministers and by the faithful, and as the one goodness of God is in reality communicated diversely to His creatures, so also the unique mediation of the Redeemer does not exclude but rather gives rise among creatures to a manifold cooperation which is but a sharing in this unique source." Thus, while on the one hand the help which we owe to our Lady is in no way comparable with, and in no way increases or diminishes, our total indebtedness to Christ, on the other hand Mary's "mediation" is but one instance, the supreme instance, of our mutual indebtedness of each to all in the mystical body of Christ. Theologically speaking, it is perhaps not so much what is specifically said of Mary in this passage that can cause difficulties to Protestants as what is said or implied about the reality of the effects of grace in redeemed humanity.*

More and more in ecumenical circles it is becoming realised that Christian unity will not come about by a simple unification of our separate streams of tradition in their phenomenal actuality. A distinction, never easy, has to be made between what each of the separate bodies holds as of the essence of the Gospel and what—however venerable and dear—is not strictly essential. It has been well said, in reference to the Catholic idea of the Church:

> We must remember that ecclesiology has often developed rather according to the pressure of circumstances than according to a substantial hierarchy of absolute values. Indeed, this is a recurrent phenomenon in the history of the science of theology, and is intimately connected with the religious life not only of individuals but of the Church as a whole. Hence we have to beware of any kind of superficial positivism of method, remembering that it is not only those points of doctrine that are explicitly expressed and developed that are basic and unanimously accepted. On the contrary, it often happens that profoundly traditional orientations remain for a long time consigned to the common conscience of the Church without being the object of specific investigation, precisely because they *are* traditional and universally received.[3]

In other words, we have to acknowledge a distinction between surface appearances and the deep underlying currents of life in the Church—and in every religious body with a long and developing history. *Aggiornamento* is a task which lies before every

---

* The above quotations from the Council documents are taken in the main from the translation *The Documents of Vatican II*, edited by Walter Abbott, S.J., Guild Press, New York, America Press, Associations Press, 1966.

[3] G. Alberigo, *La Sviluppo della Dottrine sui Poteri nella chiesa universale*, (Herder, 1964).

Christian communion that takes ecumenism seriously. And true *aggiornamento* is not revolutionary but profoundly traditional. It takes us back to our origins, back at last to the Bible and the Gospel; and if it incidentally discloses that a great deal in our current attitudes is contingent and expendable, this will not only release the deeper energies of our own communion but will remove adventitious obstacles that bar the way to our brethren in their quest of a closer association with us. If we wish to learn how serious these obstacles can seem to a most sympathetic Anglican student of Catholicism as it appeared to him five years before the opening of the second Vatican Council, we could do worse than turn to Chapters IX and X of Dr E. L. Mascall's *The Recovery of Unity*. It would be interesting to discover whether Dr Mascall would wish to couch his criticisms in the same form now that the *Constitution on the Church* has been passed, almost unanimously, by the votes of the Council, and has been ratified by the Pope. But we must revert to the task that lies before the Church herself, seen in the light of this great document.

Looking first to the possibility of a *rapprochement* with the Eastern Orthodox, we must in the first place recognise that the papacy from which, by a gradual process, our Eastern brethren became estranged was a papacy that was rapidly moving towards that kind of direct papal rule which, however convenient for the temporary needs of the Western patriarchate, was not the traditional *régime* as regards the East, involved at least some measure of neglect of the principle of subsidiarity, and was in any case not a necessary consequence of the Petrine primacy. The permanent temptation for papalists has been to see in Peter not merely the regulator of the *koinonia* and of ministerial authority within it, but the very source of all authority. Vatican I did not commit us to this view; but it gave occasion for some theologians and canonists to represent such a view as the only tenable one. Vatican II has refused to endorse this extreme position, and has reinstated the episcopate, the local Church, and the idea of *koinonia*, enabling us once again to see the Pope as one whose authority is essentially episcopal and sacramental, given to him not to exercise domination but to "strengthen" his brethren in their directly God-given authority.

The papacy is not the only difficulty as between Catholics and the Orthodox. But most of the other difficulties in the sphere of doctrine—and here I think especially of the difficulties created by the modern dogmas of the Immaculate Conception and the Assumption of the Mother of God—are susceptible to the treatment advocated by John XXIII in his opening speech to the Council, in which he bade us to be faithful to the substance of defined doctrine, but to hold more lightly to the language in which it has been expressed. The field for dialogue, in any case, is now wide open.

As regards the West, it is time for the Church, following in the wake of the dominant tendencies of the Council, to emerge finally from the polemical attitudes which have governed our practice and, sad to say, our theology for four hundred years. How many, even of the dogmas defined as a retort to Protestantism, are really very peripheral in the total organism of the faith. How greatly we need, for our own sakes, to get back to such great central truths as those which Luther and Calvin were basically seeking to reaffirm. How fruitful are such theological studies as Hans Küng's confrontation of the Lutheran and the Catholic doctrines of justification. The *Constitution on the Church,* taken along with its sister documents, the *De Ecumenismo* and the *De Revelatione* should encourage us to pursue this path. And then let us remember that in a Church which, through patriarchates, episcopal conferences or other such organs, has recovered its sense of diversity in unity, and learnt that a central focus of communion is not necessarily inimical to a vigorous life at the circumference, we shall be presenting in modern terms something far more similar to the apostolic and the patristic Church than the baroque papalism of the late Renaissance, something that must appeal with unexampled attraction to those who, like us, share the great ancestry of primitive and antique Christendom.

# The Aggiornamento of Vatican II

1966

Toward the end of its second session, Vatican Council II, bereft of the great Pope who had convened it, and seeming for the moment to have lost its bearings, took some of its precious and expensive time to celebrate the fourth centenary of the closing of the Council of Trent. The Council that ended in 1563, after a total life of about eighteen years, has gone down to history as the Council of the Counter-Reformation. It seems likely that Vatican II will be known in the future as the *Aggiornamento* Council. *Aggiornamento* was in fact the task proposed to it by John XXIII.

What is *aggiornamento*? I am no expert in Italian, but I believe the word means, etymologically, "A bringing up to date". The Church was to be brought up to date. But what should *this* mean?

Of course, any institution that lives and means to play an active, not to say aggressive, part in the mainstream of human history must from time to time, and even continuously, be making minor adaptations to its ever changing environment. Such change was already in progress long before the Council opened. We need only to remind ourselves of the striking modifications in the law of the eucharistic fast, introduceed by Pius XII after World War II, or of changes in the liturgy, of which perhaps the most striking had been the restoration of the night-vigil of Easter.

Change had been going on, and there was a machinery that made possible not only the proposal of more changes, but the deliberate study and coordination of these proposals, and the enactment of them as and when their introduction might seem prudent. The Curia existed. And there was the Pope, with an authority more practically absolute, and less liable than ever to questioning and resistance, since Vatican I had formally promulgated his universal supreme, ordinary jurisdiction and—under certain conditions, it is true—the infallibility of his doctrinal pronouncements. Has any institution in human history been better equipped for strong and pliant government than the Catholic

Church of the first half of the twentieth century? And since Rome had such dogmatic and practical competence, it could be asked: Why incur the trouble and expense of an ecumenical council?

Before the Council opened, on October 11, 1962, it was not even publicly known with any certainty how John XXIII himself viewed his task of *aggiornamento*. He had associated the Council with two other proposals: a reform of the code of canon law (which might of course mean either much or little) and a synod of the local church of Rome, of which the successor of St Peter is the diocesan bishop. The synod had been held, and its outcome had been a host of new regulations that would have made life in Rome even more difficult for Catholics if they had been observed; it was not a very hopeful augury for the ecumenical Council for which it might be considered to play the role of a pilot scheme. It is true the Pope had hinted that Catholics might look forward to the Council as to a second Pentecost. The hint was calculated to alarm rather than to encourage those who feared that the major result of Vatican II would be a firmer control of the new movements in the Church and consequent disillusionment.

Some light on the Pope's mind could be gained from the discourse with which he closed the inaugural ceremonies on October 11, although his hearers were so wearied after a long and tedious service that they were perhaps less responsive than they should have been. He spoke, said Cardinal Montini (who was to succeed to his office and to the guidance of his council), like "a teacher who loved the world". So far from urging the manning of the threatened bastions, he suggested that the Council's task would not be to repeat the old dogmatic formulas but to render the eternal truth present to the men of the present day, with due regard for modern mentalities and for the progress of research. The Church must be made present to the world, whose progress does not escape God's overarching providence, but which has no need of a Council that should find no fresh way of expressing the abiding truth. Not only did the Pope thus evoke the shades of Modernism; he dared to suggest that there was room for hope even in the seventh decade of the twentieth century, and expressed his dissent from the "prophets of woe who tell us that our age is worse than former ones and behave as though they had learned nothing from history; yet history is the teacher of life".

The crisis of the Council came in the first session when, after a long debate, but no significant vote, on the draft of the *Constitution of the Liturgy,* a secret ballot determined the demise of the draft on the sources of revelation. This vote, which showed that the Council was prepared to listen to the so-called new theology, and to the biblical scholars, was followed by a debate in which the draft *Constitution on the Church* (of which the first chapter was entitled "The Nature of the Church Militant") came under heavy fire. It was then that Bishop De Smedt made his celebrated attack on "triumphalism, clericalism, and juridicism". By the end of the session it was obvious that we were determined to consider *Aggiornamento* in depth.

May I try to explain what I mean by *aggiornamento* in depth? The Curia was able and willing to carry out surface adaptations in the life and administrations of the Church, and had in fact, as already indicated, been doing so. But the Council, it seemed, was ready to study the desirability of something more than this.

Perhaps an illustration from biology will not be too misleading.

Plant and animal species are found to include a number of varieties within themselves; they have modified a basic structure, common to all the varieties of a single species, to meet slightly differing concrete situations. But a time may come when the survival and welfare of the species' biological inheritance requires some more radical change. A species is conceived by Bernard Lonergan as "an intelligible solution to a problem of living in a given environment".[1] When the environment changes beyond a certain limit, the species ceases to be a solution to it, and the alternatives now are extinction or evolution. If evolution occurs, the resultant species is a new solution to the new problem of living. It "rises upon and takes into account, as it were", the earlier solution, and is "the sort of thing that insight hits upon and not the sort that results from accumulated, observable differences".[2]

The Catholic Church is of course not a species with varieties and specimens. It is a communion of human beings, and man,

[1] *Insight: A Study of Human Understanding* (London, Longmans, 1957) p. 265.

[2] *Ibid.* p. 265.

being not only intelligible but intelligent, is "not just a higher system but a source of higher systems".[3] The closest analogy in human history to the emergence of a new species was the Incarnation, when God the Son assumed a particular human nature into hypostatic union with the divine nature. This was certainly an entirely novel solution of the human problem of living, but it did not make man less but more himself. It was novel; it was also unique and final, within the limits of history. Yet although the Church cannot evolve into something other and higher than herself, the fact that she is a communion of human beings means that, grace aiding, she can achieve ever new solutions of the sort that "insight hits upon, and not the sort that result from accumulated observable differences".

Such new solutions will have a radical quality and will entail a searching discrimination between what is, after all, of the immutable essence of the Church, and all in her contingent existence that, however venerable, is yet—at least in principle— expendable. The Curia would have operated by gradual accumulation of observable differences. The Council contemplated the possibility of a complex of radical solutions. John XXIII had, as we have seen, hinted at a new Pentecost.

If it be asked whether *aggiornamento* in depth was really necessary, our answer may be to refer to the changed environment in which the Church has to live and function. Of this, the *Constitution on the Church in the Modern World* goes so far as to say (Art. 4): "Today, the human race is passing through a new age of its history. Profound and rapid changes are spreading by degrees around the whole world. Triggered by the intelligence and creative energies of man, these changes recoil upon him, upon his decisions and desires both individual and collective, and upon his manner of thinking and acting with respect to things and people. Hence we can already speak of a true social and cultural transformation, one which has repercussions on man's religious life as well". We are faced with a crisis of development.[4]

What, now, of the pre-Conciliar Church? Like a stratified rock to the geologist, she was a fascinating object for the historian, not to say the antiquarian. She trailed strange clouds of glory from a past growing ever more remote and irrelevant—like the three

[3] *Ibid.* p. 267.

crowns of the papal tiara. Her law was articulated on principles, not to say in a spirit, which were ultimately those of the Roman civil law. Her central administration was redolent of the *familia* of the Roman Emperors, as her ceremonial reflected that of a Byzantine court. It needed a critical eye to discern, in the action and theory of the papal primacy, what came from the gospel and what from Caesar. She had never recovered from the estrangement between Eastern and Western Catholicism, which was symbolised in the mutual excommunications of Rome and Constantinople. Lacking the counterpoise of the Eastern churches, the West had come practically to identify its local tradition with the universal tradition, so much so that the miniature Eastern churches actually in communion with the Holy See were treated as quaint appendages and exceptions to a general rule. The *koinonia* of ante-Nicene times had become the Latin *societas,* and that society, having been first imperialised, had been feudalised in the Middle Ages. Still, in the middle of the twentieth century, she seemed to be trembling from the shock of the Protestant Reformation, and following her reaction against the new theology of the sixteenth century she had reacted also against the whole general stream of progress in that area of the world's surface where she was geographically, but no longer spiritually, at home. The tremendous dynamic movement that had flung her upon the Graeco-Roman world of the early Christian centuries seemed to have taken shape in a parabolic curve, carrying her now ever further from the living, moving centre of human affairs.

A species, when no longer adapted to its actual environment, can evolve, or it can perish. The Church cannot perish. But there is a third possibility. Sometimes a species succeeds in taking refuge in a backwater of existence, where—in diminished numbers and with no further relevance except to historians of past

---

[4] Cf. F. Houtart, *L'Eglise et le Monde,* 18: "The rhythm of the development of man's potentialities is extraordinary. His mastery over nature is growing day by day and an almost unimaginable future is opening up before him. Man is becoming the basic value for contemporary philosophies and social systems, however halting their efforts may be. Men are becoming aware of great collective tasks ahead of them, involving increased interdependence, socialization and cooperation. Never has there been a more powerful consciousness of humanity's engagement in a common adventure, driving it as with irresistible force to the achieving of a goal which will mean, perhaps, man's willingness to transcend himself." Houtart was one of the "experts" of the Joint Conciliar Commission responsible for the *Constitution on the Church in the Modern World.* His influence is manifest in the passage of the Constitution cited above.

evolution—it prolongs an insignificant story. As we look back on the Church before 1962, do we not sometimes seem to be catching a glimpse of what might have become a monumental irrelevance?

It may indeed be asked: Should the Church, *ought* the Church, to adapt herself to the changing fashion of the world? Did not Pius IX condemn the proposition that "the Roman Pontiff can and ought to come to terms with Progress, Liberalism, and the New Civilisation"? Well, according to Newman, the value of the Syllabus of Errors, from which this proposition is taken, lies in its references, and Newman finds no formal condemnation of this pronouncement in the Allocution from which it is excerpted; what the Pope did say was, in effect, that the mid-nineteenth-century champions of Progress, Liberalism and the New Civilisation made use of their cause "so seriously to the injury of the Faith and the Church, that it was both out of the power and contrary to the duty, of the Pope to come to terms with them."[5] But the deeper answer to our question is simply that the Church has a mission and a message, and divine help, for all mankind; to fulfil her function she must be not only chronologically but spiritually the contemporary of those to whom she addresses herself. *Aggiornamento* in depth is thus seen to be a pastoral necessity.

The word "pastoral" has taken us to the heart of the Council. It is an old-fashioned word, but to the Council it signified something that must urgently be modern. The commission to the apostles is: to make disciples of all nations, teaching them to observe all that Christ had commanded them. We used to be warned in the first session of the Council that the Church's prime duty was to protect the faith of her actual children. But it should be observed that in the text of St Matthew's Gospel (XXVIII 19f) to which I have just referred, the making of disciples is mentioned before the teaching of the commandments. Proclamation (*kerygma*) precedes instruction (*didache*). Unless the work of evangelisation comes first, there is no one to instruct, none with a faith to be protected.

The Church is therefore necessarily outward-looking, not primarily introspective and conservative, but primarily an indomitable adventurer into new fields. What else could she be, since

[5] "Open Letter to the Duke of Norfolk", in *Difficulties of Anglicans* II 283, 286.

she is, as St Augustine taught us, the incorporation of Christian love or charity? Charity is the least introspective of virtues, calling us always to transcend the self and its immediate horizon, not feeding on itself but projecting itself thither where previously there has been a lack of love. Charity has the audacity of the great military geniuses, who know by instinct that a strategy of defence can never in the end win a campaign.

Perhaps it is not altogether fantastic to seek for this motive of pastoral charity behind a number of interests which gave the Council its characteristic colour. The widening of horizons, an inevitable consequence of the meeting of over two thousand prelates from almost every part of the world, was still further extended by the presence throughout the Council of the observers from the churches and ecclesial communities of our separated brethren. It was as though the Council became conscious, as it looked beyond the walls of the city set on a hill, of friends, brothers, fellow disciples of the world's Saviour, just outside those walls. The Church, in these separated brethren, seemed visibly to transcend its own limits. From this transcendence there springs a set of theological problems, which have left their mark not only on the *Decree on Ecumenism* but on *Lumen Gentium* itself. The Council had to turn back behind Bellarmine with his Counter-Reformation ecclesiology, behind St Thomas himself and the Fathers, to the biblical theology which governs the first two chapters of the *Constitution on the Church*.

Then, beyond the baptised and unbaptised disciples of our Lord, there was the people of the Jews, who before us had obtained the divine adoption, the visible presence and the covenant, the Torah and the Prophets: who could claim the patriarchs for their own, and of whom came the Messiah in his human nature (cf. *Rom* IX 4f). Here we owe a great debt to the German Cardinal Bea and the German hierarchy, whose successful determination to obtain a pronouncement against anti-Semitism by and for the whole Church was a blessed outcome of unhappy events in their own country in this century.

And beyond the Jews there were Islam and the great Eastern religions. It was a triumph of charity that, surely for the first time in history, an ecumenical council came to pronounce on these great faiths with practically exclusive reference to their positive values, and with unqualified respect.

And so on to secularist humanism and to atheism. Once the

question was posed, it was indeed difficult for the Council not to "reprobate" atheism, since in itself it is the professed denial of the ultimate basis of religion. But even here, in the words of Archbishop Garrone, the desire behind the Conciliar treatment of this subject (in the *Constitution on the Church in the Modern World*) was "to give a description of atheism of which an atheist would say: This is no caricature—here I recognise myself".

Charity is both cause and effect of intercommunication, or, to use our modern word, of dialogue. Throughout the Council's treatment of the themes just mentioned there is the underlying motif of dialogue; implying a respect for the interlocutor, too sincere to allow us to make compromises of truth, yet tireless in seeking points of contact, agreement and common concern.

Christian love is a love of respect, because it is an affair of interpersonal communication and communion. It therefore carries us on to another basic characteristic of the spirit and work of Vatican II. The Archbishop of Turin, in one of his notable contributions to the debates of the fourth session, said that he thought there was something valuable in modern subjectivism, properly conceived. The remark was sufficiently unusual, particularly as coming from an Italian prelate, to challenge attention. It might be said that the very hallmark of modern Catholicism has been its insistence on the order of objective truths, values and laws. In fact, this preoccupation with the objective is one reason why our manuals of moral theology have conveyed to some minds the impression of a positively algebraic irrelevance to the real drama of man's moral life. Yet it is at least arguable that precisely the ferment of the gospel has been the creative source of our contemporary concern with personal freedom and responsibility, if not of the agonies of modern existentialism. Charity, after all, being supernatural love, is always orientated toward the living person of our fellowman, and therefore to his needs and problems as they come alive in his personal subjectivity. And charity respects this person and this person's viewpoint. It respects him, and it warns us of our limited understanding of him. It is charity that says: Judge not, and you shall not be judged: who art thou, to pass judgment on another's servant? (*Rom* XIV 4). If it is a principle of law to presume that those who infringe its prescriptions are morally to blame, it is a principle of charity to presume that those who differ from us—including those who differ from the defined dogmas of the faith—are nevertheless "men of good will".

Such was the presumption governing what *Lumen Gentium* and the *Decree on Ecumenism,* as also the *Declaration on the Relationship of the Church to Non-Christian Religions,* had to say about non-Catholics. Such too is the presumption of the *Constitution on the Church in the Modern World,* when it addresses itself to all men of good will irrespective of their creeds, their ideologies or their professed agnosticism. The same presumption really lies behind the *Declaration on Religious Freedom,* though the grounds there stated for this freedom go deeper than presumed good will to the inherent rights of the human person even in error, and even in guilt. And this presumption triumphed once again, though with some difficulty, in the modest suggestion in the chapter on peace and war that civil law might make provision for conscientious objectors.

The pastoral aim, the instinct of a charity that goes beyond all boundaries, the sense of mission not so much to human nature or the abstract human species, but to human persons and the actually existing human family, demanded that our *aggiornamento* should be conceived of in depth. The consequent need to discriminate between what the Church must always be, what the gospel forever is, and the contingent elements in which, at any given moment, the Church presents herself in history, was driving the Council to some criterion. And this drive took her gaze ever backwards, behind the counterrevolutionary Church, behind the Counter-Reformation, behind the medieval synthesis, back to the Church before the estrangement of East and West, to the Church before the confrontation with Greek culture and philosophy, to the primal source: to Christ in Palestine. As Cardinal Montini said, in his speech near the end of the first session, the Church by herself is nothing. She is not so much a society founded by Christ as Christ himself using us as his instruments to bring salvation to mankind.[6] Christ himself is the fullness of the divine revelation, and the content of the sacred tradition is just revelation, the word of God made flesh. The Church's teaching authority, embodied in the ecumenical Council, is not above the word of God but the servant of that word, teaching only that which has been transmitted (*Constitution on Divine Revelation,* 10).

Thus the very need for accommodating the Church to the world of today and tomorrow, if it was not lead to compromise

[6] Xavier Rynne, *Letters from Vatican City* (London: Faber, 1963) p. 227.

263

with the world, must throw us back to our source. The *Decree on the Appropriate Renewal of the Religious Life* has its own rendering of the word *aggiornamento*: it speaks of "an accommodated renewal". The word "accommodated" here refers to contemporary adaptation. The word "renewal", however, as the text of the decree shows, does not mean "innovation" but "recovery of the initial inspiration". The more immediate source of a religious order is the "spirit and special projects" of its founder, together with "healthy traditions". But the source of the Church is the Spirit and gospel of Jesus of Nazareth, ever living in the Church he founded, but needing always to be rediscovered and relived.

Modern man has a profound sense of his involvement in the time process. For good or ill, he seems less interested in the fact that the definition of his species is *animal rationale* than that he is an existing person, caught in the trammels and the challenge of duration and therefore of change. In the realm of natural science, he is fascinated by the concept and the story of evolution. And within the general scheme of evolution he frames the history of the human race, which he studies also scientifically. If philosophy was the basic discipline of the medieval schools, history is today a basic discipline among all those that deal with man. For modern man, the return to Jesus of Nazareth must mean, at least among other things, the scientific, historical quest of Jesus. And this brings us to the Conciliar dialectic of scholasticism and biblical scholarship. Speaking as one who has taken an amateur interest in biblical studies for the greater part of my life, I rejoice that the Council's *Constitution on Divine Revelation* can be viewed as containing at least the first sketch of a charter of open biblical research. That there was much nervousness about biblical criticism in the Council cannot be denied. And perhaps we lacked the voice of some great Council orator to remind us of the already great achievements of New Testament scholarship in allowing us to penetrate, tentatively and inchoatively, behind even the primitive postresurrection formulations of the gospel to the words and person and spirit of him who spoke with authority and not as the scribes. The spirit of Jesus was not the spirit of unqualified conservatism. He took his stand within the Great Tradition of the holy community of Israel, centred in the Torah and the temple priesthood. But, in strong contrast to the Dead Sea sectarians, he subordinated law to charity and gave the impulse that was to change a predominantly national religion into one that was universal and catholic. It is that spirit which provokes audacious change in order to preserve, at a higher level and from a superior viewpoint, inherited values, which is the Spirit that animates the mystical body of Christ. In "the name of" that Spirit, Vatican II was called together and congregated. I am less doubtful than I once was that it was gathered for a second Pentecost.

My purpose here is not retrospective. If I look back upon the Council, it is not in order to contemplate it as an end achieved, but to understand it as a step toward the future. The great Council of Trent dominated the centuries that followed it, not merely by what it did but by the application made of its work by St Charles Borromeo and those who, like him, were determined that it should not remain a dead letter. Vatican II is at once a first step and, I venture to suggest, a new orientation. Fascinated, it may be, by theological rationalisations of Church history, or under the spell of Newman's theory of development, we have been too much inclined to suppose that as the Church has moved in but one direction over the past thousand years, therefore she could only so have moved, and must continue on the same line. But in fact the Church is a fountainhead of unpredictable freedom. The static element in her complex totality, the sacraments and especially the sacramental ministry, is subordinate to the dynamic moment whose immediate source is the charisms, the grace-gifts, of the Spirit of Christ, given—as *Lumen Gentium* reminds us—as and to whom God chooses, whether to pope or humble layman or woman—or, we may add, to a bushman to whom the gospel has never been proclaimed by human lips. The Spirit bloweth where it listeth, and it is impossible to foretell, from the present state and condition of the Church, what her history in the coming generations will be. But at least for the moment, without rejecting or denying her past, without any surrender of her patrimony, she appears to have changed her course.

To attempt to define this change would be hazardous, but I nevertheless would point to two moments in the Council's life and work which, between them, seem to me to be suggestive.

The first is the reaffirmation, in *Lumen Gentium,* of a genuine sacramental episcopal collegiality, which had been thrown somewhat into the background by the work of the prematurely ended Vatican I. This seems to afford the basis for a recovery of the

principle that the papacy—and now we must add the episcopate—is not the source of the actual life of the Church, but the
coordinator of that life's various and peripheral spontaneities.
This principle of subsidiarity is carried through to the point at
which the lay Catholic is seen as a genuine creative force in
the life of the People of God; and to the further point where
it is realised that the whole human family, insofar as good will
prevails, is a theatre of the operations of the grace-gifts of the
Holy Spirit, and is cooperating in the building up of Christ's
kingdom.

The second suggestive moment is the direction of the *Constitution on the Church in the Modern World* not only to Catholics,
or only to Christians, but to all men of good will. Human good
will is the liaison between the total human family and the visible
Church. Father Fernandez, Prior General of the Order of
Preachers, reminded the Council Fathers in a notable speech
that by their common humanity the members of the human race
were all bound by ties of duty to the whole of mankind, and
that this link was prior to the bonds that bind us to more
local groupings. In this fact there is found a moral constituent of
human unity that supervenes upon and perfects our biological
unity. Mankind *ought* to be morally united, to form a single
spiritual communion. The signs of our aspiration to such unity
are plain to see in past and present history. That the obligation
and the aspiration are real gives meaning to the Council's
address to all men of good will. But the past and present history show us also how halting and imperfect are the steps that
man can take in his own strength to achieve that unity without
which his own future is now more than ever clouded over with
menace. Our faith, as Christians, is that Christ came for a purpose of reconciliation: reconciling man with God, but thereby
also reconciling man with man. The Church, the People of God,
in which all hierarchy exists for the sake of service or ministry,
is the Spirit-animated mystical body of Christ and makes ever
contemporary the reality of his presence and the saving truth of
his gospel; she is the sign and the instrument of the unity of the
whole human race.

We, then, who believe these things, must study the Council's
acts. But we must do more; we must catch and embody the Council's spirit. We must be members and representations of Christ
in and to the world. And we have to show that we remember
that the heart of Christ and the heart of his gospel were directed
ultimately by adoration beyond humanity to God.

# Epilogue: Joy in Believing

1966

Faith is the basis of everything in the fully Christian life, and faith's certainty is intrinsic to itself; it does not rest on external supports. Faith, says de Caussade, has no wish for proofs: those who live by faith accept the proofs of faith not as proofs but as ordained by God.

But Christians are part and parcel of a humanity only partially converted to Christ. And even within each of us there is an unconverted residue which feels the need of the support of "proofs". Indeed, faith itself teaches us that to be a believer is the only fully reasonable way of being human: to this extent, then, even faith requires that "proofs" should be available to "justify" before the bar of reason the life of faith. The proofs are "ordained by God".

If we lived in a completely Christianised world, the proofs of faith would be fully coincident with our experience, as normal as air and sunlight. But to live fully today in the whole human environment is to live in a pluralist, and largely post-Christian world, where the proofs are hardly come by without some personal effort and are kept alive and apt only by continuing effort.

Still, they are available. Wonder, the raw material of philosophy, laughs at the horizons of sense experience and demands a metaphysical source of finite reality. Love, even before it has become reflexively the love of God, has a rational abhorrence of the absurd. Conscience brings us face to face with an absolute requirement which, in order to be absolute, must be one with the source of finite reality, *quod omnes vocant Deum*. What, then, is the meaning of this human experience itself, this "world" in which God has placed us and through which he discloses himself to us? How, in and through it, does one respond positively and concretely to the love and the will of God? Has God himself provided any indications of the way in which he wants man, individually and socially, to find and follow him in this world?

267

There are religious traditions in history which claim to rest on such divine indications. They are grouped round and appear to find their culmination in the Christian gospel. From that point the road is easy enough. In his brilliant short account of his own conversion, Evelyn Waugh contrasts (in true patristic fashion) "the local, temporary character of the heresies and schisms and the universal, eternal character of the Church". "It was self-evident to me", he says, "that no heresy or schism could be right and the Church wrong".[1] One could generalise: if there is a true religion, it is quite obviously the religion which calls itself Catholic and is known by that name wherever commonsense is not obscured by the need to defend a cause.

Thus the "proofs" of faith reach their full concreteness and their practical cogency in the "moral miracle" of the Catholic Church herself, in her existential reality—as the First Vatican Council affirmed. The years go by, experience is broadened and deepened, and the force of these proofs, this proof, increases rather than diminishes.

However, there is an important level of thought, more superficial than that of the fundamental proof, at which the state of things has been somewhat different. Of F. H. Bradley it was said that he maintained that this world in which we actually exist is the best of all possible worlds; and that everything which it contains is a necessary evil. Something similar could have been said of the Church before John XXIII: it was the best of all possible religions, and everything in it an intellectual scandal. This is an exaggeration, of course, but let us take a few examples.

The Catholic religion, firm in its proclamation that God has actually intervened in history, points to its canon of inspired literature as to a record of this intervention. The attitude of Church authority to the Bible was one of the biggest difficulties that I experienced in the last stage of my conversion. Inspiration it was said, meant material inerrancy; and when critical scholarship developed in the Church at the end of the last century, and in the first decade of this century, it was forcibly suppressed. A better climate began to spread with the publication of *Divino Afflante* a quarter of a century ago; but even just before the Council opened an obscurantist campaign was being launched in Rome itself.

[1] Cf. John A. O'Brien, ed. *The Road to Damascus.*

Again, with its realistic claim to be true, Christianity had early come face to face with Greek philosophy, and when Justinian closed the schools at Athens it could seem to have won the day. But, as had happened before, Greece in her defeat had taken her victor captive, and already in the patristic age there was a tendency to see the Christian revelation as a sort of divine appendix to the discoveries of human reason. In modern times Thomist scholasticism had been almost canonised by Church authority; and it was inevitably a debased Thomism that actually dominated in the seminaries, because philosophy—like theology—cannot live healthily in a backwater, and modern man was no longer thinking scholastically.

An intellectual backwater was, in fact, just where the Church was living. It was as though the treasures she had amassed in her early years, when she appropriated the wisdom of the Greeks and the imperial genius and laws of Rome, had become too heavy a burden to allow her to keep up with the progress of human thinking and to assimilate the new vistas of experience. Her first reactions to the advances of modern science had always been negative: witness the *affaire* Galileo; witness the fact that when I was a young Catholic it was still doubted whether it was orthodox to believe in the evolution of man from a sub-human form of life. And of course there was the same negative reflex in the face of critical historical scholarship. I have already spoken of this as regards the Bible; but it had also been true in the sphere of hagiography—and still, after the Council, we were reading the Roman Martyrology.

A society which turns its back on actual life tends to harden and intensify its own more reactionary features. The Church's reaction to modern advances was not only the Syllabus of Errors. It was the proclamation of papal primacy and infallibility (both of them, of course, absolutely true; which does not settle the question of their opportuneness, nor of the mode in which they were practically and theoretically interpreted). It was a growing centralisation and absolutism, which were draining the life away from local Catholicism and threatening to leave us with a totalitarian bureaucracy operating in a vacuum.

All this, it might be said, is very accidental to religion itself. What then, of religion itself? Take the liturgy. This, as we knew it in the preconciliar Western rite, was a public worship

269

conducted by priests for a passive lay audience, in a dead language with which even the more educated minority of the faithful were rapidly losing all contact. Of course this worship was
venerable; and of course it was beautiful—in the few places
where it was properly performed. It was even devotional, if devotion means an aura of mystery which deliberately obscures the
very signs of the transcendent Mystery incarnate for our salvation. Yet, curiously enough, the conservatism of modern Catholicism had been such that you could still read, in the liturgical texts
themselves, evidence that the liturgy had been created with a
quite different orientation.

There was one region of rapid religious change: that of devotion to our Lady. This was almost the only field in which Newman's doctrine of development was being allowed a free, indeed
uncritical, course. But development here was going on in a world
apart from the total life of theology. It was taking shape in such
phenomena as the Fatima cult and was reaching forward for
further "luxury" definitions of doctrine. If I may borrow again
from Evelyn Waugh, it began to seem that the Catholicism of
the future would approximate more and more to the condition
of an Italian tribal cult.

And this Romanised, Latinised, Italianised anachronism was
being exported by missionaries to the non-White world, where it
had made great strides under cover of the colonial powers but
was surely doomed as the old Afro-Asian cultures reasserted
themselves. It showed little aptitude for assimilating these cultures in the way in which the early Church had assimilated the
Graeco-Roman culture. In India, where an ancient tradition of
contemplation and metaphysical reflection was maintained by the
Brahmin leaders of culture, the modern Church had gone, as if
by instinct, not to these leaders but to the outcasts, and had presented itself not as the divine answer to man's metaphysical
hunger but as a provider of schools and hospitals.

At home, meanwhile, the Church seemed to have renounced
any pretension to speak to the leaders of culture and to learn
from them, or to be a ferment in social and political life. Called
to a mission universal in depth as well as breadth, it reckoned
its successes by the statistics of individual conversions, which
ran, in a good year, at a rate of about one to every three thousand
of the population. Its real effort was concentrated on preserving

the faith and practice of those who were already its acknowledged members. Millions of pounds were being spent on this
attempt, and there seemed little understanding that a strategy
limited to defence is doomed to failure in the end.

Of course, there is a real sense in which the Church cannot
fail. The gates of hell will not prevail against her. But we have
no divine guarantee that her destiny will not be that of the
coelocanthus, surviving with diminished numbers through having
taken refuge from the main current of onward-moving life. The
Samaritans still survive in Palestine.

For what was happening in the world outside the Church?
Perhaps the most tremendous forward move since the coming of
Christianity itself. Change-in-duration was not only the practical
order of the day: it was the category in which men were learning to think. There was, it is true, a defect here. What was
needed, in the field of thought, was a metaphysical underpinning.
But the kind of metaphysics offered by the current Catholic text-
books could not supply this need, since they neither faced the
modern questions nor spoke a language (I am not referring to
Latin as against the vernaculars) which modern man could
understand.

I have, of course, been exaggerating, and there were more
hopeful omens than those which I have mentioned here, in the
pre-conciliar Church. But there is not space here for a treatise,
so I must be content with a caricature.

The suggestion for these reflections was provoked by an im-
promptu remark, made in public, to the effect that, as a result
of the Council, I was more passionately convinced than ever of
the truth of Catholicism. I must, of course, explain that I did
utterly believe in the truth before the Council, as I do still. But
the intellectual relief with which I contemplate the Council
and its acts is nevertheless immense. And it is due to the activity
of some two thousand elderly gentlemen who had usually qualified for membership of the Council less by the vigour of their
intellectual life and interests than by their canonical and administrative acumen and ability and their devotion to a pastorate
somewhat narrowly conceived.

During the First Vatican Council, Pius IX is said to have

remarked that the action of the Holy Ghost would be found not outside but within the Council chamber. How else can the achievements of the Second Vatican Council be explained than as the effects of a powerful intervention of God's saving Spirit? For in virtually every one of the areas so hastily outlined above, the Council has brought about a tremendous change for the better. It all adds up, it is true, to no more than a first step. And there will surely be much suffering ahead for all of us. But Adam was a first step. The first Christian Pentecost was a first step. Conversion, for the individual, is a first step. It seems to me that the Church, the People of God, has now been invited by Providence to move forward into a great Christian Renaissance.